LAUREL

MOLECULES OF THE MIND

"A SPLENDID VOLUME!"

—Solomon H. Snyder, Director,
Department of Neuroscience,
Johns Hopkins University

"Every once in a while comes a book capable of shattering the lens through which we view the world. . . . In the deft hand of this two-time Pulitzer prize winner, the relationship between the components of a cell and the substances that stimulate it become as compelling as the drama in any novel."

—The Anniston Star

"Franklin's clear, vigorous prose and cogent arguments make this book a model of popular science writing."

—Library Journal

"Jon Franklin is an engaging and steadily interesting popularizer of a science or sciences so far advanced that the lay person knows scarcely anything of this subject which is likely to mean so much to the common life in the near future."

—Howard Nemerov

Books by Jon Franklin

Molecules of the Mind   (1987)

Writing for Story   (1986)

Guinea Pig Doctors   (1984)

Not Quite a Miracle   (1983)

Shocktrauma   (1980)

QUANTITY SALES

Most Dell Books are available at special quantity discounts when purchased in bulk by corporations, organizations, and special-interest groups. Custom imprinting or excerpting can also be done to fit special needs. For details write: Dell Publishing Co., Inc., 666 Fifth Avenue, New York, NY 10103. Attn.: Special Sales Dept.

INDIVIDUAL SALES

Are there any Dell Books you want but cannot find in your local stores? If so, you can order them directly from us. You can get any Dell book in print. Simply include the book's title, author, and ISBN number, if you have it, along with a check or money order (no cash can be accepted) for the full retail price plus $1.50 to cover shipping and handling. Mail to: Dell Readers Service, P.O. Box 5057, Des Plaines, IL 60017.

MOLECULES

OF

THE

MIND

JON FRANKLIN

A LAUREL TRADE PAPERBACK
Published by
Dell Publishing Co.
a division of
The Bantam Doubleday Dell Publishing Group, Inc.
1 Dag Hammarskjold Plaza
New York, New York 10017

Laurel ® TM 674623, Dell Publishing Co., Inc.

ISBN: 0-440-50005-2

Reprinted by arrangement with Atheneum Publishers

Printed in the United States of America

March 1988

10 9 8 7 6 5 4 3 2 1

W

To Wilma Franklin . . .

*who wound me up
and set me on my way*

ACKNOWLEDGMENTS

THE facts contained in this book, and the revolutionary perceptions about the human condition that arise from them, took more than a decade to research, compile, and reduce to comprehensible dimensions. It is no exaggeration to say that, within that decade, I was aided by hundreds of brain scientists who willingly laid aside their own work to assist me in mine. Had they not done so, this book could never have been written.

Had I known from the beginning that this project was to grow into a book, I'd have kept a list of those scientists' names, and they would be listed here—all of them, for each, in his own way, had an impact.

But as a young journalist I was interested primarily in tomorrow's story; my original notes were scribbled on copy paper and removed with the next day's trash. It wasn't until much later that

I began to realize that the individual stories I was writing about the brain, taken together, were becoming the chronicle of a revolution. And so many of the men and women who were so generous with their time and energy blend together in my faulty memory.

I remember, for instance, sitting in a leather chair in the lobby of a West Coast hotel while a neurochemist from Harvard explained to me, for the first time in terms I could understand, why it was that "speed freaks" sometimes got a temporary psychosis that was indistinguishable from schizophrenia.

Well . . . I think he was from Harvard. Or was it the University of Chicago? I remember his face as though it were yesterday, but I have no name to go with it.

Whoever he was and wherever he hailed from, I thank him. And I tip my hat, as well, to the anonymous postgraduate student at NIMH who spent her lunch hour explaining the significance of side receptors, and the postdoc who introduced me to his depressed rats. And I give special thanks to whoever it was who insisted that I had to, just *had* to, interview Paul MacLean, no matter how busy and generally unavailable his secretary insisted he was. So many names have been forgotten.

But some I will remember to my grave. Paul MacLean's, for instance.

I remember him as a wise, kind man, with a gentle face, the kind of face you trusted. It was good he was that way, since the vision he'd captured in his marvelously intuitive brain had violent and unpleasant implications about the similarities between lizards and reporters. But because he was who he was, he got through my defenses, changed the way I looked at myself and my story, and generally helped me put my head where it had to be if I was to see the strange coherence of the thinking molecules and what they meant for the human condition.

But if MacLean primed me for the story, it was Solomon Snyder who laid it in my lap. He explained it to me before the famous press conference in 1973; afterwards he never failed to make time for me when I requested it. During the mid-1970s, he patiently spent hours helping me translate the story from neuro-chemistry into English.

Those sessions gave me, among other things, a peek at how his mind worked. In a long career as a science writer I have met a lot of smart people, but when it comes to raw intelligence Sol Snyder is far and away the smartest of them all. I was impressed, so impressed that I finally bulldozed my way over two editors to make the prediction, in print, that Sol Snyder was one day going to win a Nobel Prize. Others have said it since, but I was first, and I proudly stand by it today.

And then there's Candace Pert, a different kind of genius who has become, for me at least, the key visionary of this new science. Though her philosophical perspective sometimes makes her col-leagues squirm, hers is a viewpoint that enlightens and that enables us push beyond the next likely breakthrough and gaze into the future, at all the maybes and ifs and hopes and fears that come with the new psychology she helped to create. She's the kind of scientist—far too rare in this cowardly, cover-your-tail world—who's willing to risk the leap from data to truth.

Candace is also a plain-talker and a straight-shooter. This, combined with her genius, makes her a formidable interview subject. When I interview Pert, I plan to lose the better part of a week; it takes at least four days following a Pert interview for my mind to quit vibrating on her frequencies and return to my own.

On several occasions, she's presented me with paradoxes so convoluted that they nagged at me for years before the implica-tions of what she said finally sunk in. I never will forget the time I woke up stark, staring awake, at 2 A.M., heart pounding, finally having comprehended an offhand remark Candace had made several years previously . . . and that I had been subconsciously worrying about ever since.

Many other names come to mind, some who appear in the book and some who don't. Dr. Fred Goodwin, NIMH's chief scientist, repeatedly took time out of his busy schedule to talk to me. Perhaps because of the perspective provided by his position in the federal hierarchy, he's wonderfully adept at explaining the human stakes behind the mental health research. And time after time, when he wasn't available, his public relations officer, Jules Asher, was.

Another public relations person to whom I am deeply indebted is Don Clayton, at the Washington University School of Medicine, as well as a long list of public relations people at The Johns Hopkins Medical Institutions.

My gratitude also goes to the men and women of two advocacy groups, whose efforts on my behalf were helpful time and time again. And for those many readers who have been personally touched by the diseases of the mind-brain, I list addresses and telephone numbers as well.

The first of these advocacy groups is the **National Mental Health Association,** the national offices of which are located at 1021 Prince Street, Alexandria, VA 22314 (703) 684-7722. The NMHA is a broadly based advocacy group dedicated to supporting programs for the mentally ill. With local offices across the country, it's open to all interested citizens.

The National Alliance for the Mentally Ill is a coalition of mental health patients, former mental health patients, and their relatives. The NAMI is located at 1901 North Fort Myer Drive, Suite 500, Arlington, VA 22209 (703) 524-7600. It, like the NMHA, has chapters across the country.

I am grateful, as well, to two editors of the *Evening Sun* who gave me the time and freedom I needed for the final intensive year and a half of research. With the assistance of Jack Lemmon, managing editor, and George Rodgers, assistant managing editor, this story first saw the light of day in abbreviated form as a newspaper series.

As I worked to lay out the full story in this book, there were many moments of confusion and despair. I owe a debt of gratitude to those friends who came through for me then, and without whose support I might well have lost my courage and my way.

I thank, for instance, Alan Doelp, who over the years spent many hours patiently listening as I attempted to fit my research into a coherent pattern. He oohed and ahhed when the pattern fit together, and pointed out when it did not.

Likewise, J. Tyson Tildon, a brain chemist at the University of Maryland Medical School, provided the kind of personal encouragement that allowed me to keep my chin up. And Marshall Rennels, chief neuroanatomist at the same institution and also a long-time friend, was my personal escort through the frequently daunting landscape of the brain.

As the list grows ever more personal, I thank my daughter, Teresa, for her enduring support, and my fiancée, Lynn Scheidhauer, for her tolerance and faith. On those dark days when I was clearly lost and the story foundered, along with my sanity, they were always there to lie to me, convincingly, that all was well and would obviously work out for the best. And so, with their help, it did.

Finally, as the project entered its final years, maturing into a book proposal, there came a moment when all hung on the faith of my agent, Dominick Abel. The story had not yet begun to win prizes, and the message it contained was unfamiliar, strange, and somewhat threatening; the proposal seemed doomed to bounce forever from disinterested publisher to disinterested publisher.

An agent puts himself and his judgment—which is to say, his whole stock in trade—on the line every time he submits a manuscript. And when it's rejected, he's the one who is there, in the author's place, to absorb the blow in all of its immediacy. And yet Dominick kept the faith with this book until the day when the newspaper series that preceded it began winning the legitimacy that comes with national prizes.

And the tide, when it turned, carried me finally into what is an author's dream of safe harbor: a first-rate editor at a first-rate publishing house.

Now there are certain relationships in this world that are by nature intimate and intense, and fraught with potential for disaster. Man and wife, for instance. Soldier and foxhole buddy. Mentor and apprentice. Executioner and condemned prisoner.

And, of course, editor and writer.

Trish Lande is the almost mythical sort of editor that every writer hopes, someday, to find.

For one thing, she has the inner security that allows her to resist competing with the writer in the artistic process. Instead she becomes an ally, actively joining with the writer in the conspiracy to create that strange fabric of fact and derivative pattern that engages the reader and, by means of the engagement, provokes growth.

She is the kind of editor, in short, who can get out of the writer's way when he's working well and, when he's not, can step in and figure out not what *she* would say in those circumstances but what the *writer* needs to say. Thus the books she edits retain that magical coherence that comes from consistent point of view.

Another way of putting it is that, with an editor like Trish Lande, a writer comes off sounding a whole lot better than he is.

Truthfully, of course, Trish is more than Trish. An editor, in addition to editing, serves as a link to the infrastructure of the publishing house. And so the roses I throw at her feet are intended, as well, for those others who have assisted, with such professional style and care, in the birth of this book.

In particular I thank Harry Ford, production/art director *extraordinaire*; Robert Anthony, the artist who designed the cover; Barbara Campo and her department, fine copy editors who made the story flow ever more smoothly; and the dozens of sales people without whom this book would never have reached your hands. As a writer who has worked with a variety of publishing houses I can testify that, together, these people make a very classy act.

The final responsibility for a book, of course, devolves to the writer whose name is on the cover. I accept that responsibility. But insofar as this book succeeds—insofar as you find it entertaining, enlightening, and amusing—these are the people who deserve not just my gratitude but yours as well.

Jon Franklin
Baltimore, 1986

xiv

CONTENTS

INTRODUCTION—
A MILLENNIUM DAWNS   3

THE WORLD IS CRAZY   11

A DESPERATE NEED   26

MOTHS TO A FLAME   39

THE CURE FOR EVERYTHING   50

THE MAGIC MOLECULES   60

BREAKTHROUGH   74

GOLD RUSH   82

A TARGET OF OPPORTUNITY   97

A LESSON IN HUMILITY   107

THE CHEMICALS OF SORROW   119

TWISTED MOLECULES   134

THE BAD SEEDS   147

THE NATURE-NURTURE THEORY   160

A Tantalizing Clue 170

The Scanners 183

The Mechanism
and the Mechanics 199

The Devil Below 219

Of Ancient Yearnings 227

The Apple Is a Persimmon 251

Brave New World 265

A New Nightmare 280

At the Crossroads 290

MOLECULES

OF

THE

MIND

Introduction

A

MILLENNIUM

DAWNS

EARLY in this century, an obscure patent office clerk in Switzerland concocted a theory that flew in the face of common sense. According to his equations, for instance, space could stretch like a rubber band and time was a dimension, like height or width. The theory fascinated physicists, but practical people paid no attention. There was business to attend to, shopping to do, children to bear and rear. Life went on, as it always had.

Then, early one morning in the New Mexican desert in the summer of 1945, just before dawn, the theory produced a kind of fruit that could not be ignored. It began with a point of light that, in less than a heartbeat, grew into an embryonic star. The star vaporized the tower that held it, turned the desert sand to glass, and sent a mushroom cloud boiling angrily into the stratosphere. The sun, when it appeared a few moments later, rose on a new age.

As the months, years, and then decades passed, we began to perceive that moment as the most important technological watershed since we learned to control fire. Certainly our generation, we were sure, would never see the like of it—such incredible things do not happen twice in the same century.

But, as the story you are about to read will illustrate, we were wrong about that. Even as we were struggling to grasp the implications of the atomic age, a small group of researchers in the only scientific discipline stranger than physics were laying the groundwork for an even more powerful revolution.

These scientists, surrounded by an obscurity as effective as the secrecy of the Manhattan project, thought the unthinkable and tested hypotheses that not so long ago would have been categorized as heresy.

At first their efforts came to little, but with the passage of time they were more successful. Finally, in the 1970s, the scientists began producing formulas that accurately described a set of forces more fundamental than gravity and electromagnetism, relationships far more profound than that between E and mc squared.

This new science's equivalent of the atomic bomb has not yet exploded, but the moment rapidly approaches. And as it does insiders have begun to recognize the implications of what is about to happen—and to tremble at the prospect.

A thousand years hence, when our descendants look back on this time, it will not be the name of Albert Einstein that comes to their lips. For while the forces contained within the nucleus of the atom are truly powerful, and though the hydrogen fires may burn hot and bright, they pale when compared with the energy contained within the human mind.

The story of the coming release of this energy, and the birth of the millennium, has unclear beginnings. As far back as the 1800s there were hints of what might come, as when certain chemicals were discovered capable of altering the beat of a frog's heart. But the manner of thinking about the mind in those days allowed no glimpse of the truth—or if it did, the visionary who was smart enough to see it was also bright enough to keep his mouth shut.

Modern experts on the mind, tracing the roots of their discipline, select different moments to mark its beginning. Some point to the postwar years, and the accidental discovery of a molecule that could prevent schizophrenic visions. Others point to a chain of insights about the brain that occurred to a number of different scientists during the 1960s.

But as a storm gathers over time, so scientific revolutions are built of small discoveries, observations, and insights by many scientists. As Einstein himself remarked, heroes are selected later, from among the candidates, by those of us who have trouble grasping the impersonal accretion of knowledge. The exact moments and names that we decide to inscribe first in our memories and later in our almanacs are rather arbitrary.

My preference is for the date 1973 and the name Solomon Snyder. In that year he and a doctoral candidate, Candace Pert, performed the experiments that converted a theoretical notion about the nature of the human mind into an undeniable fact.

But as one who is about to weave for you a rather incredible tale, I owe you the admission that Snyder's discovery was also a pivotal point in my own life. It almost had to be that way, for this is not the kind of story in which even the most objective reporter can long remain truly detached. This story, for all the technology it must traverse, is in the end about me . . . and about you, and about us.

As a science writer for the *Evening Sun* in Baltimore, I was one of the first outsiders to become privy to the revolution. What I was told, and what I observed, triggered a chain of insights that profoundly changed my attitude about the nature of the human condition.

The psychological jolt was heightened by the fact that, when I walked into Snyder's office on that bright and pleasant June day, I was totally unprepared for what I was about to discover.

5

I was a young man then—very, very young in hindsight—and my scientific background was in astronomy, geology, physics, and the other "real" sciences. I had the hard scientist's distaste for biology: in my mind it was the muddling science, the guesswork science, the sort-of-a-science science. I kept my mouth shut and covered biology, because medicine is one of Baltimore's chief exports. But I privately yearned to be where the important things were happening, like down at the cape with Walter Cronkite.

So I hadn't been overly impressed when a Johns Hopkins University public relations woman called me and said that a guy over there had just made a major discovery about the brain.

The way I figured it, brain scientists were pretty pathetic characters. Maybe in ten thousand years or so someone would figure out how the brain worked, and how it produced the mind. But in the meantime, brain scientists were a bunch of blind men writing tortured descriptions about this horribly complicated elephant. They didn't know what they were looking for and wouldn't recognize it when they found it. Science might have gone to the moon, field-stripped the atom, and built the computer, but in seeking to unlock the secrets of the mind it had broken its sword.

My idea of psychology, like that of most other people in the beginning of the Age of Aquarius, was a tumbled-up mixture of Freud, Jung, Skinner, Hitchcock, hypnotism, EST, psychodrama, and all the fringies out in California. The most important thing about the psyche, in my opinion, was its mysteriousness.

So I walked into Snyder's office a total innocent. I was in effect a six-year-old child who was about to be told, matter-of-factly and with logical proofs and Polaroid pictures, the Truth about Life. There was no Santa Claus. Ditto the tooth fairy. God was highly debatable. Daddies fantasized about running away, mommies occasionally considered murdering six-year-olds, and babies were conceived not in love but in hot lust. In two hours Snyder turned my world upside down.

So rational and yet at the same time so unacceptable were the implications of what Snyder told me that my mind, after that

interview, simply wouldn't function. I attended the press conference, but I was a sleepwalker. My notes, sentence by sentence,
made perfect sense . . . but when the sentences were combined,
the result was gibberish.

I had no context for what I had learned, no way to file the data
short of rearranging my entire mental framework and rethinking
everything I thought I knew. With the passage of years I would
do precisely that, but in the meantime it was all I could do to get
the facts of the story down on paper, and get that paper to the
city editor.

The result was a report that, while factual enough, was totally
devoid of the implications. My only consolation, looking back,
was that most of my colleagues didn't even write the story at all.

And so what was probably the most important story of the
twentieth century ran for one day in a few newspapers and was
entirely ignored by television and radio. And then it disappeared,
replaced with easier-to-understand and more acceptable phenomena like ax murders and political scandal.

But I couldn't forget what I had learned—there are some
things you can't unsee. It nagged at me, tugged at the back of my
mind, assaulted me with its implications. I began to analyze the
actions of people around me on the basis of what Snyder's experiment had implied. I'd get flashes of insight at awkward moments.
For instance, it might occur to me during the act of sex why a
certain emotion suddenly boiled to the top of my mind.

I couldn't forget it, so I pursued it. I read everything I could
get my hands on about neurochemistry—which wasn't very much.
I taught myself to understand the language neurochemists spoke,
memorized the difference between an agonist and an antagonist,
puzzled out how the brain reacts by inhibiting an inhibitor that
inhibits an inhibitor. I started hanging out with brain scientists
and neurosurgeons and putting together what I slowly became
convinced was the most important story of our lifetime. The
problem was, though, that the neurochemical story just wasn't
very believable.

Over and over I tried to explain to editors what people like

Snyder were doing at places like Johns Hopkins, and where they were going, and what it meant. The editor would listen to me, politely, and then go about his business. He had even less background than I, that day when I waltzed into Snyder's office.

I wrote several stories, but my editor handed them back to me. He simply didn't believe it and nobody else would either, he explained to me in a fatherly way that made me want to jam the typewriter down his throat.

But the story had lodged in my mind like a blackberry seed in a cavity of a tooth. What Snyder and Pert were doing was so incredible that I couldn't quit worrying with it, couldn't quit talking about it. I wanted to grab people by the lapels and shake them, but I was learning more and more about psychology and had started to notice that my crusade was beginning to earn me some funny sideways glances.

As the months passed, and then the years, the revolution blossomed. Yet very few people wrote about it; those who did concentrated on fragments. No journalist or scientist seemed prepared to risk his reputation and lay out the whole story, all in one place, so that the nature of what was happening would be revealed.

This was personally frustrating, of course, but in time I began to worry about it in a larger sense. The revolution in brain science has the potential to make the world a much better place to live, but at the same time it carries with it some dangers that make the threat of nuclear war seem almost manageable. We went blindly into the atomic age, and look at what it got us. Were we going to go blindly, as well, into the age of mind control?

So what had been a driving interest and a personal passion became, finally, a mission. I collected relevant scientific papers, filed and cross-filed them, and tried this way and that to explain how the chemistry worked. Finally, though the guts of the matter still seemed to defy the newspapering trade, some of my fringe stories began to get attention.

In 1978, for instance, I set about to demonstrate to my readers the fact that while the brain was a mechanism far more complex and delicate than the finest of clocks, it was nevertheless a mechanism. To make the point I decided to take them into a brain surgery operating room and show them the gray organ, laid bare.

The literary vehicle I chose for doing this was a story about an intrepid brain surgeon who performed a delicate and dangerous operation in an almost desperate gamble to save a woman's life. The story was calculated to let the reader "see," through my narrative, a living, throbbing human brain.

A few months later, that story won a Pulitzer Prize, and a few months after that I agreed to do a book on the same subject.

Then, in the very appropriate year of 1984, after more than a decade of research and literary practice runs, I finally undertook to lay out the entire story in this book. As a warm-up exercise, and to make certain my explanations worked and were on target, I did a series of articles for the *Evening Sun*.

In that series for the first time I felt that I was really addressing the substance of the story that had so long captivated me. Though the narrative was compressed, in typical news style, I felt that the articles at least began to convey the startling nature of the new science that I had named molecular psychology.

There were so many requests for copies that the newspaper reprinted the series in tabloid form. They quickly ran out and printed more. Then the series won the Carringer Award from the National Mental Health Association, and, finally, as I sat down to begin this book, the series won me a second Pulitzer Prize.

Times, of course, have changed dramatically since June 1973. We have all read bits and pieces of the new psychiatry, printed in magazines and newspapers, and some hint of it has even appeared on television. Even if you know nothing of the biological sciences, you are probably better able to grasp the truth than I was in 1973. It will seem, in the present climate, somewhat less alien.

Still, the reality of what we know, what that means, and what we will be able to do with it at first seems very alien. We are used to living in a moralistic world.

The paradigm of good and evil is, after all, a comfortable one, engraved into our minds and into our social behavior by a million years of practice. It is probably even programmed into our genes.

In our day-to-day, moment-to-moment existence, it is good and evil, right and wrong, like and dislike, that govern our attitudes toward our fellow human beings. We are good, the Soviets are bad. The Democrats (or Republicans) are right, the Republicans (or Democrats) are wrong.

Yet at the same time, if you are a thoughtful person you understand that the world's problems just don't lend themselves to such a simple interpretation. The dilemmas we confront aren't the product of a few evil people with pig faces and beady little eyes who dream of disrupting our lives. No, our problems stem somehow from the honest efforts of good men and women, well intentioned, who are doing their dead level best to make the world a better place to live.

But something goes wrong and what we get, instead, is . . . well, take a glance at today's headlines.

1

THE

WORLD

IS

CRAZY

"The whole world is crazy except for me and thee . . . and sometimes I wonder about thee."

—Old Quaker farmer

D E E P in the secret files of your mind and mine, down in the dark caverns of our psyches where we wall off forbidden perceptions, there lurks the suspicion that the mythical old Quaker speaks the truth—that there exists around us an insanity so fundamental, a dementia so indelible, an illogic so embedded in our society that it defeats everything good and worthwhile that we attempt to accomplish.

It is an uncomfortably hopeless thought; worse, in itself it's a little schizophrenic and perhaps even paranoid. If I suspect the world is crazy, might not the diagnosis apply, mirror fashion, not to them but to me? So we speak of the thing only to friends. Even then we find it necessary to chuckle and, by the chuckle, we fuzz up the truth by implying that we don't really mean it.

Outside the realm of dark humor we rarely see the thought put into words (except, perhaps, by the gnomes who spray paint it on the walls of underpasses and the sides of subway cars). It never, never gets printed in the *New York Times* or *Newsweek* since the message is not, as editors like to say, "responsible." Yet it's the media that keep the evidence before us.

In Beirut, a young man or woman, full of life but also of hatred and maybe something else, some madness, drives a truck packed with explosives into the portal of an embassy.

In Pittsburgh, a successful career woman and mother of two, married to a handsome and dynamic young executive, awakens one morning when her husband is away and, taking the pistol he left for her protection, kills first the baby, then the toddler, then herself.

In Washington, representatives of the most powerful nation on earth, possessor of enough nuclear weapons to destroy the human race a hundred times over, vote to cut aid to education and to put the money, instead, into a new missile. In the White House the most popular president in a generation hails the decision and calls the missile "Peacekeeper."

The cacophony of craziness goes on, and on, and on.

In California, a half-dozen major celebrities lose several fortunes on an investment scam so obviously fraudulent that it makes us laugh.

In Baltimore, a minimum-wage helper in a doughnut shop hits the lottery for a cool million bucks. But a few months later the money's gone (he's not sure where), and he's back making doughnuts.

In Detroit, a major automaker announces it is recalling several thousand cars so that faulty brakes can be fixed—while at the same time denying that there's anything wrong with them in the first place. Meanwhile, in Washington, an industry lobbyist argues for tariffs against Japanese imports.

The Census Bureau tells us that the divorce rate is the highest in history; a poll indicates that Americans are increasingly against sex education. From New York comes the story that the theory of evolution is being watered down in still another junior high school textbook, lest it fail to sell in Texas. Elsewhere, a group of parents and educators release a report pointing to all-time low literacy rates among high school graduates and decrying the quality of public education.

Writers and commentators carefully analyze each event, taking pains to crank in the cultural, economic, and religious factors. A liberal appears on the television screen, explaining in reasoned syllables that the answer, as anyone can see, is more liberalism. A conservative face comes next, arguing that a free market is the real panacea. He is replaced by a new-right preacher who tells us that the answer is God and a return to old values. It is all very balanced. Then the talking heads are followed by a computer commercial, and that is followed by ninety seconds of gunfire in Beirut, sixty seconds devoted to the Brazilian debt and the danger to New York banks—and then comes a three-minute feature on drunk driving in which the narrator never once mentions seat belts.

And so, as Kurt Vonnegut once observed, it goes. Day follows day, a little bit of bright no-nonsense rationality and a little bit of something else, something murky and frightening that lurks behind the news and haunts the edges of our minds.

Psychiatrists have a variety of names for it. They make distinctions between psychosis and stupidity, for instance, or between homicide and war. But in the lay vernacular only one will do; it is craziness, all craziness. Jesus! We chuckle nervously, turn the page, change the channel, and open another beer.

And then, every so often, a lightning bolt of unadulterated insanity explodes so brilliantly across the national psyche that it fixes our attention. For a while we stare, mesmerized, at the television set.

The videotape runs for the hundredth time, showing us a confused scene outside the Washington Hilton. A madman moves through the crowd, unnoticed by the press corps at the time but now, in the hindsight of video replay, pointed out by an arrow provided by the network artist. The commentator's dulcet voice tells us the madman's name is John W. Hinckley, Jr.

Hinckley, Hinckley, Hinckley.

Deep in his convoluted mind a young man we never heard of has drawn discordant and grandiose conclusions about the ways of love. Now, rebuffed by the actress he adores, he stalks a president and bides his time, seeking a clear field of fire. Finally, as Ronald Reagan and his entourage emerge from the hotel, the stalker's patience is rewarded. The gun comes up and discharges sharply, again and again. The president's press chief falls, as does a policeman; a secret service agent pushes Reagan, looking more surprised than injured, into the armored limousine.

That night the madman smiles hideously at his lady love from the red-hot medium of the television tube.

A day passes, and the story dies down, replaced by the humdrum everyday sequence of world events. There are riots in South Africa. The Soviets shoot down an unarmed passenger aircraft. A political figure in Central America is discovered dead in a pool of blood. In America, a bomb reduces an abortion clinic to rubble. A newspaper prints a series of stories about the homeless rabble who, turned out of closed-down insane asylums, now haunt the alleyways and sleep on park benches. There is famine in the Sudan, flooding in India, poison gas in Afghanistan, yellow rain in Southeast Asia.

And then, amidst the torrential downpour of craziness, another lightning flash.

A man in San Ysidro, California, tells his wife he is going out to "hunt humans" and, weighted down with three guns and several pounds of ammunition, leaves the house. A few minutes later he walks into a crowded McDonald's restaurant. He bags twenty-one humans and wounds eighteen more before he, too, lies dead on the blood-slick tile.

His name is James Huberty.

Huberty. Huberty. Who the hell is James Huberty?

Why? we ask ourselves. Why?

For anyone who understands the many faces of craziness, that one, at least, is easy. As the media scour the man's hometown for every lurid tidbit, talking to those who once employed the hunter and those few who seemed to have known him, we assemble a story of withdrawal coupled with weirdly incoherent political convictions and delusions of grandeur. Those facts, added together with the terminal act of nonsensical violence, bear the mark of a special kind of craziness called schizophrenia.

There is no McDonald's murderer left to try, of course—he is as cold dead as his victims. But at the Hinckley trial, the same word surfaces. Schizophrenia. Schizophrenia. Schizophrenia.

Law-and-order aficionados are livid at the insanity defense strategy put forward by Hinckley's lawyers, but the judge won't strike it. No, schizophrenia, and schizophrenia alone, makes sense. A jury hears it all, deliberates, and concurs.

Schizophrenia.

Hinckley is hustled off to St. Elizabeths Hospital.

There is a certain satisfaction in the diagnosis, a certain order in being able to put a name to it. All too often the great craziness is unspeakably amorphous, intangible, unreal—that's what makes it so difficult to deal with directly. But schizophrenia is something you can discuss intelligently.

Superficially at least, there's nothing foggy or abstract about schizophrenia. With its distinctive symptoms of withdrawal, hallucinations, delusions, paranoia, idiosyncratic belief systems, and incoherent thought processes, it was, in the early days of this century, the first mental illness to be described in specific, clinical terms.

Schizophrenia is the very cliché of madness; in its full-blown form it can be identified by even the most amateurish psychologist. Newspaper medical writers, as well as others who for one reason and another attract the attention of schizophrenics, learn to identify their letters instantly by their characteristic, margin-to-margin writing style.

In fact, the disease is rather common. It strikes about one in every 100 people, and perhaps two more are borderline cases—

schizoid personalities. In a country with a population of 250 million, that means that perhaps five million schizoids find it impossible to bring their minds totally to bear on reality. Two and a half million more full-blown schizophrenics are cursed with the certain knowledge of things palpably not so.

This certainty has many different manifestations. One victim is pursued by devils, another by extraterrestrials, another by communists, still another by the CIA. They all share with you and me that secret, forbidden thought that the rest of the world is crazy—crazy or evil. But in their case the thought will not be suppressed. We call such people "paranoid."

The hunted may hide in alleyways or retreat into dingy rented rooms where dead mothers and fathers appear before them, accusingly.

Trees talk, ceilings weep, animals laugh. Thoughts bend back upon themselves with the logic of the Möbius strip, producing tangled contradictions, mutually exclusive facets of truth that the human tongue can't express.

Yet the tongue, being human, must try. Humans crave communication, and so schizophrenics, despite their strange disease, struggle to tell us what they see—they try desperately, accosting us on the street, grabbing us by the lapels, staring into our faces, trying to tell us, trying, trying, trying . . .

We edge away from them, pull free, and flee.

The schizophrenic withdraws, then, but he can't escape from the truth, from God, no . . . not from God.

Or is it the devil?

Whoever He is, His booming voice echoes imperiously in the brain, dispensing righteous commands that no one would dare refuse. Obediently, fervently, the schizophrenic preaches the Holy Gospel from street corners.

By and large, schizophrenics are the most harmless of people. But there are a lot of schizophrenics, and when the madness of one of them leads to violence, that violence is often spectacular.

A schizophrenic, when he fights, knows no limited objectives. He takes his stand for Right and Survival. The armed men beyond his barricade may wear blue uniforms and may identify themselves as policemen, but they don't fool him. He knows they are evil and perhaps even alien, and he fights like the cornered animal he believes himself to be. As a result, law enforcement officers universally fear the violent schizophrenic; headline writers, on the other hand, love him.

Despite the impression left by the headlines, though, schizophrenia is by no means the most violent form of madness to threaten us. Far from it. Other kinds, too, occasionally furnish fodder for the tabloids. For instance:

MOM KILLS TOTS, SELF.

The story explains that the young mother in question had everything to live for. She was college educated, lived in middle-class suburbia, had two perfectly normal children, and was married to an upwardly mobile lawyer who, according to the neighbors, treated her with love and respect.

So why, the question screams at us from between the lines of the story, did she wake up one morning, take the pistol, and methodically kill first the infant, then the toddler, and then herself?

Why?

The editor seems not to know, but for a psychiatrically astute reader a glance at the headlines is sufficient for a diagnosis. The story, revealing that the incident occurred in the morning, confirms it. The woman had good and sufficient reason for what she did, and that reason is called depression.

As a victim of depression, the dead woman was exceptional only because she made the headlines. Depression is responsible for far more bloodshed than is schizophrenia, but because the depressive's aggression is primarily directed inward, he (or more often she) rarely makes good copy. The exception, of course, is when she precedes her self-destruction by killing her children or when she chooses some spectacular means of suicide, like jumping from a tall building or a well-known bridge.

If she chooses a bullet in the brain, carbon monoxide, or poison, her obituary simply notes that she died "suddenly," or "unexpectedly." If she is astute enough in her final agony to choose the automobile as her instrument of death, she simply disappears into the maw of statistical reports and her insurance company pays off double.

Depression is not only more violent than schizophrenia, it is also more common. It strikes about 6 percent of the population. Yet in the minds of most of the rest of us who are not so afflicted, it's difficult to conceptualize it as a disease.

Schizophrenia is easier to deal with in that respect—few of us have experienced hallucinations, so it's easy for us to think of them as abnormal. But we've all been depressed. Depression is natural. Why, we ask ourselves, don't people like that mother in the headlines just pull themselves out of it?

In its milder forms, depression is in fact an everyday fact of human nature; when its cause is dramatic, as when death claims a family member or we lose our livelihood, it can be profound and relentless. But even death loses its sting with the passage of time and, when the mourning is done, our psyches return to normal. The thing that identifies normal depression is that it goes away.

But for fifteen million Americans, depression settles over the mind without cause, or, if there is cause, it refuses to lift. It bears down, crushing the will and smearing out the identity. Then it becomes, in psychiatric terms, clinical depression.

Such depression, having no logical rationale for its existence, classically metamorphoses into self-hatred. It then becomes one of the most painful conditions known to man. Depressive people who have also experienced excruciating physical pain, such as kidney colic, unanimously report that the psychic pain is far, far worse.

This being the case, and the mind being a malleable thing, it is perhaps understandable that most depressives learn to wall off the psychic agony at a level the Freudians like to call the subconscious. Eventually the pain begins to manifest itself in other forms. Insomnia is common, as are impotence and appetite disturbances. Often the symptoms eventually emerge on the physical level in the form of fatigue, "ghost" pains in the abdomen, and intractable back pain.

The frequency with which depression is translated into something else is illustrated by the story of a research team recently assigned to test a new drug for depression. The scientists advertised for volunteers in the local paper, offering free treatment for depression in return for participation in the experiment. But they got few takers.

Then one of the scientists had a brainstorm. Another ad was composed and printed, but this time it didn't ask outright for depressed volunteers. Instead, it included a simple checklist of symptoms: Have you lost interest in sex? Do you feel hopeless? Do you have trouble with insomnia? Do you often feel that you are a bad person?

The laboratory telephone started ringing as soon as the newspaper hit the streets. It didn't stop for days.

One of the researchers was Dr. Joseph Coyle, now at The Johns Hopkins University Medical School in Baltimore. He remembers that many people became very upset when they found out they were calling a psychiatric clinic.

"They didn't perceive that they had a psychiatric problem. The mind plays tricks. Different people do different things. A lot of people don't think psychologically . . . they don't put all these symptoms together and say, 'Well, I must be depressed.'

"In fact, they may be depressed. If they think about it, they may even acknowledge that. But then they ascribe the depression to the fact that they're physically sick—rather than the other way around."

The ability of depression to mimic physical illness presents a real problem for family doctors whose waiting rooms are filled with people whose pain, quite literally, is all in their heads. But the doctor rarely knows which complaints are purely psychological until he or she has completed an exhaustive, and often expensive, work-up. Then, when a diagnosis is reached, the

19

patient usually rejects it. Angrily, he or she stomps out of the office and goes to another doctor.

Because clinical depression is so common, this problem is huge, and it contributes significantly to the nation's health bill. One result is that doctors have, in recent years, established special clinics for patients who have intractable and undiagnosable pain. A few patients who end up in such clinics do indeed turn out to have physical pain that is correctable by surgery. Most of them, however, respond best to psychiatric treatment.

Beyond schizophrenia and depression, we come to another broad category of mental illness called "the anxiety disorders," a catchall term for a long list of common psychological ailments. Included among them are the phobias, panic disorders, and obsessive-compulsive behaviors.

These conditions often involve intense and uncontrollable fears —fears of heights, or bridges, or animals, or insects, or highways, or open spaces, or confinement . . . or sometimes just fear, pure and simple, attached to nothing, or even phobias of developing phobias.

As we have all been depressed, likewise we all have our fears. We are afraid, and legitimately so, of poisonous snakes and stinging bees. If we are rational, we are afraid of mobs that surge screaming through the streets and muggers who lurk in the alleyways of the darkened city; we are afraid, if we are rational, of bankruptcy and lost love. We all have our allotment of shyness, stage fright, and things that go bump in the night. But if we are healthy these fears, like our episodes of depression, know limits.

For some 8 percent of us, however, those limits do not apply. For them, the fears blossom.

Focusing on an object or creature, such as bees or snakes or even other people, such fears can severely restrict the victim's productivity. They are also frequently responsible for serious accidents—a bee-phobic driver is very likely to lose control of his vehicle if a bee flies into the window.

The phobic does not need to be faced with the object of his fear, however, for it to rule his mind. He is always on the lookout for it, and will actually seek it out—rationalizing that if he knows where the bees or the spiders are, he can better avoid them. If he can't find them, they may appear, almost as hallucinations, in his peripheral vision.

Even when there is absolutely no possibility that the object of the phobia will appear, the victim finds himself thinking about it, rehearsing possible phobic scenarios in his mind in an agony of fearful anticipation. Eventually, many phobics confine themselves to the perceived safety of their homes.

Other manifestations of anxiety focus not on objects but on situations; those fears, too, can bend the personality to its will. Fear of failure can drive a businessman to the point where he becomes incapable of distinguishing between the means to an end and the end itself, and he loses all sense of moral limits. Fear of success, an anxiety that has won much attention in the women's movement but that afflicts men as well, can lead to self-destruction.

Fear of bad health can lead to a life so intent on vitamins and exercise that there is no life left worth having. Fear of impotence can be self-fulfilling, fear of the opposite sex can lead to self-hatred (since one continues, somehow, to desire), fear of relationships can lead to estrangement from all of mankind.

Fear, fear, fear—we've all felt it, but for some twenty million of us, fear rules with a dark clammy hand that renders its victims miserable and unproductive.

Then, continuing on down the list of madnesses endemic to our society, we come to one that many people still have difficulty viewing as a disease at all: drug addiction. Another 7 percent of us are pathetic slaves to chemicals.

The common perception of this drug madness focuses on chemicals like PCP, cocaine, and heroin. But perhaps 80 to 85 percent of America's drug dependence problem involves one of the most addictive, and yet traditionally legal, drugs known to man: alcohol.

The "disease" status of drug addiction, and particularly alcoholism, is difficult to accept in part because so many of us use drugs with apparent impunity. Almost all of us drink alcohol, and most of us, statistics indicate, have at least dabbled in illegal drugs. Yet we control it. If Uncle Joe doesn't, we reason, the pitiful state he's in must have something to do with will power, or moral fiber. Recent research has made such an interpretation scientifically untenable, but our moral feeling about drug addiction embodies an ambivalence so deeply ingrained in our attitude and our society that it refuses to die.

Yet there can be no disagreement about the damage done to our social fabric by the 17.5 million Americans who are addicted to drugs and alcohol. They cause at least half the automobile accidents, account for more than half the crime, and contribute substantially to the phenomenon of sick-leave abuse—though the sick-leave problem may be a blessing in disguise. It might be better if they all stayed at home. Popular wisdom counsels the consumer to avoid, if at all possible, buying an automobile that was manufactured on a Monday.

Beyond the classic addictions, of course, there's the almost unmentionable matter of tobacco. Nicotine is one of the most addictive substances known to man, more addictive by far than heroin; nicotine addiction is not yet considered a mental illness, though estimates of its death toll, considering only lung cancer and heart disease, run as high as 500,000 a year.

And so it goes, one form of mental illness piled on another, inexorably adding up. One percent of us are schizophrenic and another 2 percent are schizoid. Six percent suffer from depression, 7 percent are addicted to drugs (not counting Camels, Winstons, and Carleton 100s), 8 percent suffer from anxiety disorders. . . .

Add them up, as scientists with the Alcohol, Drug Abuse and Mental Health Administration did in 1984, and you arrive at the inescapable conclusion that in any six-month period one out of every five Americans suffers a serious psychiatric episode.

But we are far from done.

The list so far includes only the classic conditions that, with the possible exceptions of alcoholism and nicotine addiction, are generally recognized as mental diseases. But research psychiatrists are in the process of discovering that another category of mental problem, once held quite separate from insanity, may not be so separate after all. We are talking now about personality disorders and criminality.

In one sense this perception reflects commonsense findings. If half of all automobile accidents are attributable to alcoholism, it shouldn't be surprising that half of all violent crimes are also committed by alcoholics. It is also common knowledge that addiction to so-called hard drugs supports an underworld prone to both violence and theft and thereby accounts for another significant percentage of lawless behavior. So there is a long-recognized overlap between mental illness and crime.

Most criminals are, nevertheless, adjudged sane—not only by the courts, but also in the minds of most citizens. But are they?

Whatever the law and cultural traditions may say about rapists, for instance, and however strong our urge to lock them up and throw away the key, many of us harbor an almost secret suspicion that rapists are not sane in any supportable sense of the word. The same can be said of mass murderers.

And what of the petty criminal who steals small items of little value and steals them so clumsily that he is caught, again and again, until he winds up doing hard time as an incorrigible recidivist? Is he sane? Are there truly differences between psychiatric madness and personality disorders, or have we separated the categories so that we won't have our sense of guilt and innocence complicated by our knowledge of mental illness?

As subsequent chapters will make clear, there are increasing indications that such questions are indeed quite valid, even insightful. Recent findings indicate that there are many categories of mental illness that manifest themselves in behaviors that traditionally have been called criminal but that, when pried open by the crowbar of science, look increasingly like insanity.

A significant number of violent criminals, for instance, are turning out to be the victims of a disease characterized by abnormal electrical discharges in the emotional layers of their brains. These discharges, and the associated violence, can in many cases be abated with the same class of drugs that are effective for epilepsy. Other research indicates that certain forms of criminality may be due to genetic influences, and still other forms may involve a disease akin to depression.

As a result, a steadily increasing number of psychiatrists are convinced that criminality, like alcoholism, will eventually come to be recognized as a cluster of specific mental illnesses. If they are correct, then the base of perceived madness in our society will expand still further.

After all, at any given moment half a million Americans are in prison. Since most criminals do not go to prison, this again represents but the tip of the iceberg. So to schizophrenia, depression, addiction, and the anxiety disorders we now add, at least tentatively, criminality.

But as we have compiled our roster of psychological pathologies we have delicately skirted what is arguably the twentieth century's most serious mental health problem.

We are talking now about a cluster of mental infirmities so pervasive, so common, so "normal" in modern life that they often escape our attention. Most of them do not even have names, and only those few of us who can afford a psychotherapist to relieve the pain ever think of calling them by the old name "neurosis."

We simply endure them without thinking, innocently assuming them to be harmless or if not harmless at least unavoidable, the same way citizens of the twelfth century once accepted contaminated water, body lice, rats, fleas, bedbugs, mosquitoes, and intestinal worms.

Today we suffer, with no more complaint, the constant manifestations of illogic, emotionality, and so-called human nature run amuck.

We see this pandemic, episodic madness all around us. We see it in the entrepreneur who labors to establish a business and then, having become successful, loses it all in a series of uncharacteristically stupid decisions. We see it in the executive who destroys his career by falling in love with his secretary. We see it in the husband who destroys his marriage by chasing women he doesn't really want to catch.

And, speaking of love, we see this everyday madness flicker too in the woman who marries an alcoholic, divorces him only to marry another alcoholic, whom she then divorces to marry still another. We see it in the woman who allows herself to be beaten, again and again, by a long series of sadistic husbands and lovers. And what of the men who beat her? Are they sane?

What of the person who lives beyond his means? Who speeds, yet refuses to wear seat belts? Who struggles with his boss for no reason? Who jogs, and then runs, until it dominates his life? Who talks too much? Who is pathologically shy? What of destructive jealousy, and avarice, and possessiveness, and impulsiveness, and compulsive manipulativeness . . . where lies the thin line between the frankly insane and the merely stupid?

Or, indeed, does such a distinction exist? And if it does not, then what do we have left of the concept of sanity? What about me, and thee?

So add the craziness up, according to your own perceptions, and draw your own line. Again, one of every 100 of us is schizophrenic, two more are schizoid, eight are phobic, seven are addicted, six are depressed, perhaps five are criminal. Perhaps another five are destructively irrational at any given moment. . . .

Add them up, beginning with the 1984 federal study and adding in all the factors they conservatively left out. When you are done you have a number, depending on your personal inclinations and prejudices, that at any moment encompasses up to a third of the population.

It is a number to stare at, a number to evoke memories of the all-too-human truth writ on the subway walls: the world, then, is to a large degree crazy.

2

A

DESPERATE

NEED

IT's easy to understand why we are so stubbornly reluctant to stare directly into the maw of the great craziness. Like death it is too awful, and too personal. We are all too aware it's there, why should we look at it? We must live each day as though we were immortal, even though we know otherwise; likewise we must, for the sake of whatever sanity we have, assume a certain constancy of mind.

Anyway, the great craziness isn't exactly something you can escape. Like death, it comes to us on its own, uninvited. Mental illness is so common that most of us, including me, have it in our immediate families.

We really don't have to be told what it's like to stand by helplessly, witnessing the terror of a husband or wife, or a parent or child, as the mind slowly disintegrates. We've seen it firsthand. We've seen how the victim, sinking further and further into the muck of insanity, tries desperately to understand what's happening to him and to fix blame, as humans must, somehow, on someone. . . .

Few of us have to be told what it's like to hold our hand out to a loved one or a friend . . . and be rewarded with a cannon blast of that mad blame.

And we know, in excruciating and intimate detail, of the burning shame that accompanies mental illness, isolating not only the primary victim but the family as well—and we know how depression or schizophrenia, sealed off, festers like a hidden sore. We know what happens to the children of a phobic or an alcoholic, or the husband of a depressive, or the father and mother of a schizophrenic, or the friend of a miser or a recluse.

We know that the measure of the great craziness is not a clinical description or a government agency's tabulations but individual tragedy, heart-rending tragedy, inchoate, unreasonable, inexplicable, unquenchable tragedy multiplied 250 million times.

And yet as the echoing numbers grow in our minds, they also become meaningless. On the scale of human comprehension, a thousand faceless suicides bear far less weight than one—if that one is your mother.

In this respect we are peculiar creatures, uniquely fitted for living side by side with the obvious and yet never perceiving it. We can count the apples in a basket or even a truck and produce an understandable number, but as human beings we totally lack the ability to sum up the pain contained behind the chain-link fences of a single mental hospital. Perhaps nature, in denying us this ability, has been kind.

Yet at the same time the great craziness does require some multiplication, some quantification of the aggregate of individual tragedy. We don't want to think about death, either, but we compile statistics on it and calculate the number of coffins that will be necessary in 1998. Likewise we must compute the need for mental hospital beds, quantify the future need for psychiatrists, and make the other arrangements for dealing with the unthinkable.

Our propensity is to hire experts and statisticians to sit in clean offices, far enough removed from the anguish to be able to think abstractly about it, to design methods of quantification. Naturally they seek to sum it all up in a way that is consistent with our society—a way that meshes with the fluctuations of the stock market, the unemployment rate, the national debt, and the outpourings of the Census Bureau. In short, they put a price on it.

In one sense that strategy itself defies reason. It is tragedy we're dealing with, not money. And yet the measure of dollars does give us a certain muted, computeresque sense of the magnitude of the thing.

One of the more comprehensive attempts to quantify the costs of mental illness was undertaken recently by the Research Triangle Institute in North Carolina. There, after several years of research, experts concluded that the classic mental illnesses, combined with drug addiction, cost the country $250 billion a year. That figure, a thousand dollars for each man, woman, and child in America, is roughly equal to the annual budget deficit.

Though the number is itself large enough to defy human comprehension, its importance can be seen in the anguished jockeying of congressmen and senators as they try in vain to cut that same amount out of the federal budget. Two hundred and fifty billion dollars worth of debt is a tidal wave of money, capable of swamping the economy of the most productive nation on earth.

And yet, to anyone who studies the problem, expert or casual observer, $250 billion is a gross and misleading underestimation of the problem. A breakdown illustrates why.

About $50 billion of the computed mental illness price tag goes for what statisticians call "direct core costs"—doctors, nurses, hospital rooms and drugs, disability payments, and lost employment. Roughly four times that figure, or $200 billion, is attributed to clearly documentable secondary costs, including social welfare programs aimed at the mentally ill, automobile crashes laid to alcoholism, and direct losses to the victims of crimes clearly attributable to drug abuse and mental illness.

The omissions are glaring.

Perhaps the most obvious one involves criminality. Criminality directly attributable to alcoholism, say, is included in the statistics. But the figures do not include the broader costs of criminality on the rationale that most crime is not committed by mental patients. However, as evidence accumulates that criminality is as legitimate a category of mental illness as, say, depression, those costs must also be factored in.

Americans suffer direct crime losses in the neighborhood of $25 billion a year. It costs billions more to catch criminals and process them through the court system. About $50 billion goes to pay for prison systems—and most criminals don't go to prison; they are dealt with by such means as probation programs. Such programs, while less expensive per individual client, cost more in aggregate than prisons.

But criminality aside, the numbers compiled for mental health and addiction are fundamentally conservative simply because they're skewed—dramatically skewed—in favor of the documentable. There is simply no way to estimate, or even put a value on, the broad economic impact of the great craziness.

There is obviously a monetary cost attributable to the secretary who shows up for work on Monday preoccupied with her husband's weekend drunkenness and, her mind elsewhere, forgets to give her boss a critical message from an important client. We all pay for her mistake, but how much?

And what sliding scale can pinpoint the economic damage done by a Detroit engineer who, racked by groundless jealousy of his wife, overestimates the efficiency of brakes that will ultimately appear in a quarter of a million automobiles?

And what is the cost, in economic terms, of a brilliant writer who might have produced revolutionary insights but who instead dies before his artistic maturity from an overdose of drugs?

The brutal fact is that even if you are in perfect mental health, and even in the wildly improbable event that your mother, father, spouse, and children all share your good fortune, you are nonetheless a victim. The great craziness is so pervasive, and so disruptive, that no one can escape.

You may meet the mentally ill person almost anywhere you go. You may meet him on the street, in the guise of a thug—or a policeman given to brutality. You may meet him in a hospital, where he is a brain surgeon or a pharmacist. If he is an alcoholic you may meet him, head on, on the highway.

Each time you write out a check for automobile insurance, a majority of the payment is earmarked to indemnify the victims of alcoholism and suicidal drivers. Health insurance payments are likewise dramatically inflated by illnesses like pancreatitis which, while physical, are direct results of mental illness; an even larger percentage of health payments goes to pay for the endless tests and attention lavished on patients whose fundamental complaint is not physical but mental.

A large chunk of our federal and local taxes is destined to support social welfare bureaucracies and law enforcement agencies whose primary responsibilities are not officially mental health—but which, on careful examination, turn out to be precisely that.

We pay, and pay dearly, each time we buy a product inflated by the effects of sick-leave abuse and hospitalization insurance—costs attributable, in the main, to mental illness.

But we have still not reached the bottom line. The bulk of our automobile insurance payments goes to the secondary victims of mental illness, and is duly calculated by the statisticians and added to the mental health bill. But insurance doesn't pay the cost in full. Rarely do insurance settlements adequately compensate the family for, say, a dead father—and nothing compensates the rest of us for the loss of that father's skill and knowledge that, had he not been broadsided by a drunk, would have been applied over the course of a full lifetime.

And what of the mind-shattering effects on the children of alcoholics, of depressives, and of schizophrenics? What of the children whose mentally ill fathers lead a life of crime with periodic and perhaps even long-term incarceration?

The economic costs of criminality, in addition to the obvious expenses both to the victims and the state, also include the economically disruptive costs of fear. They include the manu-facture, installation, and maintenance of burglar alarm systems and the wages of tens of thousands of security guards.

The impact of fear also includes the price of the thousands of handguns purchased each year for family protection—handguns that, statistics show, are more likely to kill a family member than an intruder and that, therefore, add another grim convolution to the impossible task of computing the costs of mental illness.

No discussion of the costs of crime is complete without an acknowledgment of the generalized climate of fear that slows down and sometimes even partially paralyzes our everyday lives. It's not even a totally rational situation: the cost of crime itself is magnified by the cost of our crime phobia. The effect of fear is again impossible to quantify, but it plays an undeniable role in our economic system.

Middle-class flight into the suburbs is at least partially at-tributable to fear of violence on the streets and in the schools. In New York City many of the commuters who choke the high-ways with their cars and fill the air with their exhaust twice a day might well prefer to commute by rail, were it not for their fear of being threatened and intimidated. Many citizens who stubbornly continue to live in the city are effectively prisoners in their own homes after sunset, so great is their fear of the streets.

Although the perception of crime focuses largely on urban environment, crime itself does not; as statistics show, suburban and rural crime is a real and growing problem. Burglar alarm companies do a booming business on the city fringes, as do gun shops and firing ranges that capitalize on such fear. And it appears as though the boom in vacation property, which promised to add so much to the rural economy in the 1960s and early 1970s, has been effectively squelched by the rise in off-season burglary and vandalism; thanks to the predation of a small minority of the rural population, second homes have become virtually uninsurable over the past decade.

And what, we ask ourselves, was the real cost of the bullet a young schizophrenic fired into President Reagan's chest? What was the cost, per hour, of having the world's most powerful political figure out of action?

And so it goes, on and on and on and on and on. There aren't enough prisons, there aren't enough policemen, there aren't enough psychiatrists, there aren't enough mental institutions, there aren't enough halfway houses, enough understanding, enough emotional energy . . . it saps us, individually and collectively, and still there isn't enough, there isn't enough, there isn't enough.

And still we are only talking money, only dollars and cents. We are only talking the accountants' language, devoid of human feeling, a measure that compares to mental illness the way sex compares to love. The real issue cuts deeper, into the heart.

The real issue is contained in the ancient fear of a young wife when her husband comes home late again, drunk again, and abusive. The real issue is contained in the tears of a family around the coffin of a victim of what we so euphemistically call an "accident." The real issue is in the hopelessness of a mother who watches a child sink deeper and deeper into the abyss of schizophrenia. The real issue is these things, all these things, multiplied that incomprehensible but nonetheless brutally real 250 million times.

As we consider the depth and breadth of the craziness in our society we finally come to see mental illness for what it is: a tumor. It's a tumor with tentacles that extend into every facet of our lives and economies. Its costs, whatever they are, are by orders of magnitude greater than has ever been officially estimated.

It is a terrifying and deadening notion. We respond, or at least we always have responded, by turning our backs on it, by telling ourselves that it has nothing to do with us or if it does it's better not thought about . . . and, anyway, hasn't it always been so? Haven't the insane always been with us, since the memory of man runs not to the contrary?

The superficial answer is yes but the deep answer, the real

answer . . . the answer that may impinge on our very survival . . . is no.

Today is different.

It's the nature of modern society to magnify the significance of otherwise minor mental aberrations. Hundreds or even thousands of lives may depend on the clarity of mind of an air controller. An error of omission committed by an anxiety-ridden computer designer in California will replicate itself, through the marvels of mass production, a quarter of a million times. Captains of nuclear submarines are carefully screened for latent seeds of madness, but, we are reminded, psychological tests are far from perfect.

Further, as our society becomes more interdependent, more specialized, and more technological, we become more vulnerable to the madness in our midst. In the day of the horse and buggy, an alcoholic could fall asleep and old Maggie would get him home just fine, thank you. Today the homebound drunk drives a two-ton, high-performance automobile or even a thirty-ton eighteen-wheeled steel rig. A paranoid schizophrenic with a gun always posed a danger to those around him, but when he forces himself into the cockpit of a jumbo jet that danger is awesome.

The assassination of a chief of state, an act that in many minds automotically marks the perpetrator as insane, was once a relatively minor political inconvenience. In a more leisurely era, others had time to pick up the reins of government and to close ranks before the impact was felt. In a more leisurely era, there were no MXs or missile submarines.

But the 1981 shooting of Ronald Reagan was immediately followed by an apparent confusion as to exactly whose finger was on the button—was it Secretary of State Alexander Haig, at the White House, or Vice-President George Bush somewhere on an Air Force airplane, or . . . or who? In the modern era, those questions, whether real or perceived, echo resoundingly in a geopolitical situation rife with potential for international tragedy.

Terrorism capitalizes on precisely this growing vulnerability to the well-calculated act of madness. Terrorist groups reportedly have no trouble recruiting mentally ill young people, primarily schizophrenics, for suicidal missions. American foreign policy in Lebanon was blunted and ultimately thwarted by madmen who willingly drove truckloads of explosives into the portals of embassies and barracks. What does that bode for the day, which analysts tell us is rapidly approaching, when a miniaturized nuclear weapon can be carried, unobtrusively, in a suitcase?

We of the modern world are simply more vulnerable to madness. And to make matters even worse, some experts believe there is evidence that the incidence of madness is itself beginning to increase. When adjustments are made for age and other factors, new cases of schizophrenia, depression, anxiety disorders, addiction, and criminality appear to be growing faster than the population.

The reason for this trend is not clear, but most guesses focus on a broad rise in levels of stress that accompany the development of our postindustrial society. Implicit in this view is the idea, repeatedly documented, that while some of us are emotionally stronger than others, none of us is immune to madness. Subjected to enough stress, each of our psyches, depending on our individual vulnerabilities, will collapse into schizophrenia, depression, anxiety, or criminality.

If a rising level of stress is the key to the increase in madness, there are some grim implications. Stress can be in part a function of crowding, lack of control over one's destiny and similar factors, *but it is also increased by precisely the social distortions caused by rising rates of mental illness.*

As a majority of us know all too well from firsthand experience, the mental deterioration of a family member has a pressure-cooker effect on the family as a whole. The psychological problems of a child can add stress to the lives of its parents, who are therefore more likely to pitch into fullblown schizophrenia, depression, or alcoholism themselves. The child's delinquency, in turn, will be dramatically increased by the appearance of mental illness in the parents—and the child's delinquency will, as the screw turns again, further increase the stress on the parents. Mental illness also leads to financial instability in the family unit and that, too, is a prescription for further emotional damage.

Similarly, neighborhood crime increases stress among the non-criminal residents of that neighborhood and that, in turn, increases the alcohol and drug consumption, which, in starkly circular fashion, raises the odds that the psychologically weaker members of the community will crack.

Ironically, in modern times the situation has become further complicated by a dawning realization that the insane, the addicted, and the criminal are victims as well as victimizers. They are human beings like ourselves and there, but for the grace of God, go we. This has led to the enlightened notion that our own humanity if not theirs demands that we provide them with decent care and treatment.

As a result, the insane and the criminal, once written off and relegated to remote insane asylums and pigsty prisons, are now perceived as having rights. A schizophrenic is entitled to food, to such treatment as is available, and to a roof that doesn't leak. A criminal is entitled to just treatment, to medical care, and a small cell of his or her own. In theory at least, the children of criminals and madmen are also entitled to economic benefits sufficient to raise them above the status of animals.

These advances, as minimal as they may be in practice, conspire to make the problem of mental illness more expensive and, as a result, more acute. The upgrading of mental institutions and prisons must ultimately have a deleterious effect on the economy, which, in turn, adds stress to those who produce—and immeasurably increases the odds that they, too, will succumb to madness and join the growing army of social dependents.

As we ponder the broad effects of mental illness, and consider its potential for malignant growth, and read the daily newspapers, we remember that the society we now enjoy is unlike any other in history.

Never before has any society been so closely interlinked, so intricately controlled, so sophisticated in all ways as our own. And never before has the human animal been subject to such continual stress.

Our world is, in short, an experiment.

Can it be sustained? Or as the stress levels continue to rise, will we reach a critical point at which mental illness, in all of its forms, begins to feed on itself, creating still more madness, and that in turn creating more madness yet, and then more and more and more, in a self-fueling chain reaction destined to bring down the whole house of cards? And if so, is that critical point dead ahead? Or have we already reached it?

Those are questions that hang in the mind, demanding answers—and once they are asked, and examined, the rules change.

It is no longer possible for us to ignore mental illness, as we have done in the past. We can no longer afford to close our eyes, to look the other way, to assume it will only happen to the other guy. No longer can we tolerate the moralistic, political, and religious interpretations of insanity that have allowed us to discount the diseases of the mind and their effect on our society. No longer can we afford to suppress the dark suspicion that there is a craziness in the land. There is.

And, by the same token, we can no longer afford to make the practice of psychiatry the butt of our jokes. By all indications there is a plague on our society, and if our lack of support results in those psychiatrists failing in their efforts to stop it, our children's children may have precious little to laugh about.

In truth, of course, one of the reasons we have doggedly refused to face the mental health problem is that to do so seemed futile—nothing much could be done, anyway, aside from worrying about it and carrying leftovers and canned goods to bedlam at Christmastime.

Since the days of Sigmund Freud the practice of psychiatry has been more art than science. Surrounded by an aura of witchcraft, proceeding on impression and hunch, often ineffective, it was the bumbling and sometimes humorous stepchild of modern science. If we laughed, perhaps it was because we had no alternative.

But in the past ten years, while we sniggered over couch jokes and scoffed at the notion that the mind might be understandable, there has incubated a strange new science: a science I call molecular psychology.*

The basis of this new discipline is the perception that human thought, emotion, and behavior result from the interplay of molecules across the surface of brain cells. The corollary from which the science grows is that mental processes are therefore quantifiable in chemical terms.

For a decade and more, molecular psychologists, in pursuit of the molecular basis of behavior, worked quietly in the laboratory, dissecting the brains of mice and men, communicating primarily in highly technical papers published in unfamiliar journals. As a result, only fragmentary accounts of their odyssey have been published in the popular press; for the most part, their discoveries have been made and their theories shaped behind a cloak of obscurity reminiscent of the Einsteinian revolution in the 1920s and 1930s.

The results promise to be even more portentous. The new sci-

---

* Though most scientists approve of the way I've christened their discipline, several have asked me to make a specific distinction between "molecular psychology," as a legitimate frontier science, and "orthomolecular psychiatry." The latter is a crank pseudopsychiatry stressing the discredited but still much touted role of vitamins and diet in mental illness. Quackery is fed by hopelessness, so this and other forms of psychiatric quackery will probably vanish as legitimate cures and treatments become available.

I should also note here that while I once tried to shift between "molecular psychology" and "molecular psychiatry" to conform to the old distinction between psychology and psychiatry, I no longer do so.

While the practitioners of mental medicine are still divided into those two warring camps, the science upon which they base their therapies is rapidly unifying. As a result of the breakthroughs described in this book, the distinctions between psychology and psychiatry are dwindling both in number and in importance. As a result, I found that my attempts to distinguish molecular psychology from molecular psychiatry were often confusing and sometimes downright silly. I have therefore (and with no offense meant to psychiatrists) arbitrarily chosen the phrase "molecular psychology" throughout the book.

ence, though little more than a decade old, has proved astonishingly productive. Already researchers have identified many of the interlocking molecules that produce human thought and emotion, and others are being discovered almost daily. Already there are scanners that can trace the flickering web of personality as it dances through the brain. In the near future experts may map out the terrain of what we once were pleased to call the human soul.

The objective of this new science, of course, is to cure the classic forms of madness, dramatically decreasing human suffering and sparking an incidental rise in productivity. This is the stated goal, but the potential of molecular psychology extends far beyond the confines of classical psychiatry.

Many molecular psychologists believe they may soon have the ability to untangle the ancient enigma of violence and criminality. Others believe that molecular psychology, when combined with new discoveries in anthropology, may lead as well to the solution of the problems of "normal" craziness, of broken marriages and adolescent emotionality.

Further, there is the very real promise that current technology will lead to the development of drugs capable of expanding the workings of the normal mind, enhancing memory, heightening creativity, and perhaps, one day, even increasing intelligence. Ahead lies an era of psychic engineering.

But this revolutionary science holds a promise even more important than the cure of mental illness, even more useful than smart pills, memory enhancers, or love potions. It may solve the most ancient and enduring enigma of all and lay out for us, to understand and appreciate, the fundamental truths about who we are and why we are that way.

3

MOTHS
TO
A
FLAME

O F all the primary emotions, curiosity is the one that is the most . . . well, curious. Since it's not notably present in lizards or birds, it apparently evolved along with the mammalian brain, which is to say the brain most capable of learning. Curiosity is in effect nature's schoolmarm, compelling animals to try this or that new thing, and to stick their noses into various places where they might or might not belong, collecting knowledge that might or might not be useful in the future.

The schoolmarm of course is a pretty tough lady, teaching as she does from the syllabus of hard knocks, and much has been made of curiosity's potential for causing trouble. It was curiosity, or so it's said, that killed the cat. But the likelihood is much greater that it killed not the cat but the kitten—the emotion, in cats, dogs, rats, spider monkeys, and almost any other mammalian species you can name, is principally confined to the juvenile. Its risky ways are somehow replaced or suppressed by the changes in the brain that accompany sexual maturity.

It is only in the human that the compelling *craving to know* persists into adulthood, to be linked with the sexual drive and capsulized in such powerful and frightening myths as that of Pandora and her box—or to be converted to the cold, double-edged sword of science.

But even in the human species, curiosity burns especially bright in the young. I, for instance, had traveled the tree-lined path along the power line corridor many times that winter and had somehow failed to notice the huge cocoon in the maple tree. But Cathy, my youngest daughter, saw it the first time I took her along.

The cocoon hung, just out of reach, from the branch of a bare tree. Intrigued, I pulled the branch down with a stick and, standing on tiptoes, plucked it free so we could examine it.

It was a full three inches long, and it all but covered her small hand. She stared at it, fascinated.

What was it? I didn't know, but I did know how to find out. So we carried the cocoon home and looked around for a container to put it in. It had to be large, I explained to the children, to give whatever was inside the cocoon room to unfold its wings when it emerged.

We settled on an oversized peanut butter jar, the kind that holds enough to satisfy two growing daughters for weeks. That, I was certain, would adequately contain any moth or butterfly in existence. We poked holes in the lid and set the jar on the back porch.

The winter passed. Christmas came and went. There were snowmen to build. Groundhog day. School. Life went on and, as it did, the cocoon lay motionless in the bottle, doing nothing; it was easy to forget, and so we forgot it.

Then one warm spring day there was a shriek from the porch that brought us all running. Cathy, the source of the shriek, was staring wide-eyed at the jar. There, inside, was a huge red, brown, and black moth.

Our joy was dampened, though, by the fact that the jar, while large, had not been quite large enough. The moth hadn't been able to completely spread its wings to dry and as a result their tips were bent and wrinkled.

Trying to make the best of a bad situation, I explained that the moth wouldn't have lived very long anyway. Moths don't have mouths, you see, so they can't eat. They breed, lay their eggs, and then die.

But the children, staring at the crumpled wings, didn't buy my logic. A beautiful thing had been deformed by our ignorance. There were tears in their eyes.

In an attempt to turn their thoughts away from the damaged wings, as well as to satisfy my own curiosity, I took down a field guide to moths and butterflies, and together we looked it up. The exquisite thing in the jar, the book told us, was a cecropia moth. It was a member of the family of giant silkworm moths, and one of the largest moths on earth.

The children seemed interested in this information, but they still stared, sadly, at the moth's damaged wings.

Maybe, I said wishfully . . . maybe it could fly anyway. So we took it outside and tossed it gently into the air. It fluttered valiantly, but sank softly to the lawn. I picked it up and placed it on the trunk of a tree in the back yard. There it remained, throughout the day.

Then that evening, as I was about to call the children inside for the night, Cathy came running into the house with the news that our moth had company.

Sure enough, there were now two moths on the branch. The newcomer was different from our moth, though, in that it sported two huge, bushy antennae. It was a male, and our moth was a female. Love, or what passes for love in an insect, had found a way.

How had one moth found the other? the girls wanted to know.

Even at their ages, they understood that there couldn't be very many cecropia moths in our neighborhood, and that it was unlikely that one would find the other by accident. That piqued their curiosity.

The trick, I explained, had to do with a chemical called a pheromone. It was sort of like a perfume; the female released it, and it attracted the male.

That satisfied the children, but not their father. After they went to bed, I wondered how the male detected the pheromone in what must be vanishingly small quantities—too small, certainly, to smell. How, considering the limited brainpower of a moth, did it know which way to fly?

In the human species curiosity mellows some with age, experience, and the growing understanding of mortality. I no longer feel compelled to stick my hand into dark holes to see what's there, and I haven't climbed an active volcano for years.

But once an enigma lodges in my mind, it clings with a tenacity it never used to have, and as the weeks passed I found myself wondering about this strange ability of moths. The question nagged at me mercilessly until one day, in the course of my science writer's routine, I happened to find myself in a conversation with a University of Maryland entomologist. He got the third degree.

For openers he assured me that the explanation I had given the girls was for the most part correct—except, perhaps, for the comparison of pheromone with perfume. Strictly speaking, pheromones don't have a smell. For one thing, they exist in quantities too minute to add up to anything resembling an odor. And even if they did, moths have no noses.

I also learned that scientists were as fascinated as children with the giant silkworm moths—a bit of intelligence that reveals something not about moths but about humans, and their preference for things of beauty even in ostensibly intellectual undertakings. In any event, the big moths like the one we hatched are among the best understood of any insect species.

This knowledge was accumulated painfully over the decades

by basic scientists laboring in what seemed to most of us, at the time, to be a particularly obscure branch of science. Yet the information they collected guides us into a labyrinth that opens, if we follow it far enough, through a hidden trap door and into the psychological basement of human history.

To understand the significance of what the scientists found, we must first follow them down the long echoing staircase of scale. We must let our imaginations shrink, leaving the familiar world of humans, dogs, cats, elephants, and gnats in favor of things almost infinitely smaller.

As we pass from the kingdom of the naked eye and into that of the light microscope, animals break up into individual cells. We can't see animals through the microscope, any more than we can see a forest from the middle of it.

The critters that populate the world we now see are skin cells and muscle cells and liver cells—cells of the bowel, of the pancreas, of the blood, of the spleen, of the reproductive organs, and of the brain. Each cell is a living entity with a separate life and a set of imperatives different from our own, yet together they make up the community of organ and organism.

And still we descend, now passing through the resolution of the light microscope and into that of the electron microscope. Now, as we settle into an expanding landscape, the cells themselves can be seen to be composed of many organs—or, to be scientifically correct, "organelles."

Still we descend, down, down, down beyond even the resolution of the electron microscope.

As we proceed, the organelles break up into their component parts until finally these unnamed parts break up into structures that themselves come apart as we descend, down, down, down, until finally we find ourselves in the mechanistic realm of the living molecule.

The "life molecules" themselves aren't really living, of course. But they are often called that, because they are at least *biological*

43

—and at this scale, that gives the human mind something to cling to.

These molecules are as small as the galaxies are large, and on the great scale of things they represent the last, tiniest frontier of biology. One step further down the staircase and they break up into their component atoms, and, in the process, the laws of nature dictate a surrealistic shift.

The individual atoms of the molecules that compose the genetic acids, for instance, bear no more significance for the messages they carry than do the individual letters of the words on this page.

The atoms of the life molecules are nothing special; they are interchangeable with the atoms in rocks or fire or even the solar wind. A carbon atom in a protein would serve as well in the crystalline matrix of a diamond. Beneath the molecular level, biology drops away and there is only physics.

Since our interest here is in moths, not mesons, we halt our descent at the molecular level. We stop, catch our breath, and look around at this strange and almost mythical world, the ultimate limit of biology, the inner edge of life, a frontier only recently opened.

Until the past decade, we could have traveled here only in our imagination, on the magic carpet of theory and speculation. But we come today not as dreamers but as tourists: science has blazed the path for us.

So we stand here now, and, if we have a soul at all, we gawk. If anywhere in the universe there is ground that can be considered sacred, this is it. For it's here, at the shimmering edge of physics, where life began.

It happened when the world was young and hot and shrouded with methane. Then, for reasons that are only vaguely understood, under circumstances that lend themselves more to speculation than knowledge, certain atoms of carbon, phosphorus, oxygen, and hydrogen combined to form the first self-replicating molecules.

In time those molecules evolved into different shapes and sizes that, interacting like so many magnetic Tinkertoys, snapped together to form the membranes and the organelles of cells that, themselves evolving, would eventually give rise to the organs that would form the creatures who build houses, write books, direct traffic, design computers, run for president, and wonder ceaselessly about enigmatic things like the love lives of moths.

And so it is that now, four billion years later, we (and our guides, the bioscientists) encounter the ultimate truth about ourselves. If we are to truly understand who we are and what we are about we must comprehend, first, the molecule and its world. Here, and only here, can we see the pheromone of the cecropia moth for what it truly is.

It is a molecule that, like other molecules, is composed of atoms. It has a certain specific shape and, with the shape, characteristic magnetic properties. Certain parts of its surface carry a positive charge, and other areas are negatively charged. It also happens to be the sort of molecule that vaporizes easily into the air. This quality of being "volatile" enables it to be carried on the wind.

The other defining characteristic of the cecropia pheromone is that all the molecules are precisely identical. The pheromone molecules produced by each cecropia moth are exactly like those produced by every other cecropia moth. At the same time they are different, both in shape and in magnetic properties, from those produced by other moth species. They are noticeably different even from the pheromones produced by the cecropia moth's first cousin, the green luna moth.

The reason for the species specificity of the pheromone molecule is that they are in effect magnetic keys—keys to the metaphorical heart of the male. And the metaphorical heart of the male moth, like that of the human, beats of course not in the breast but the brain.

If the pheromone is a key, then, in what lock does it fit? To find that out, we shift our attention from the female to the male. In doing so we take a small detour, ascending back up the staircase of scale to the level of the light microscope.

Like the much larger and more complex brain of man, the nervous system of the moth is based on gray cells called neurons.

In fact, the moth neurons, at least on cursory examination under the light microscope, are chillingly similar to the ones found in the human brain.

Biology being what it is, of course, a neuron isn't a neuron isn't a neuron. It, like other cell types, is best thought of as a theme with many variations in size and shape and function, even in the limited brain of a moth.

There are certain identifying features, though. For one thing, the neuron almost always has an axon, a tail-like structure that is the biological equivalent of an electrical cord. The axon may extend only a few centimeters or it may stretch all the way across the brain (a vast distance on this scale). Wherever it travels, it ultimately splits into many branches—each of which ends in a barnaclelike "bouton" that lays up against the surface of a sister neuron.

Electrical charges generated in the cell body are transmitted down this tail at a rate of one to sixty pulses per second, depending on how "excited" the cell is. Scientists can monitor individual cells in the moth brain by inserting microscopic electrodes into them. The aggregate of millions of pulses ultimately gives rise to the brain's overall electromagnetic aura and produces the "brain waves" captured by the squiggling pens of the electroencephalograph, or EEG machine.

The fundamental purpose of this electrical activity has been broadly obvious for many decades. The neuron's function involves producing electrical charges, which it fires off to other cells through its axon. It, in turn, is the recipient of similar messages from other cells all over the brain. Simply put, the purpose of brain cells is to excite one another.

So intricately interwired is the brain, even the brain of the moth, that the average neuron isn't visible in its natural state. It's completely covered by the barnaclelike boutons of other cells. The connections are so dense, in fact, that many neurons have evolved a set of treelike antlers, called dendrites, to increase the area available for bouton contact.

All of this is true for man as well as moth, but in the male moth the dendrites in one of the brain's sexual centers have under-gone a dramatic evolutionary change. Instead of remaining micro-scopic they grow wildly, madly, until they protrude through the head and into the outer world, where they form a latticework filagree of tissue exposed to the raw environment. This filigree, the antenna, is nothing less than a dendritic extension of the brain itself. Its sole purpose is the detection of pheromone molecules.

To understand how it does this, we end our detour and descend, once again, to the level of the molecule.

Here we can see that the substance of the cells, including those that produce the antennae, is composed of interlinked molecules: big ones, little ones, medium-sized ones, proteins, acids, fats—the same general mishmash, with some minor varia-tions, as goes into the building of all cells.

Some of these molecules compose the machinery of the mito-chondrion, where chemical energy is produced. Molecules of another shape change that energy, battery fashion, into electrical charges. Others form the cell's skeleton. Still other molecules, sticking together, compose the membrane that shields all the others from the hostile outside world.

Floating in that surface membrane, like a lily pad on the surface of a pond, is a complex molecule about which biologists have long theorized, the thing that embodies the true meaning of moth love.

It is called a receptor, and insofar as one molecule has meaning without its fellows, it is perhaps the most important gizmo in all of biology. If there is magic in the mind, if there is a ghost in the machine, if there is philosophy in physiology, if there is poetry in the act of love, it is to be found here.

The typical receptor is a large molecule, consisting of hundreds of thousands of atoms. The exposed section, the "lily pad," floats on the surface of the cell membrane, while the "roots" extend deep into the cell. There, by means of various molecular linkages reminiscent of Rube Goldberg cartoons, they are tied to the inner workings of the cell. Most often they are linked to the cell's metabolic throttle.

47

The exposed end of the receptor, the lily pad, is in truth not so much a pad as a cup. In the case of the cecropia moth's antennae, the cup is the mirror image (both in geometry and in magnetic properties) of the pheromone molecule. The pheromone of the female cecropia moth fits it perfectly; no other molecule fits at all.

The final critical aspect of the receptor is that it is spring-loaded. When a pheromone molecule settles into it, it suddenly and forcefully changes shape. Inside the cell, the roots move. The movement triggers a reconformation in another Tinkertoy molecule, which in turn disturbs another, which in turn disturbs still another. The reaction travels, domino fashion, down the antenna until it enters the head and reaches the cell body deep in the moth's brain.

Suddenly, spurred by the change, the cell's metabolic rate increases. More electrical charges race down the axons, exciting other cells. Then they, too, begin to fire more rapidly.

Milliseconds after the pheromone molecule settles into the receptor cup on the cell's antenna, the reaction spreads into the network of cells that control the moth's mating behavior. In seconds these cells, quiescent throughout the insect's previous life, are embroiled in an ecstasy of electrical excitement. In their excitement, they override other brain centers, exerting control throughout the entire nervous system, taking absolute command of the moth.

The moth, of course, knows nothing of this reaction that boils up from the molecular level; it lacks the equipment to be aware of anything.

But awareness is not necessary. It doesn't need to know that, in its random fluttering, its antennae have snared a messenger molecule from a potential lady love. All it needs to do is respond. And respond it does.

As the awakened sexual behavior center takes over the moth's navigation cells, the fluttering undergoes a change. Previously random, it changes now into a purposeful search pattern, sifting the breeze to find other pheromone molecules. As it does, the sexual behavior center in the brain becomes ever more excited. The search pattern becomes yet more distinct, moving the creature upwind . . . where it finds still more pheromone molecules.

In some primitive sense, not knowing what it wants but wanting it nonetheless, wanting it with all the intensity that his tiny brain can muster, the moth craves more pheromone molecules, yearns for them, aches for them. It wants more, and more, and more, and more.

As he flies upwind, seeking a greater and greater density of pheromone molecules, his course carries him up the gradient of pheromone until, finally, he finds himself—wonder of wonders—in the intoxicating presence of a female.

Then, prompted by visual patterns and perhaps other pheromones that are active only in higher densities, more explicit urges take over and the mating ritual begins.

Cause, effect, and reproduction. From Tinkertoy molecule, back up the long staircase to the realm of the familiar, to cocoons and peanut butter jars, to the world of wide-eyed human children and the curiosity of scientists.

The tale of the pheromone and its receptor is rich with its many levels, laced with variations and implications . . . yet elegantly straightforward. It would be easy to forget that it took a hundred years and more to puzzle out, and that in the process it consumed the careers and lives of hundreds and even thousands of some of the most brilliant and above all curious men and women to ever to become ensnared by the mystery of biology.

But their effort was well spent for, at the end of the technical maze, the story itself becomes a key—a key as magic as the pheromone, a key that changes the shape of the universe as we perceive it and unlocks that trap door I promised you earlier.

It springs open, and we step through into one of the most sorry, sordid, and bizarre themes in all of human history.

There is, as it turns out, at least one chemical that attracts humans as powerfully as the pheromone attracts the moth.

In its variations it is called opium, morphine, or heroin.

4

THE
CURE
FOR
EVERYTHING

THE sweet principle of opium was known by witch doctors at the dawn of Western civilization: it cured whatever ailed you. If gout had swollen your foot, if you had diarrhea, if you were tortured by kidney or gallstones, if your head throbbed, if your bones ached, if your tooth hurt—why, the pollen of the magic poppy was just what you needed. As the Renaissance physician Paracelsus so succinctly put it, opium dissolved disease the way fire dissolved snow.

Opium even cured the ailments of the spirit. If what ailed you was lost love, or depression, or malaise, or a lack of opportunity, or a low social status, or even just boredom . . . opium was the stuff to fix you up. The stuff was so good, in fact, so incredibly, wonderfully, dazzlingly effective that *it even cured you if there was nothing wrong at all.*

There was just one peculiar side effect. As it felt bad to be sick, so it felt equally good to be cured. Opium made you feel so good that you wanted to go on feeling that way. On and on and on and on.

But if you did, a strange paradox sometimes occurred. You lost your appetite and grew thin. You lost interest in your work, your mate, your children—even, in a peculiar way, in yourself. All you were interested in was being cured, and cured some more, and cured some more, and some more, and more, and more, and more, until the cure metamorphosed into something else and you got so well you died.

That was indeed a strange thing, all the more puzzling because it didn't happen all the time—just occasionally. As a rule, the more opium that was prescribed, the more likely the patient was to become addicted, but that was just a rule of thumb. Some patients could use a lot of opium, then walk away from it. Others took one small dose and BAM, they were goners. It was a lot like alcohol, that way, except it was more dramatic.

For some millennia the magic cure, and its terrible single side effect, was common knowledge among physicians and other casters of spells. But it was in China that the ultimate danger was driven home in such dramatic form that the whole world could see.

The story varies, depending on whose account you read. But the Chinese apparently got their first sweet whiff of opium from Arabian traders toward the end of what the Europeans would one day call the Middle Ages.

The Arabians stood on the docks of Shanghai, Foochow, and Tientsin and extolled the virtues of their wares. It made you strong, smart, virile, well—whatever you wanted, this was the stuff. The Chinese crowded around and peered at the powder. It looked innocuous enough. A few tried it. It was good, they reported . . . really, *really* good. A few more tried it. Merchants inquired about wholesale prices. Slowly at first, then with increasing speed, a trade developed.

The trade grew some over the centuries, but the growth wasn't dramatic. The Arabians, for all their strengths, lacked genius in the field of marketing. Their successors, the British, did not.

The British knew a good thing when they saw it and set about in logical fashion to put their insight to work. First they sought exclusive rights to Indian opium, and, once that had been gained, they took over the trade and put it on a solid commercial footing. In the process the agents of the crown became the world's first large-scale drug pushers.

Chinese officials, always suspicious about the activities of the foreign devils, soon became specifically alarmed by the growing popularity of opium. They could see—who couldn't?—that there was something about opium that enslaved people without the necessity for chains. Many customers of the British trade gradually lost their will and ambition, becoming worthless as laborers and vassals. So in 1729, though only a small percentage of the population was addicted so far, the authorities issued an edict banning the stuff.

The British East India Company, resourceful as always, responded by establishing its own smuggling operation—and the confirmed opium smokers kept right on smoking the stuff. But the signs came down from in front of the opium dens and, inside, the prices went up. For a while the alarming growth in addiction seemed to slacken.

The British, however, were superb merchants. They already had their foot in the door, and, best of all, they had the advantage of a product that, once sampled, tended to sell itself even better than rum. So, faced with the disadvantage of an official ban, they tried harder. After an initial pause, a few more opium dens opened, and then a few more, and then a few more.

So it was for a century. Chinese rulers, disorganized and impotent against the British Empire, watched in horror and disgust as the problem grew like a cancer. Finally in 1820, in a desperate and almost convulsive move, the Chinese authorities issued an order that prohibited any vessel containing opium from entering the Canton River. Opium shipments, financed by British merchants, were seized and destroyed.

A century and a half later the same tactic would be tried by the American government, with the same effect. The price went up. More shipments were seized and destroyed, increasing the need for bribery and stealth and further corrupting drug officials. Still, addiction in China grew. The Chinese enforcement officers put on more heat. Finally in 1839 the British struck back militarily.

The war was short and, from the point of view of the British, gratifying. The spoils included the island of Hong Kong, a whopping reparations settlement calculated to reimburse the smugglers for their lost opium, and unlimited trading rights. Within a few decades, one-quarter of the citizens of China would be prisoners of the poppy.

From the American point of view, the Chinese affection for opium was just the sort of repulsive behavior one might expect from heathens. It was first and foremost a Chinese problem, separated from American life by the Pacific Ocean. Few Americans gave much thought to it at all until Chinese laborers, imported to work on the railroads, started opening opium dens in San Francisco—and even then, in the view of social critics of the time, opium addiction remained largely confined to the Chinese.

But the brutal truth was that by the mid-1800s America had spawned a significant opium problem of its own.

The American addict, like the Chinese opium smoker, was the victim of commerce and profit—but the American culture wrought the gray dragon in a different form. A quarter of a million Americans, typically upstanding citizens who looked with disdain on the despicable Chinese addicts, got their daily fix from the fathomless elixir in the unlabeled patent medicine bottle. Addiction to laudanum was so common that it was considered a minor weakness, like cigarette smoking in the 1950s and 1960s.

As China was bowing to the power of British opium and

America was learning to like Dr. Smith's Backache Cure, biological scientists in the Western world had entered the golden age of analysis and purification. Every interesting substance known to science was being studied to ascertain its active ingredient, and the magic extract of the opium poppy was high on the list of interesting substances.

The first breakthrough in opium science came in the early 1800s when Friedrich Sertürner, a German chemist, isolated from opium an alkaloid that did everything opium did—only better. He named the extract morphine.

Physicians, carrying on Sertürner's experiments, discovered that morphine could be injected directly into the muscle and that, administered in that fashion, it was a much more powerful pain reliever than opium taken orally. This discovery came in time for injections of morphine to be widely used during the Civil War.

The immediate result was a merciful release from pain, unknown in previous wars. The long-term result was that thousands of men returned home from the war carrying the invisible scars of addiction. In time they introduced their friends to the habit, and their numbers grew.

Eventually morphine addiction came to be known as "the soldier's disease." The use of the word *disease* was a euphemism, though, to be used around children when referring to Uncle Bob. Almost nobody believed it was a disease. Clearly, it was a moral weakness.

The risk of addiction had always troubled physicians who used opium, and it wasn't long before it became obvious that morphine addiction posed an even worse danger. For one thing, more people seemed susceptible to morphine addiction. For another, the addiction, once it took hold, seemed to be infinitely stronger. At the same time morphine, in its guise as a painkiller, was one of the most humane drugs ever developed. How could a physician withhold it?

To chemists, the solution was obvious. What was needed was a compound that was as potent as morphine but not nearly so addictive. So medicinal chemists began tinkering with the morphine molecule, adding a few atoms, taking a few away, changing a few around, seeking a nonaddictive painkiller.

The eventual result, produced by the Bayer laboratories, was a morphinelike compound with the name "diacetylmorphine." By all reports diacetylmorphine was as good a painkiller as morphine and yet, unlike morphine and opium, it was not addictive.

Bayer marketing experts, in preparing to advertise the breakthrough analgesic, knew that a name like diacetylmorphine would never fly. They needed something catchier, something easier to remember. The publicists went to work. So it was that the nonaddictive painkiller made its commercial debut in 1898 under the trade name "Heroin."

On the other side of the world, in the meantime, the merchants of England had achieved such success that their opium was threatening to anesthetize the entire Chinese culture. Slowly at first, and then with gathering speed, humanitarians of all nationalities began to express their revulsion.

Embarrassed by the unanimity of opinion against them, the British tried to backpedal, but the egg of addiction is far easier to break than to unbreak. The market for opium was tenacious and demanding and, when the British swore off the opium trade . . . nothing happened. The smugglers they had once financed simply went into business for themselves.

The Royal Navy, which had conquered the Orient for the opium trade, was now assigned to interdict the smugglers. But in this it failed miserably.

In the United States, the moral outcry against the opium trade in China led to the horrified discovery that the stuff was also in widespread—and legal—use in American patent medicines. The result was a series of congressional actions, most notably the passage of the Harrison Narcotic Act of 1914. The act itself was rather weak, but in subsequent decades it would be the basis of court interpretations and regulations that would require the listing of ingredients on patent medicine labels.

As this happened something occurred that, at the time, seemed like a testimony to America's moral fiber—but that, half a century hence, would have scientists scratching their heads. The strange thing that happened was that in the United States, unlike in China, the crackdown worked.

As opium became illegal, and therefore difficult and expensive to get, the businessmen, grandmothers, and salesmen who were addicted to it simply . . . quit. They suffered through an initial period of withdrawal, of course, but when the misery passed, the whole thing was over and done. The ex-addicts went on with their lives almost as if the opium hadn't been that big a deal.

At the same time, as the national process of detoxification ground on, there emerged a stubborn group of apparently incurable addicts—people to whom it was obviously a very big deal indeed. Unlike the vast majority, they couldn't break the habit. Ultimately they were confined to prisons and mental hospitals, where doctors tried everything they could think of to treat them.

What were the differences between those addicts and the ones who put their laudanum aside with such apparent ease? Nobody knew. In the vacuum of knowledge the obvious presumption gained strength: it had something to do with will power. Most Americans dismissed the addicts as being weak at best and, at worst, criminal.

Doctors in treatment centers like the one at Lexington, Kentucky, didn't have the luxury of dismissing addiction and so, as doctors always had, they studied it.

The first and most obvious truth to emerge was that addiction had two parts, the first physical and the second psychological.

The physical aspect was the easiest to study and also to understand. Physical dependency built up over a period of time, and, when the drug was withdrawn, the result was a period of physical pain and disruption. The addict sweated, his heart pounded, his skin crawled, and he writhed in agony. But contrary to popular myth he rarely died. After a few days he emerged from the experience as good as new—physically, at least. In this, the incurable addict was no different from those who had successfully kicked their addiction to laudanum-laced patent medicines.

It was the second aspect of addiction, the psychological one, that was clearly the key. The people who successfully broke the laudanum habit seemed to have no long-term psychological effects at all. The "pathological addicts," in sharp contrast, never lost their craving. Though they might be "clean" for years, in the end almost all of them succumbed to the craving.

The doctors did what they could. They tried Freudian psychotherapy, group therapy, behavioral therapy, and even religion. Nothing worked until, finally, a definitive cure was found: "maintenance" therapy with the new nonaddicting drug, Heroin.

Early in the American detoxification effort, most problem addicts had originally picked up their habit basically by accident —through patent medicines, for instance, or the prescriptions of unscrupulous or careless physicians.

But there were also pockets of willful resistance to the new drug laws. One such group came from what was then called the "Bohemian" counterculture, and another included young urban blacks.

These groups at first used opium and then, as time passed, morphine became the drug of choice. Eventually they learned, from the addicts released from treatment centers and prisons, of the glories of Heroin. In time, Heroin lost its trade-name status as Bayer officials ceased to claim it, and the word was no longer capitalized.

This was the situation as it remained, rather stable, through the Depression and World War II. Then came a boom in chemical technology, and by the 1960s, a number of new "psychoactive" drugs became available.

Amphetamine, first marketed as a "diet pill" to a waistline-conscious culture, moved into the street trade as "speed." LSD fascinated first the Army chemical-warfare experts, then the flower children. Barbiturates went from the bedroom, where they were prescribed as a sleeping pill, into the hands of dropout teenagers in Haight-Ashbury. Valium, dispensed by psychiatrists, became the new opiate of the suburbs. The acrid smoke of marijuana wafted above audiences at folk concerts and antiwar demonstrations.

As the multicolored rainbow of pills flooded through the counterculture, citizens of the movement shunned "heavy" drugs like heroin. But to many inner-city blacks, who were attempting to generate their own revolution, heroin was their history, their balm . . . and their master.

But they were black, and they didn't matter that much. White heroin addicts, never very plentiful by comparison, went to Lexington for the cure. Black ones were far more likely to end up in state prisons. The white world sipped its martinis, clucked, shook its head sadly, hired more police officers, and went on about its business.

Slowly, inexorably, ever larger numbers of young blacks (mostly men) were drawn to the chemical that solved their problems much more directly and efficiently than any Great Society program ever could.

As the postwar culture grew ever more dependent on mind-altering drugs and the addiction statistics crawled steadily upward, drug treatment specialists became increasingly alarmed at the figures. As impotent as the Mandarin rulers of China, they watched helplessly as a generation gravitated to drugs like so many moths to a flame.

Equally alarming was the blithe social denial of what was happening. The importance of the drug culture just didn't seem to sink into the minds of the only group empowered to do something about it—suburban, middle-class America.

By 1970 the reason for this denial had become abundantly clear. Drug treatment experts had documented that addicts often shifted from drug to drug—when one was denied, another was substituted. And in the end most addicts gravitated to the most popular drug of all, the one drug that was comparable in its psychological effects to heroin.

That drug, of course, was America's favorite: alcohol.

As drug treatment experts and alcoholism therapists increasingly began to compare notes, the grim truth fell into place. The American middle class was too drunk to worry about what was going on.

When alcoholism statistics were combined with those on illegal drugs, and these figures were added to those on addiction to prescription drugs like Valium, it appeared that perhaps one in every five Americans was hopelessly addicted to something— and another one or two were steady users. The reason Americans couldn't get excited about drug use was that it was "normal."

What was needed, the experts decided, was a new attitude toward drug use—and toward addicts. The fact that most people could use drugs, even "hard" drugs like heroin, without becoming addicted, indicated that there was something different about addicts. They had some pathology, somehow . . . they shouldn't be viewed as scum, or weaklings, or moral failures, or potential criminals. They were mentally ill.

In an almost desperate attempt to press this point home, advocates of this new attitude lobbied newspaper reporters, went on talk shows, and churned out millions of pamphlets.

The problem was growing critical, they harangued us, and to combat it society needed to lay aside its traditional judgmental attitude toward addiction. In this way they sought to open the hearts (and the wallets) of the American people to research and innovative treatment programs.

They were wasting their breath, of course. Alcoholism experts had been saying the same thing for fifty years. They even had studies showing that drunkenness tended to run in families. But most people, including doctors, continued to ignore the problem.

For one thing there was a deep and abiding resistance to any explanation that required people to look at misfits and weirdos of any ilk with a "could just as easily be me" attitude.

Besides, in our heart of hearts most of us knew that there was a solution to the drug problem—and it had nothing whatsoever to do with new attitudes. The answer was for the addict to straighten up and behave himself, like the rest of us. Failing that, there was prison.

So it had always been and so, regardless of what the so-called experts were saying, it remained.

5

THE

MAGIC

MOLECULES

B Y the early 1970s, researchers and clinicians had reached the inalterable conclusion that drug addiction, alcoholism, and insanity were but different facets of the same problem. Virtually no knowledgeable scientific authority doubted this. But for the average citizen, truth in this matter has never been as important as perception—and the perception was one defined principally by moral revulsion.

The result was a stigma against the mental patient and his family, a stigma so strong that it often caused more trouble than the disease itself. Society, in effect, was too crazy about craziness to do anything about it.

As anyone closely associated with the issue knew, the first and most urgent need was to do something about the stigma. Only when diseases of the emotions were accepted as bona fide illnesses, no different from kidney stones or varicose veins, could the problem be approached rationally. Only when the moral taint had vanished, only when the mental patient was seen as victim and not villain, would we find the collective interest and the resources required for real progress.

Alcoholism therapists, for instance, had devised treatment programs that were finally working. Alcoholics Anonymous had never obtained cure rates much higher than about 5 percent, but modern group therapy methods were effective in a third to a half of all patients.

The key was getting those patients early. That meant judges, police officers, and ministers had to view the alcoholics they came into contact with as ill, as suffering from a curable disease instead of a moral weakness. We look the other way when we see moral weakness, but we send sick people to a doctor.

As for the alcoholic himself, the stigma was an especially difficult problem. Like everyone else, he (or she) had been trained to view alcoholism as a moral weakness, and his own knowledge of his compulsion brought with it, naturally enough, an overlay of self-hatred. In the end, the diagnosis of alcoholism sounds to most patients more like an accusation, to be defended against. And so, instead of confronting the problem, the average alcoholic and his family deny it until it's too late. The disease, in other words, had to be made acceptable not only to those who came into contact with it but also to those who were afflicted by it.

A growing appreciation for the similarities between alcoholism and heroin addiction didn't help matters any. The heroin addict, after all, was widely perceived as being the scum of the earth. Even gutter alcoholics despised the heroin mainliner. So what good might be undone, what evil might come, if the public realized how little difference there was between the junkie and the middle-class drunk?

The fear that scientific truth might wreak havoc with tangible progress in public enlightenment was even more pronounced among the mentally ill, their families, and the physicians and counselors who treated them.

Of the three groups, it was this one that had made the most

progress at removing the stigma. By 1970 the mentally ill and their friends and therapists had sparked a dawning perception that mental illness really was a disease, and that the victim was fault-less.

It couldn't really be called a victory—not yet. It fell far short of that. The perception was new, it was fragile, and it was shared only by an enlightened minority of citizens. We still laughed at schizophrenics in the park and shook our heads in disgust at the "laziness" of depressives. But there was a glimmering of hope, a hint for the first time that the impossible dream might come true.

It's difficult for an outsider to comprehend the emotional force, the desperation, the spent lives that were invested in that precious hope.

Throughout history the mentally ill had been the most despised and abused of all groups, and the crusade for humane treatment had been one of the loneliest and least popular ever fought. Spanning centuries, it had fed on terrible suffering by millions of victims and their families. It had consumed the lives of generations of advocates—most of whom had died with every reason to suspect their work had been for nothing.

And now, finally, this effort was about to bear fruit. Society was toying with the idea of accepting the mentally ill as ill, instead of evil, or stupid, or willfully bad. There was a light, as they say, at the end of the tunnel. So people were reluctant to risk things by making common cause with druggies and winos.

In sober truth, the victory was tentative at best. The idea that certain people should be forgiven for their failure to exercise control over their lives, and excused from punishment, ran directly counter to human nature.

Moral and religious explanations for madness fit more com-fortably into the mind—and this attitude has prevailed since prehistory. Depression, and the guilt that helps define it, was clearly a mark of degeneracy. The schizophrenic was a witch, or his soul had been expropriated by demons.

It was in this context that the insane were subjected to exorcism by priests and, when that didn't work, to whippings and other forms of torture. This, in the belief system of the time, was treatment, not cruelty. What's more, it was thought to work: medieval drawings depict demons emerging from the mouths of madmen under the lash. Men and women with violence disorders were put to death on the gibbet or, as the ages grew increasingly civilized, the gallows.

Slowly, as the Middle Ages faded into the great Enlightenment, attempts to cure the mentally ill became more humane and, by the standards that then existed, more "scientific." As we look back at the tiny confinement boxes, the isolation booths, and the other implements of "treatment" common to the psychiatry of the 1800s, they seem barbaric beyond description. And yet, like the whippings, they sometimes produced results—pain and isolation, like the whip, could sometimes clear and focus the mind for at least a brief interval.

Then at the end of the nineteenth century and the beginning of this one there came a series of introspective giants, the best known of whom was Sigmund Freud. They began the long transformation of psychic medicine that, they hoped, would lead from religion to science.

As with any science, the age of modern psychology began with classification. In the early 1900s, retarded people and those suffering from the tertiary effects of syphilis were separated from the other asylum patients. Their infirmities were physical.

In Germany, Emil Kraepelin wrote the first objective, clinical description of schizophrenia. The hallmark of depression, including the loss of appetite, diminished sexual drive, and self-revulsion, began to appear in textbooks.

The Freudian era revolutionized our way of thinking about the mentally ill and produced therapies at least marginally useful for dealing with what would later be called the neuroses. But the "talk therapies," when tried on the frankly insane, proved singularly useless.

More drastic methods were called for, it seemed, and in the mid-1930s they began to arrive. Within just a few years of one another, European doctors made a series of critical observations.

63

Manfred Sakel, working in a small asylum in Germany, became interested in schizophrenic patients who were also diabetic and, at the same time, hypersensitive to insulin. Such patients often depleted their blood sugar and went into shock; when they regained consciousness, they sometimes also regained their sanity—at least for a while.

At about the same time L. J. von Meduna, a Hungarian, heard a rumor that schizophrenia rarely occurred in epileptics and, when it did, it seemed to improve following an epileptic seizure.

Thus were born the two varieties of shock treatment. Chemically induced shock was produced by injections of insulin, which depleted blood sugar and produced a short-lived coma; a similar coma was achieved by shooting electrical currents through the brain.

The introduction of insulin and electroconvulsive shock treatments was followed by the development of the most drastic treatment in modern psychotherapy, the prefrontal lobotomy.

The lobotomy was developed in 1935 by Egas Moniz, a Portuguese physician who learned that animals and humans who had become aggressive following brain damage or tumors often lost that aggressiveness when they subsequently experienced injury to the prefrontal lobes, or forebrain.

Egas Moniz undertook to intentionally induce such injuries in the forebrains of violent schizophrenics. He achieved this by forcing a thin, ice pick–like instrument through the patient's eye socket and then waving the point around in the brain.

Though these treatments would seem primitive and cruel to a later generation, they were not without scientific merit—and, what's more, they seemed to work when nothing else did.

Shock treatments did sometimes restore patients to rationality, at least for a while. And while insulin shock treatment is almost never used today, a modern version of electrical shock remains the best treatment for severely depressed patients.

Prefrontal lobotomy, despite its dehumanizing effect on the personality, seemed to suppress hallucinations and allowed doctors to free violent patients who, earlier, had been held in straitjacketed seclusion. In a more precise surgical form, it, too, is still used occasionally—not for schizophrenia but for severe obsessive-compulsive illness.

But both treatments were mysterious and admittedly primitive. Even if they worked, they really didn't make much sense.

Then in the late 1940s a dramatic breakthrough emerged from what, for most people, was an entirely unexpected quarter: anesthesiology.

Since ancient times, chemicals like alcohol and morphine were known to have profound effects on the brain, and by the 1940s physicians and surgeons were commonly using ether and chloroform for general anesthesia. But the action of these substances was very general. They dulled the mind nonspecifically, by generally mucking up the works.

One result of this nonspecificity was that the anesthetic agents had serious side effects, and the medical community was always on the lookout for new chemicals. There was a clear need, for instance, to find ways to calm patients without impairing their breathing or heartbeat.

As part of this search a Paris neurosurgeon, Henri Laborit, discovered that a weak antihistamine called chlorpromazine had the ability to calm patients before surgery—and, at the same time, did not seem to make them more likely to die on the table. After using it for some time, he was so impressed with the tranquility it induced that he wondered if it might not have other uses as well. In a conversation with two psychiatrists, Jean Delay and Pierre Deniker, he suggested that it might be used to calm the hyperactive, difficult-to-manage patients they were always complaining about.

The psychiatrists tried it, and Laborit's suspicion proved correct. Chlorpromazine had a dramatic sedative effect on a broad range of mental patients. It made them calmer and easier to manage, creating less bedlam as a result.

But there was one surprise—a surprise that was to revolutionize psychiatry.

For the most part, the mental patients who received the drug didn't get any less crazy, they just grew quieter in their craziness. But there was one exception: the schizophrenics. Many of them actually got better as well as quieter. Their hallucinations vanished, and, within days, they were seeing the world more or less as it was.

The psychiatrists almost couldn't believe their own findings, so they repeated the experiment . . . and got the same results.

The full implications of the discovery would not be clear for a generation, but at that moment the torch of psychology passed from the philosophers to the scientists.

Mental disease had always been amorphous, with the various syndromes blending into one another. Even the definition of the common diseases differed radically from expert to expert. Yet here was a drug that had a very specific effect on a very specific and unmistakable symptom. It quelled hallucinations. At the same time, it did nothing specific for the victims of other diseases.

Science, by nature reductionistic, works its magic on just such specifics. Now scientists finally had something they could get their hands on, something that could be measured, weighed, analyzed, tinkered with: the chlorpromazine molecule.

There was something special about that molecule, and if scientists could figure out what that something was they might have a bold new prespective not only on mental illness but also on the mechanism of the mind in general.

In the meantime, there was a specific drug therapy to test and develop, and the work went forward quickly. By the end of the 1950s, chlorpromazine, released under the trade name Thorazine, had revolutionized the treatment of schizophrenia. It was so much better than anything else, so much more effective than whipping, so much less barbaric than isolation or cold packs or prefrontal lobotomies, that it was hailed in the popular press as a wonder drug.

The discovery of the neuroleptics, as they were called, alerted doctors to look for other compounds that might be effective against a variety of mental illnesses. The result was a series of interrelated

66

observations that, once scientists started comparing notes, yielded the first antidepressants.

As the revolution picked up momentum, a unifying theory began to sprout. In this emerging new thought, the first lapping of a historic tide against ancient prejudice, the minds of moths and men were beginning to look increasingly similar.

The key was the receptor.

By this time scientists in other fields like entomology and endocrinology, by nature less puzzling than the science of the mind, had discovered that the surfaces of many cells, and perhaps all of them, were studded with receptors.

Hormones were shown to be a pheromone of sorts—a pheromone that stayed within the body, carrying messages from one cell to another. Insulin, for instance, carried a message in its shape. When a molecule of insulin settled into the receptor of a cell in the arm, or leg, or kidney, it triggered a series of Tinkertoy reactions that allowed the cell to begin feeding on the glucose in the blood.

Other hormones, using the same basic mechanism, told the sex organs when to grow, the intestines when to digest food, and the adrenal glands when to produce adrenaline (which, in itself, was a hormone). Receptors allowed the immune system to recognize viruses and bacteria, receptors caused hair to grow (and, in male-pattern baldness, to eventually fall out), receptors controlled the kidneys, the lungs, the heart—once they began looking, scientists found everywhere the effects of receptors, receptors, receptors, receptors, receptors, receptors.

As biologists began to appreciate the role of receptors, their perception of the nature of organisms began to change. Moths, mice, and men were at bottom but colonies of cells, intricately coordinated ecologies in which the various functions were controlled by an almost infinitely complex traffic in chemical messengers—messengers that, like the pheromone, carried their information in their shapes and magnetic properties.

This new perception fit, as well, into the emerging theory of mental processing.

For a century and more, neuroscientists had focused their attention on the brain's electrical properties—electricity was something they could measure and chart. By means of probes inserted in individual cells, for instance, they had discovered that the gray neuron, at rest, sent about one pulse of electricity down its axon every second; when excited, the neuron could send up to sixty pulses a second.

By using induction devices called electroencephalographs, neuroscientists had learned to measure the combined electrical activity from outside the skull and to relate the resulting tracings to certain diseases, like epilepsy, and states of mind, like sleep.

But the brain's electrical activity had the disadvantage of being more or less homogeneous throughout the brain. Scientists could study an individual cell with a probe, and the entire brain with an EEG, but there didn't seem any practical way to learn much about how the different populations of cells—the various "centers," each involving millions of neurons—kicked in and out during the process of thought. One might as well try to deduce the function and program of a computer by monitoring the electrical disturbances produced around the outside of the terminal.

But the electrical view of the brain did present one interesting question, a question that would prove central to the new psychology: How did the charge of electricity jump from the tip of the axon to the surface of the receiving cell?

Early in the history of neuroanatomy, researchers assumed that the tip of the axon made contact with the surface of the receiving cell's membrane, and that electricity passed directly from axon to cell surface. But the age of electron microscopy had made that assumption untenable. The boutons, though they lay very close to the receiving cells, never quite made contact. There was a gap, ever so small but still a gap, between the bottom of the bouton and the surface of the receiving neuron.

How did the electrical impulse cross the gap? Certainly, in the wetness of the brain, no spark could jump! If the electrical impulse didn't cross from bouton to neuron, what did? What carried the message?

There was only one answer: pheromones, as the entomologists would have put it. Or, in the language of the endocrinologists, hormones.

Brain scientists, rejecting both names, called the hypothetical chemical carriers "transmitters." Or, to be more specific, "neurotransmitters."

Somehow, the electrical charge ran down the axon and, by triggering some as yet mysterious reaction in the bouton, released neurotransmitters. The transmitters crossed the gap, or the "synapse" as it was called, and played up against the cell surface. Obviously, that implied that the surface of the brain cell was studded with receptors.

Throughout the 1960s, this theory developed, bit by bit, drawing its energy from discoveries elsewhere in biology. By 1970, a number of candidate transmitter molecules had been isolated in the brains of animals. There was a deep suspicion that norepinephrine and serotonin, which were apparently involved in depression, were neurotransmitters.

One of the best illustrations of how chemicals mediated the transfer of messages within the brain came with the study of a fascinating but somewhat obscure disease called myasthenia gravis.

Victims, who included the late Aristotle Onassis, lost the ability to control their muscles. Their arms and legs grew weak, their eyelids drooped, and finally, when the disease progressed to the point where their diaphragms would not respond to impulses from the brain, they suffocated.

Scientists studying this and similar diseases discovered that nerves activate muscles by releasing microscopic sprays of a transmitter chemical called acetylcholine. The acetylcholine is directed onto sensitive structures called "end plates," which are located on muscle cells. The end plates are studded with receptors that, when activated by acetylcholine molecules, trigger a molecular linkage inside the cells that results in muscle contraction.

Myasthenia gravis, it was learned, occurs when the victim's immune system goes haywire and attacks the receptors on the end plates. With the receptors gone, the muscles no longer respond to the pulsing sprays of acetylcholine from the nerve endings.

Chemists, in their search for more effective drugs to combat mental illness, reasoned that similar transmitter-receptor processes must be going on in the brain itself. By the time the secret of myasthenia gravis was untangled, in fact, scientists had uncovered evidence that there were several transmitters—including variations of acetylcholine—in the brain.

A strange new thought took shape. Might mental illness somehow result from damage or defects in such transmitter-receptor systems? Extending the thought, might it be that the neuroleptics worked because they happened to correct some such deficiency in the brains of schizophrenics? Perhaps the antidepressants similarly corrected some chemical problem in the brains of depressed people.

With these thoughts, hypotheses, and speculations, the foundation for molecular psychology was laid down. What was needed, now, was some way to trace the specific locations of receptors in the brain and to monitor the flow of chemicals onto them.

Meanwhile, advocates of more humane treatment for the victims of mental illness were for the first time achieving notable success in their efforts. For one thing, the idea that drugs could help treat insanity added new credibility to the contention that the mental patient was fundamentally innocent. For another, a few mental patients actually began to return to their communities, apparently cured, to assume their former lives. They were the examples of the new order of things.

The changes in mental institutions during this period were startling. As drug therapies were developed and improved, there was less and less need for chains, strait jackets, or isolation rooms. Mental hospitals were still little better than prisons, but at least they were calm now, and less offensive to visitors. It all helped.

Times were definitely changing, and a symbol was needed. Shackles and chains, destined for the junk heap and the museum, were collected by volunteers of the National Mental Health Association. They were melted down and cast into a bell. Today the bell is rung at each meeting of the organization in a ceremony that never fails to bring tears to the eyes of many participants.

But though times may have been changing in the 1960s, they were changing ever so slowly.

It was true that the word *crazy* was very seldom used to describe schizophrenics—at least not in print. And true, no one ever talked about "insane asylums" anymore. They were mental hospitals now. But the changes, such as they were, were cosmetic. In the eyes of most people, insanity had always been a moral condition, and by any other name it so remained.

There was much left to do; the crusade continued, merging now with the march of science. And still, despite the development of antipsychotic drugs, public opinion seemed as implacable an enemy as the diseases themselves.

One source of trouble came from within the psychiatric community. Psychiatric dogma, to which most practitioners subscribed, held that mental illness invariably was caused by environmental factors. Schizophrenia, for instance, was due to poor mothering.

This view, along with many of the new-Freudian psychiatrists who held it, was threatened by the success of the neuroleptics in treating schizophrenic hallucinations. If the neuroleptics really worked, that made schizophrenia look suspiciously like a physical disease. Many psychiatrists addressed this heresy by challenging the competency, and the honesty, of their drug-oriented brethren.

Perhaps, they claimed, it was the tranquilizing effect that got results—in which case chlorpromazine wasn't very specific after all. Drug trials of broad-spectrum tranquilizers produced only more relaxed hallucinations, but the controversy raged on, fueled by bias, conflicting reports, and the dawning knowledge that some of the drugs might have serious side effects.

The conflict between the drug therapists and talk therapists was not as legitimate as it seems on the surface. The talk therapies had never been useful against schizophrenia or severe depression anyway, and there was no specific drug therapy effective against the neuroses—they were, and remained, the turf of the Freudians.

71

Many Freudians, in fact, more interested in their patients than in public squabbles, were quite willing to use drugs whenever it seemed they might work.

But in this as in so much else involving the history of psychiatry, public perceptions were more at issue than realities.

Although Freudian psychiatry had dominated the field for decades, it had never been as accepted by the public as its advocates thought it should be. Psychiatrists, then as now, were not taken seriously by most people. They were the butt of merciless jokes. They were "shrinks" who went to sleep listening to their patients ramble on. Most mentally ill people avoided going to them until they were almost terminally ill, and it was a rare patient who actually *admitted* to being under the care of a psychiatrist.

So the perceived conflict involved much more than science. It involved egos, philosophies . . . and money. Psychiatry was already among the most highly trained and at the same time the lowest paid of all the medical specialties. And if the public got the idea that they could cure their miseries by taking pills, why would they consent to spending thousands of dollars and many years of their lives lying on the couch?

The conflict might have amounted to no more than a footnote in the medical history books had it not coincided with the rise of The Revolution and a romantic new public perception of mental illness.

Like the old prejudices about mental illness, this new vision of insanity had its roots in moral thinking. But as the revolution was wont to do, the old bias was turned on its head. To the flower children and the new left, it wasn't the mentally ill who were at fault, it was society. For that matter it was society, and not the schizophrenic, who was crazy.

Schizophrenia, in particular, was seen as a rational response to an insane world. A series of plays, movies, and books, most notably 1962's *One Flew Over the Cuckoo's Nest*, portrayed psychiatric hospitals as prisons equipped with chemical strait jackets and diabolical "treatments" wielded by a staff intent on forcing patients to conform.

By the late 1960s, the lines had been drawn sharply. A molecular psychologist with a paper to present often showed up to find the meeting place besieged by chanting lines of "Science for the People" protesters waving signs and chanting, "Nazi, Nazi, Nazi!" Newspaper articles about molecular psychology drew dozens of angry rebuttals in the letters-to-the-editor columns. Congress, reflecting the mood of the times, cast a jaded eye on requests for money with which to follow up the dramatic new discoveries.

The social situation had a profound effect on the birth of molecular psychology. Scientists working in the field grew first reticent and then secretive, often refusing to talk to the press. Meeting announcements, if released to the public at all, were carefully worded and low-key. Increasingly, discussions of the new discoveries were couched in the mumbo-jumbo of the neurobiological journals. In many respects, the new science went underground.

6

BREAKTHROUGH

D U R I N G the late 1960s, at the peak of the civil rights movement, America at large professed concern for the plight of blacks. A central feature of that plight was heroin addiction, which had reached epidemic proportions in the ghettos and was destroying the economic future of a large percentage of young black men. Increasingly, it was affecting black women as well, and through them their babies. By the end of the decade, the phenomenon of the black infant who went into heroin withdrawal immediately after birth had become commonplace in city hospitals.

But heroin addiction was an issue with which few Americans could identify, and, though urban drug therapists struggled valiantly to spark national interest in innovative new drug programs, the issue never quite caught fire.

In the suburbs, most people continued to see heroin addiction not as a tragedy in itself but as a precursor to crime. The heroin addict was black, probably armed, and bent on breaking into middle-class homes in search of stereos, jewelry, and other booty that, translated into money by the inner-city fence, could be used to support his habit. The black addict, like the schizophrenic of old, was not a patient—he was a criminal.

So the agony of the inner city did not lead to a rethinking of the problem of addiction or to efforts to understand its nature as a disease. It might never have led to that. The effort in that direction, when it finally came, was catalyzed by a parallel surge of heroin addiction among American soldiers in Vietnam.

There, reportedly with the help of the crafty Vietcong, America's draftees discovered that heroin was the perfect drug for rendering tolerable the demoralizing, day-to-day discomfort and frustration that characterized the unpopular war. As they returned to the United States they naturally brought their craving home with them.

Blacks made up a disproportionate number of combat soldiers, and their heroin use was, if anything, greater than that of whites. Their return prompted an outcry from black leaders, but the brutal fact was that, by 1970, black neighborhoods were all but resigned to the heroin epidemic.

When young, middle-class white men returned to their homes and families with the heroin monkey on their backs, though, it was . . . well, somehow different. It brought the agony home.

No one, of course, knows just how many heroin addicts there are in the United States at a given time. Almost by definition, addiction proceeds in secret. Nevertheless, there is an indicator of addiction trends: overdose rates.

Opiates suppress breathing as well as physical and psychic pain, and so a certain percentage of addicts will inevitably end up in emergency rooms, dying of overdose. The rate at which they die gives experts an idea of whether the overall addiction problem is stable, subsiding, or growing. And as the 1960s drew to a close, this indicator was dramatically on the rise.

The patient, usually a young person and increasingly one with white skin, would be brought in either by ambulance or by friends. He would generally arrive in a coma. A resident would observe the pinpoint pupils and the shallow breathing and pronounce the familiar diagnosis.

If the victim arrived soon enough after taking the overdose, and if the medical team could get him on a respirator quickly enough, he might live to mainline again. But frequently it was too late; the shallow breathing, in denying precious oxygen to the brain, would already have damaged the delicate neurons. If the gods were merciful, death followed quickly. If not, brain swelling secondary to shock destroyed the higher centers and the family had a vegetable on its hands.

At first, the sole hope for the overdosed heroin addict was the respirator, which, with luck, could preserve brain function until the drug wore off. But as the 1970s opened, hospitals began to receive allotments of a powerful new drug, called Naloxone, which was an effective antidote for heroin poisoning.

How the stuff worked was a mystery, but the emergency room doctors didn't really care. Assuming the patient's brain was still alive—a substantial assumption, since most heroin addicts inject themselves in private and aren't found for hours—Naloxone was a miracle. A few minutes after the injection, the patient was sitting up, rubbing his eyes, and groggily trying to figure out where he was and how he got there.

There was some hope that Naloxone could be used to treat addiction itself. In theory, at least, the drug would make the patient immune to the effects of heroin; no matter how much he injected, he couldn't get high.

But the effects of Naloxone turned out to be extremely short-lived and, to make matters worse, the drug had serious side effects. It would be more than a decade before the problems could be solved sufficiently to allow clinical trials with addicts. In the meantime, while Naloxone did decrease emergency room fatalities from heroin overdoses, it had no effect on the rising addiction rates among middle-class whites.

As increasing numbers of soldiers returned from Vietnam

addicted to heroin, the alarm grew. Politicians now *had* to pay attention, and Nixon administration officials focused on the problem. A law enforcement crackdown ensued but, despite public relations statements to the contrary, the narcs didn't have much more luck than the Chinese had had. The most notable thing that happened was that the price of heroin went up, which meant that addicts had to steal more to get the drugs they needed.

The only other solution was to figure out some way to deprive the pushers of their market, which meant curing addicts. But how? For an answer to that question, officials naturally turned to the medical sciences.

The answers from psychiatrists, and from traditional treatment authorities, were vague and not very practical. Group therapy sometimes worked. More halfway houses were needed but no, there was no guarantee of cure. Methadone maintenance worked, said some, but already bootleg methadone was being sold on the streets as super-heroin. It was an enigma. More research was needed, but there wasn't even any consensus on where to start.

Only one group of scientists seemed to speak with authority— and didn't contradict one another or squabble among themselves over philosophy. These were the molecular psychologists, the materialistic advocates of the mechanical mind, last seen in this narrative facing new-left picket signs, dodging rotten eggs, and trying to keep their research teams together in the face of dwindling financial support.

Their theories about the chemical nature of the mind were no more acceptable to outsiders in 1970 than they were in the 1960s, but few laypeople associated addiction with mental illness. Besides, heroin was a chemical, wasn't it? And the talk therapies had already hit the addiction problem and bounced off, hadn't they? So who else was there to turn to but the chemists?

So it was that there was suddenly new funding for neurochemistry. In the great scheme of big-time research it wasn't much —a few million, that was all—but to the neurochemists it was a bonanza.

One of the scientists who eagerly applied for the new money

was Dr. Solomon Snyder, a young neurochemist at The Johns Hopkins Medical School in Baltimore.

Snyder's background illuminates the mindset of his profession. Originally he had wanted to be a psychiatrist, practicing in the Freudian tradition. He had pursued that goal to the point of receiving his medical degree, but then, confronted with the murky imprecision and seeming ineffectiveness of his chosen field, he had rebelled. It was too vague, too subjective, too wishy-washy. So he'd switched to something he could quantify—biochemistry.

His new specialty had suited him, and he did well in it—well enough to win the attention of a high-powered mentor, Julius Axelrod, the Nobel Prize winner at the National Institute of Mental Health.

Dr. Axelrod's principal interest was in the then-mysterious chemical events that took place in the "synaptic cleft" between the bouton and the receiving neuron. Snyder did his postgraduate work in Axelrod's laboratory before coming to Hopkins.

Like his colleagues, Snyder had long been intrigued by the specificity of the opiate-morphine-heroin reaction in the brain. Alcohol, by contrast, was a very weak drug—it took a lot of Scotch to make a person drunk, and, once intoxication had been achieved, it seemed to affect the entire nervous system equally. But comparatively tiny amounts of opiates had profound and specific physical effects. The pupils contracted. Breathing grew shallow. Bowels ceased to rumble. Pain damped out.

The specificity of the opiate reaction, in light of the new theory of molecular psychology, naturally led Snyder to suspect that opiate molecules found, and snapped into, a specific receptor in the brain.

Perhaps, his thinking went, there was in the brain a natural transmitter molecule shaped something like the morphine molecule. Perhaps morphine or heroin, injected, somehow mimicked that molecule, achieving its effect by snapping into the receptors and activating them.

The idea wasn't original with Snyder. Others had had it before him and had attempted to identify and label these receptors.

In principle, the experiment was simple. If indeed there *was* an opiate receptor in the brain, and if the morphine or heroin molecule snapped into it, then the parts of the brain that contained such receptors ought to be very selectively "sticky" with regard to morphine molecules.

The experiment that was required to prove the existence of opiate receptors was obvious. Morphine, labeled with radioactive tracers, should be mixed with fresh brain cells—they had to be fresh, since the receptors were probably delicate and came apart shortly after death. Once the mixing was complete, the brain cells were washed and checked with a radiation detector.

If the brain cells were "hot," that would mean some of the radioactive morphine molecules had stuck tightly to them. That would mean there were receptors. If the brain cells weren't radioactive, on the other hand, that would mean all the radioactive morphine had washed off—and that there were no receptors.

It was a straightforward experiment, and, if a generation's thinking about the matter was valid, the morphine molecules ought to stick. Unfortunately, they didn't.

The scientists scratched their heads and groped for explanations. Perhaps . . . perhaps the problem was that the morphine molecules didn't stick very tightly in the receptors. Perhaps a stronger drug, like heroin, would stick. So the researchers attached radioactive tracers to heroin molecules and tried again.

Nothing.

It was maddening and, more than that, deeply alarming. Because the experiment should have been simple and straightforward, its failure cast doubt on the basic theory. It made it look suspiciously as if the receptors of the mind were but a figment of the dreamy imaginations of neurochemists.

Maybe . . . but the neurochemists, of course, didn't warm to that possibility. They weren't willing to walk away from their test tubes and their brain slices—not yet, anyway. Certainly not at the precise moment the Nixon administration was promising to drop some big money into the science.

At Hopkins, Snyder used some of his share of that money to

79

hire a bright young doctoral candidate named Candace Pert. Together they carefully went through the steps of the standard experiment. Morphine was labeled, poured over fresh cells from rats, mice, and guinea pigs. But the Hopkins team got the same results as everyone else: nothing.

There was either something wrong with the theory or with the experiment.

They tried again. And, like everybody else, they failed again.

Snyder, casting about for another approach, found himself thinking about Naloxone, the drug that so effectively woke up patients in heroin-induced comas. How, he asked himself, did it do that? He puzzled it through, following the theory.

Perhaps Naloxone, though not an opiate itself, somehow fastened onto the opiate receptor in such a way as to pop the heroin molecule out of its place—without activating the receptor. Or perhaps, clinging tightly to the edge of the receptor, it prevented the morphine molecule from snapping in.

Either way, one had to assume that Naloxone was so effective because it clung to the receptor very, very tightly—more tightly, even, than heroin.

Why not, he asked Pert, label some Naloxone and mix that with the brain cells instead of the morphine? They certainly had nothing to lose.

So it was that in May 1973 Pert, under Snyder's direction, repeated the experiment using radioactive Naloxone. This time, it worked: the radioactive molecules clung tightly to the brain cells.

The theory was right!

There *were* receptors, after all!

Suddenly, in hindsight, the reason that earlier experiments hadn't worked became clear. Morphine was never meant to stay locked in the receptor. It snapped in, did its work, then snapped out. Naloxone snapped in and stayed, which was why it was so good at waking up people who were unconscious from opiate overdoses.

As the excitement died down, another Hopkins scientist, Dr.

Michael Kuhar, took the next logical step. He labeled an especially potent opiate with radioactive tracers and injected the material into rats. He killed the rats, removed and sliced their brains, put the slices between sheets of photographic film, and put the result in the freezer.

The hope was that the radioactive opiates would stick to the areas of the brain where the receptors were and that, over time, they would burn their impressions into the film.

Several days later Kuhar removed the brain slices from the freezer and developed the film.

There, in the emulsion, were dim outlines of the brain slices— punctuated by brightly lit areas where the radioactive opiates had stuck tightly to the tissue.

Those areas, rich in opiate receptors, marked precisely those centers of the brain that scientists already knew were suppressed by heroin overdose. The respiration center was lit up, for instance. So were the centers that controlled pain.

But that wasn't all.

Deep in the brains of rats and men, hard on the shores of the straits through which spinal fluid passes from the third and fourth ventricles, there lies a small rind of ancient tissue called the "periaqueductal gray."

The periaqueductal gray had long fascinated brain anatomists. When electrodes are placed there in living rats, and the rats are allowed to stimulate themselves by pressing a bar, they quickly became hopelessly addicted to the trickles of electricity.

The periaqueductal gray, many believed, might have something to do with psychological pain and its suppression. When stimulated, it produced happiness and bliss.

And, on the Hopkins negatives, it was lit up like a neon light.

Kuhar, Snyder, and Pert stared at the films, and in them they saw the millennium.

7

GOLD

RUSH

MODERN scientific revolutions are the products of many minds, many perceptions, many discoveries. But it was the Snyder-Pert experiment that crystallized the new view of the mind and held up, for all with the vision to see, the promise of biopsychology in general and neurochemistry in particular.

As time passed and the practical usefulness of the information sank in, thousands of the best biologists of the twentieth century would come to work the gold fields first opened up by the two young Hopkins scientists. And the particular discovery of that watershed experiment, the chemistry of pain, would one day be deemed so important as to rate the cover of *Time*. Discussions of receptors and transmitters, starring the legendary Solomon Snyder, would ultimately attract huge audiences that would pack the Turner Auditorium across from the Johns Hopkins Hospital.

But that was far in the future. In 1973 the message of the

receptors wasn't an easy one to square with the prevailing romantic view of the human mind.

Most of the big national publications didn't send reporters to the press conference on Snyder and Pert's discovery, and the science writers who did show up found the technology difficult to grasp. What the hell was a receptor? How did it relate to the real world? And who cared? And if this story was so damned important, why hadn't they ever even heard about it before?

The fact was that even the best medical science writers in 1973 lacked the background to put the Snyder-Pert discovery in context and make its implications clear. Reporters learn from the stories they research and write, and the stories they wrote about psychology in those days focused almost universally on environmentalism or behaviorism.

The public was in an even worse position to understand: legitimate stories on psychology were far outnumberd by reports on spiritualism, acupuncture, reincarnation, faith healing, hypnosis, and similar intellectual fads of the early Aquarian age. The human mind was almost universally considered not only inscrutable but also spiritual, and evidence based on contrary assumptions was more likely to provoke confusion than understanding. In the public mind, the Snyder-Pert breakthrough was but a footnote to the daily stream of events.

The result was that molecular psychology, perhaps the most important cascade of scientific events in all of human history, would proceed with its revolution shrouded in an obscurity so profound that it might as well have been a state secret.

Even most scientists outside the narrow field of neurochemistry missed the significance of the discovery. Researchers themselves are laypersons once they move far from their own specialties, and even many biologists who worked in more traditional fields like immunology and blood flow dynamics shared the unconsidered perception that the mind was somehow spiritual.

Besides, from a certain routine point of view the Snyder-Pert discovery was but a technical milestone. Receptors in other parts of the body had already been labeled and analyzed, so the fact that they existed as well in the brain came as no real surprise. Even the fact that there was a receptor for morphine in particular only bore out current thinking.

The only people who fully grasped the implications of the experiment were those who had the training to read the technical report in *Science* with ease—Snyder's fellow neurochemists. They more than anyone were aware, excruciatingly aware, of the deep abyss between the theory of receptor-transmitter interaction and proof of such interaction.

Proof that there were indeed receptors in the brain provided for the first time the confidence that such experiments could be done. Experiments with neuroreceptors were practical. That encouraged other researchers to push ahead with a whole list of secondary questions, some of which had broad implications for the human condition.

The Snyder-Pert experiments, in short, had knocked over the first domino.

The fact that the opiates derived their potency from a receptor effect in specific parts of the brain, for instance, implied a great deal about how the brain worked. Presumably it manufactured a neurotransmitter that was very much like the opiate molecule. After all, the receptor wouldn't be there if there weren't something for it to receive.

That meant that the normal brain had the capacity to administer, to itself, a morphine high. It could become addicted . . . to itself!

What was the purpose of the natural high?

Well, if the effects of morphine and heroin were any clue, the most straightforward thing it did was kill pain. Perhaps that was the reason why a person injured in an automobile accident, for instance, often felt very little pain until an hour or two later. In this sense, the theoretical natural morphine was nature's own mercy chemical.

But the Snyder-Pert receptor maps clearly indicated that there would be effects, as well, on the brain centers that processed psychological pain. Those psychic pain centers had evolved from the more basic physical pain centers, and they apparently used the same receptors.

In that part of the brain, the effect of the natural morphine was to anesthetize the cells that process mental anguish and induce pain's opposite, bliss. The natural morphine, as Pert would later phrase it, was the "good feeling chemical."

From a slightly different perspective, it was the "mother molecule."

Perhaps a mother's smile, processed through the visual cortex of a baby, resulted in an administration of a "fix" of natural morphine. Perhaps the infant became addicted to the morphine and, not incidentally, to the smile of approval that induced it.

Perhaps, when a toddler defecated in his diaper, his mother's displeasure initiated a sequence of reactions in the toddler's brain that cut off the flow of natural morphine. Perhaps the toddler went into mild withdrawal as a result. Perhaps, next time, it would do anything to avoid that misery—including learning to move its bowels only while sitting on the toilet.

Perhaps, after that, the morphine came as a result of learning to tie one's shoes, and then a good report card. A "B" in arithmetic earned a mild fix, mediated by Mommy and Daddy's pleasure, and an "A" earned an ecstatic high. Perhaps by that time the mere anticipation of an "A" made one feel good.

The psychic balance between elation and depression was controlled by the natural morphine system. Perhaps our basic habits, our urge to learn and achieve, our very morality, was no different from a heroin addict's craving for another fix, and then another, and another. . . .

Drug addiction, as one considered the Snyder-Pert work, also made sense. Apparently an addict learned to use artificial chemicals to induce the good feelings that the rest of us got naturally.

The human brain, of course, was not designed for a steady flow of good feelings. In time it adapted to the heroin stimulation, perhaps decreasing the number of receptors and shutting off the flow of natural morphine, so that more and more heroin was needed to achieve the same effect. The result was tolerance. When the heroin was withdrawn, the result was a short-lived misery that was alleviated when the brain readapted to a normal flow of natural morphine.

Presumably something like this happened when laudanum-laced tonics became first difficult and then impossible to get during the crackdown of the 1800s. Most people who had been addicted were able to break their habit very quickly and, after a brief period of withdrawal, to return to normal lives.

The same phenomenon, so alien to the common view of addiction, was now emerging among middle-class veterans who had become heroin addicts in Vietnam. Most of them, contrary to expectations, seemed to be successfully kicking their habit. Only a small minority were becoming hard-core addicts.

Clearly the normal brain, even after having its morphine receptors artificially stimulated by heroin for months or even years, could readjust to a normal flow of the natural good-feeling chemical.

What of the brains that could not readjust? For this, too, the Snyder-Pert work suggested a straightforward explanation—an explanation that dovetailed nicely with a perception then emerging from the more classic disciplines of psychiatry. The answer, apparently, was that the addicts had a preexisting brain disease characterized by deficiencies in the natural morphine system.

It was easy to imagine a variety of scenarios that would lead to such damage. Some people might be born with defective systems, a result either of genetic faults or submicroscopic malformations in the womb. Others might be born with normal systems, only to have them stunted by a lack of the proper psychological stimuli.

The mechanism by which a healthy physical system in the brain might be damaged by strictly psychological events was suggested by a classic neuroanatomical experiment with kittens.

In the feline, the optical cortex develops during a genetically programmed period early in life. This period lasts no more than a few days. If one of a kitten's eyes is covered during that period, so that no light can get in, the part of the brain that processes vision through that eye will never develop. Although the eye itself will be normal, the brain that serves it will not, and the cat will be forever blind in that eye.

Stimulation, in other words, is necessary for normal brain development. Though such experiments could not ethically be done on humans, the results of sensory deprivation were all too obvious in neglected children. And certainly a child who received intellectual stimulation early in life seemed to grow up to be more intelligent than the child who didn't.

So it was compelling to assume that a mother's love, say, could have a similar stimulating effect on the development of receptor fields in the centers that controlled psychic pain. Perhaps some people, failing to get the proper amount of love during some critical period of growth, never developed the ability to quench their own psychological angst.

Or maybe it wasn't a mother's love that was important. Maybe the receptors failed to develop properly because of some fundamental dreariness in the environment, or lack of hope.

In any case, whether the damage was genetic or environmental, the victim would never develop the capacity to feel good about himself. He would, in short, be in constant psychic pain.

He wouldn't be aware of it, of course. The mind is notorious for its ability to mask such pain. He would endure it, below the level of his consciousness, and think nothing of it—unless he took a shot of heroin. Then, for the first time in his life, he would feel . . . well, "right."

Though his friends might remain casual users of the drug, capable of undergoing withdrawal and then leading a normal life, the susceptible person would be instantly and forever addicted. If he withdrew, he would know, now, what he was missing. Like his friends he would return to normality but to him, normality would be intolerable. He would inevitably return to the drug.

In the parlance of more classical psychiatry, such an addict would be "self-treating" for a mental illness. Psychiatrists had discovered that many confirmed addicts were indeed capable of resisting heroin if they were treated, after withdrawal, with anti-depressants.

It was not, of course, going to be all that simple—and no one who knew anything about the complexity of brain and behavior thought that it would. But, overly simplistic or not, the speculations raised by the Snyder-Pert work pointed up the potential impact of neurochemistry.

Put simply, there had always been speculation about the nature of the mind. But now, in experiments like those at Hopkins, scientists were in the position to convert speculations into hypotheses. And a hypothesis, unlike speculation, could be subjected to experimentation in the laboratory and could ultimately be either proved or disproved.

Psychology, in short, had just taken a giant step toward becoming a science. And in doing so it had crystallized what to most laypersons would appear to be a totally new perception of the brain, the mind, and ultimately the human condition. This view, for all practical purposes, constitutes a new theory of psychology.

Because "theory" is one of the most popularly misunderstood words ever to emerge from the scientific discipline, and since it will figure prominently in the following narrative, its use in this context merits a digression.

In the hard sciences, such as physics, a theory consists of a precisely and almost always mathematically defined description of how things are—the theory, for instance, that E equals mc squared. In the biological sciences, in which complexities far surpass those in physics, theories tend to be perceptions of processes. Darwin's theory of evolution is the best example.

Theories, whether physical or biological, are not exactly the same thing as truth. Oddly enough, their truth is almost irrelevant. A theory is a way of looking at the universe, and all that matters in a practical sense is that a theory is more useful than the theory that came before. Newton's perceptions of the universe, though they would one day be shown to be woefully imprecise by Albert Einstein, in fact served science well for centuries. And, despite their many faults, they produced the technology of the industrial revolution.

A theory is really a coherent model, a useful thing that guides one's thoughts—a set of perceptions that can be modified, tinkered with, realigned, and eventually discarded when a better paradigm comes along. As Newtonian physics fell, so, presumably, will Einsteinian physics. And the current theory of evolution, while still identified by the name of the wise old genius who laid down its foundation, would be almost unrecognizable to him.

And so the new theory of the molecular nature of the mind, as it has developed in the past decade, is notable not because it is the last word in defining human psychology but because it is incredibly useful. It amounts to a complex proposition, an approximation (one hopes) of the truth, but most of all a set of perceptions that can be pursued, experimentally, by laboratory scientists.

In this new view, the brain is a biological computer that, as one scientist phrased it, "secretes thoughts the same way the kidneys secrete urine." The brain and the mind are therefore one, inseparable, mechanistic, and—at least in principle—understandable.

But if the mind-brain is no more than a biological computer, neither does the theory suggest that it is any less. The new view might be mechanistic, but it is no less rich or awesome than the spiritual model that it is destined to replace.

As an information processor, for instance, the brain is intrinsically more powerful, by orders of magnitude, than any man-made supercomputer ever conceived.

The most sophisticated man-made computers, for instance, function in classic "digital" fashion: at any instant, a circuit is either off or on.

At the most basic level, the brain functions digitally too—each transmitter molecule represents either an on or an off command, depending on the configuration of the receptor it happens to snap into. The morphine molecule, for example, may stimulate a cell involved in producing good feelings and depress one that processes alertness.

But while the variables in a man-made computer are confined to that digital code, the digital model represents the human brain only at a most superficial level. In the new view of the brain as a biological computer, it has overlay upon overlay of variable complexity.

The individual cell of the brain, for instance, isn't either off or on. It generates a changing rate of charges from one to sixty pulses a second down its axon. In effect, the vocabulary of the gray neuron consists not only of "yes" and "no" but also "perhaps" and "maybe" and "sort of," and "if you say so, I'll consider it."

The second function of the neuron is to produce neurotransmitters, sometimes of more than one variety, and pump them down its axon. Ultimately the transmitters are stored in the boutons, where they are sprayed against the receiving cell with each electrical pulse. This function admits to another level of variability, insofar as the cell can produce more or less of a given transmitter.

Still another variable involves the receptors that stud the cell's surface. The receptors, like almost all component parts of living cells, are constantly being manufactured and degraded. The cell can produce more or less of any given receptor, thus changing its overall sensitivity to the neurotransmitters that are constantly spraying against its surface. The cell can also change the linkage between its metabolic throttle and the receptor so that a given receptor will either accelerate or slow down the metabolic process.

The brain cell, then, is like the basic chemical "chip" in the computer, responding in variable fashion to the constantly changing flux of neurotransmitters against its surface.

There are by some estimates perhaps as many as a trillion such cells in the brain, each changing its status and activity by the moment, exquisitely sensitive to the outside environment, storing, processing, changing, changing, ever-changing, ever embedded in the rich chatter of chemical messages that alter their meanings and contexts in accordance with complex transformations and feedback loops. At any instant a cell's variables offer choices more numerous than the total number of all the elemental particles in the entire universe. The result of this interplay is the multiplex structure of human thoughts and emotions that we refer to as personality.

This emerging picture of the brain, its processes, its hierarchies, and the complex properties that arise from it amounts to a wonderfully coherent way of looking at the mind and brain as one. And as psychiatrists ponder it in light of the Snyder-Pert work, nature's use of chemical transmitters appears increasingly ingenious.

At the most basic level, for instance, there is only one kind of electricity—but there is almost an infinity of different shapes that can be assumed by living molecules.

By using such molecules as the basic unit of intercell communication, nature effectively divides up the great human computer into hundreds or perhaps even thousands of parallel-processing subcomputers. Those individual systems, because they recognize only certain transmitters, are by definition immune to "cross talk" from other systems. A stray morphine molecule, sloshing over into a system using a different transmitter, has no effect whatsoever.

But the thing about the new vision of the mind that makes the scientists' hearts pound and their hands shake is the implication for medicine . . . and, beyond medicine, for psychic engineering.

"As you roll this perception around in your mind," one excited scientist told me in the late 1970s, "the thing that strikes you is all the moving parts. There are thousands and thousands of different types of molecules involved—not just transmitters and receptors but also the enzymes that manufacture and degrade them. Modulating molecules. Effector molecules. Messengers, inside the cell. Second messengers. Feedback chains from the body to the brain.

"And—think about this!—each time we discover a molecule we have discovered the potentiality for at least two diseases. Some people will surely have too much of that molecule; others will have too little.

"Granted, there are probably back-up systems and patchthroughs that allow the machine to correct for errors. Even so, it doesn't take a genius to understand that the next century is going to see a dramatic process of discovery in which molecular defects are connected, one after another, to mental illnesses. It's difficult, looking at what's on our plate, not to be dumbfounded, paralyzed by the possibilities."

The excitement was compounded by the assumption that, once a given transmitter-receptor system was understood, it could be tinkered with by chemical engineers.

But as the possibilities blossomed in the minds of scientists who understood the implications that flowed from the Snyder-Pert discovery, their actions were directed at the straightforward practicalities of experiment.

The most obvious first objective was to find the molecule that fit the Snyder-Pert receptor—that strange and mysterious chemical, that natural form of morphine, that flowed through the human psyche. In neuroscience laboratories all around the globe, lights burned late into the night.

At Hopkins, Snyder and Pert had a head start, but they were not fated to monopolize the new science. The prize went, instead, to Hans Kosterlitz and John Hughes at the University of Aberdeen in Scotland.

As had been expected, the business end of the natural opiate molecule turned out to be similar in shape as well as magnetic properties to the morphine molecule. The natural opiate eventually became known as "endorphin," from the Greek for "end plus morphine," or "morphine-ended."

As the science progressed, so the perception of the mind-brain grew and became more inclusive. One by one, logical-sounding explanations for human behavior presented themselves.

When physically stressed rats were shown to have unusually high levels of endorphin in their brains, for instance, scientists made the leap from that to a puzzling phenomenon reported by many joggers—a sort of intoxication that came from long-distance running.

The "runner's high," whatever it was, was a powerful thing, powerful enough to keep the runner running on a sprained and even broken ankle. Suddenly, that made sense. The high, in terms of molecular psychology, was probably endorphin. Long-distance running produced pain, pain stimulated production of the body's natural painkiller and . . . well, people who said they were addicted to running apparently WERE addicted. They were addicted, as surely as a heroin junkie, to increased levels of their own natural morphine.

The research also shed light on the puzzling effects of pencyclidine, the suddenly popular drug known on the streets as PCP or "angel dust." It induced a new kind of high, one that sometimes led to a form of temporary madness accompanied by incredible physical strength. Police officers quickly learned to fear PCP abusers, and, in the laboratory, neurochemists went looking for a receptor.

It was there, all right. Initial experiments indicated that it might have something to do with creativity. The source of the superhuman strength was a little fuzzier, but the drug apparently stimulated the system that drove muscles to great feats of endurance.

What was the purpose of a natural drug that bestowed such strength? The most obvious possible answer presented itself in the occasional news reports of people who performed seemingly impossible feats under great stress—fathers, for instance, who singlehandedly lifted automobiles off the bodies of their children.

As the 1970s waned and the 1980s began, discovery followed discovery followed discovery. The pattern, as it developed, underscored the dawning awareness that the mind was directed by chemical phenomena.

A valium receptor was discovered. When activated, it generated a feeling of peace and security.

Amphetamine, the diet pill that moved to the street as "speed," turned out to get its effect by stimulating the production of two transmitters, one called dopamine and the other norepinephrine.

There was also something called "substance P," which appeared to mediate pain.

Some transmitters, apparently, were modulators. Their effect was indirect; they made certain receptors more or less sensitive to other transmitters.

Sometimes such discoveries and observations were reported by the popular press, and sometimes they were not. But in the small, closely knit fraternity of molecular psychologists each new development echoed like a thunderclap. It wasn't only that the individual developments were important, but that for the first time in the history of psychological research, they all fit!

In the meantime, the Snyder-Pert report in *Science* became one of the most cited scientific papers in all of modern biology. Snyder was named the director of a new department of neurosciences at Hopkins. He also founded a drug research company, Nova Pharmaceuticals, which made him an instant millionaire—at least on paper.

A few years later he, Hughes, and Kosterlitz won the Lasker Award, an honor traditionally marking them as prime candidates for a Nobel Prize.

Some science-watchers were outraged that Candace Pert wasn't chosen to share the Lasker, but her future nevertheless proved bright. Almost before the ink was dry on her new doctorate, she had moved to the National Institutes of Health to take over her own laboratory.

All over the world, scientific insiders saw immediately what others would fail to comprehend in a decade. There were receptors. They could be labeled. And if they could be labeled, they could be specifically altered.

In a historical instant, psychology had been converted from a form of witchcraft into a laboratory science and ultimately an engineering discipline. The human condition was up for grabs. There were money, power, and Nobel Prizes at stake.

The news of the revolution, at first confined to the neurochemical laboratories, spread to other fields. Neuroanatomists and neurophysiologists increasingly became involved, relating already-known structures and functions to the newly discovered transmitters and receptors. One by one, other biological disciplines became involved as well.

As the floodgates of discovery opened wide, brain chemists all over the world laid aside their research and jumped on the bandwagon. Francis Crick, who had won the Nobel Prize for his part in cracking the genetic code, turned his back on his former field and joined a team of neuroscientists in California. An increasing number of the best and brightest science students, always searching for new worlds to conquer, chose molecular psychology as their field of study—and even in an era of shrinking scientific budgets, there was money to finance their work.

By 1980 the literature was full of reports of new receptors, and of possible neurotransmitters. With a suddenness more characteristic of science fiction than the trudging progress of real-life science, a dream began to turn into reality.

Throughout previous human history, psychoactive drugs had been discovered and developed almost entirely by accident; the process typically had taken decades of work by dozens of top-flight scientists. Now, as the knowledge about the brain accumulated, it became possible to engineer psychoactive drugs in a more straightforward fashion.

The power of this new technology, along with the era of psychic engineering it heralded, was underscored by an almost off-hand development in Baltimore.

Scientists had long used a caffeinelike compound in their experiments with animals. Snyder decided that it would be nice to have a stronger version of the drug and assigned a junior researcher to the project. In less than two years, that young scientist, working alone but using the techniques developed in the Hopkins laboratory, produced the desired result.

The substance he produced, when tested, proved to be 500,000 times more powerful than the original.

Although the achievement had no clinical significance, the six-digit number seemed to foreshadow what was to come. Neuro-chemistry was already leaping the gap between science and the engineering discipline. The mind balked at the prospect of a drug a half-million times more powerful than, say, Valium. Or heroin. Or PCP.

8

A

TARGET

OF

OPPORTUNITY

As the new view of the mind-brain coalesced, the blizzard of confusing evidence about mental illness began to make sense. The various systems in the brain, though visually and electrically quite similar, were chemically distinct. It was easy to see how a disease might affect one, while leaving the others intact—and equally easy to understand how bizarre and unreasonable behavior might result.

The first mission of the new science, then, would be to determine which chemical systems were malfunctioning in patients with various phobias, neuroses, addictions, criminality, depression, manic-depression disease, and schizophrenia. Different scientists chose to zero in on different diseases, depending on their backgrounds and inspirations, but most experts saw schizophrenia as the target of greatest opportunity.

One of the reasons for this enthusiasm was sheer exuberance.

By the mid-1970s, it was clear to anyone watching closely that something truly remarkable and historic had happened in the brain sciences. The sudden emergence of the new psychology, based on biology instead of philosophy, was at least as profoundly important as the splitting of the atom or the breaking of the genetic code.

At the same time, the research so far was mostly fairly complex. One result was that the public at large was almost totally oblivious to the fact that something had happened. The scientists, if they were to parlay their breakthroughs into the big budgets that the revolution required, needed a highly visible and clearly important clinical breakthrough. They needed, in short, to demonstrate that they could actually cure something.

And what better candidate for that cure than schizophrenia?

Certainly no other mental disease was so visible. Schizophrenia, with its characteristic hallucinations and thought disorders, was the archetypical form of insanity. It was the "index" disease, the epitome of madness even among laypersons. It was an obvious target for molecular psychologists with a point to make.

There were also humanitarian, economic, and social motives for focusing on schizophrenia. Although the disease is by no means the most common of the severe mental illnesses, it is arguably the most devastating—not only to the schizophrenic, but to others as well.

For one thing, schizophrenia tends to strike young people, preferring the teenage years or the early twenties. This converts the disease from an individual tragedy into a family one, and it strikes at the moment when the family typically has other children who are also trying to get a foothold in the world. So its agony is far greater than statistics might otherwise indicate.

In addition, schizophrenia is unlike the other mental illnesses, which tend to come and go. Schizophrenia persists. Even though drugs can reduce or eliminate the hallucinations, the underlying disease is chronic, progressive, incurable, and debilitating. Perhaps eight out of ten schizophrenics never return to normalcy. They sap the strength of their families and then, when that resource is exhausted, become lifelong dependents on mental health and social welfare agencies.

The urgency of the schizophrenia problem was further increased by what might be called the public relations factor involving schizophrenic violence.

Though schizophrenics may often be arrested on charges like loitering, they are probably less prone to violent lawbreaking than the rest of us. One of the symptoms of schizophrenia is extreme passivity, a condition generally not compatible with violence. For another, seriously ill schizophrenics usually are incapable of even the minimum amount of planning and preparation required for successful lawbreaking. All in all, schizophrenics are as unsuited for crime as they are for honest labor.

But schizophrenics aren't all alike, and the few who are violent can be very violent indeed. Such people are usually responding to paranoid impulses—they're trying desperately to protect themselves from dangers that only they perceive. This "cornered rat effect," coupled with the fact that the violent schizophrenic is responding to his comic-book hallucinations and not to reality, makes him very unpredictable—and makes the crimes he commits tend to be bloody, spectacular, and senseless.

Incidents like the attempted assassination of President Reagan and the McDonald's killings paint the mentally ill as villains instead of victims, giving false credence to the notion that the insane are generally dangerous. Bluntly put, violent schizophrenics give crazy people a bad name.

If molecular psychologists could understand the chemical nature of schizophrenia in a precise enough way to have it lead to improved diagnosis and treatment, schizophrenic violence might be kept out of the headlines. This would aid immeasurably in the effort to remove the stigma from mental illness as a whole.

Whatever outsiders might perceive, the question of the stigma that attaches to mental illness isn't just a question of sensibilities. True, the shunning hurts. But the stigma is an integral part of the problem, and, in one sense at least, it is the problem. In the chronically underfunded mental health field, public hostility and indifference toward the mentally ill works out to be a self-fulfilling prophecy.

The effects of this can be seen in even the most superficial histories of schizophrenia. Schizophrenics, the sickest of the sick, the least acceptable of the unwanted, the most despicable of the despised, were kept hidden even in bedlam.

If anything, they were less curable than other patients, and, as they reacted to their sometimes terrifying hallucinations, they were a threat to order and discipline. Even when they weren't howling and banging on things, they were often paralyzed by a physical (and apparently mental) condition called catatonia. So, until the second half of the twentieth century, they were generally warehoused in the back wards of mental hospitals. If they had any place at all in this world, that place was well out of sight.

Theoreticians of mental illness, though, have always been fascinated by the disease. In fact, it attracted the early Freudians for precisely the same reasons that it now caught the interest of molecular psychologists.

The Freudians, following their theory, settled on the idea that schizophrenia probably resulted from a poor family environment in early life. Mothers in particular were singled out as being at fault, and while that blanket indictment was usually presented in the smooth, euphemistic language of psychiatry, the family generally got the message: Mama did it.

In the midst of tragedy, as each family member searched for a way to be absolved of guilt, this kind of explanation added an icing of blame that often triggered the final disintegration of the stricken family.

But, as mentioned earlier, the Freudians' ability to provide a facile answer and a ready scapegoat was not matched by any successful therapy—and the therapies that were even marginally useful, such as prefrontal lobotomy and electric shock, were total mysteries. And, in the end, it couldn't honestly be said that any-thing really worked.

That being the case, news of Thorazine's development in the

1950s burst like a bright bombshell of optimism over this land-scape of utter hopelessness. Schizophrenia was hallucinations, wasn't it? And Thorazine cured hallucinations, didn't it? There was no question of that. Therefore, Thorazine cured schizophrenia —or even if it didn't, some new drug, modeled after it, soon would.

Unfortunately, of course, Thorazine did no such thing. In stopping the hallucinations it only uncovered that deeper complex of symptoms that characterize the schizophrenic today—the profound withdrawal, the terrible shyness, the indelible alienation that leaves the patient socially incompetent.

As the years passed, it also became obvious that the neuroleptics (drugs like Thorazine) could produce serious side effects.

Early in the course of treatment, for instance, many patients developed a Parkinson-like slowing of bodily movements accompanied by awkward posture. Sometimes the eyes rolled up into the head. These early effects could be treated with anti-Parkinsonian drugs, and, if all else failed, they subsided if the neuroleptic was withdrawn.

But a longer-term set of side effects, termed tardive dyskinesia, also appeared. TD, as it came to be known, was characterized by rapid, involuntary twitching or writhing of the mouth, lips, tongue, arms, legs, or even the entire torso.

TD was anything but subtle. Its symptoms were frequently serious enough to be crippling in and of themselves. Even when they weren't, they were repulsive enough to make it impossible for the schizophrenic to ever live a normal life. Further, TD was very common—in the early days up to 40 percent of those who took Thorazine developed TD.

Those patients were taken off the neuroleptics, of course, but it didn't help. The drugs quelled hallucinations only as long as they were being administered, but TD was permanent. Somehow the drugs damaged the part of the brain that controlled movement, and that damage, whatever it was, was irreparable.

The situation was made immeasurably more tragic by the conditions that existed in most of the chronically underfunded mental hospitals. These conditions, alluded to in an earlier chapter, ran the gamut from lack of privacy and exercise to malnutrition. In truth mental hospitals had always been as bad as, or even worse than, prisons.

But the 1960s and the early 1970s constituted the era of the underdog, and mental patients were at least as qualified for that title as blacks, American Indians, and political prisoners.

The result was a series of highly effective media exposés documenting conditions in the country's mental institutions. Those exposés seemed to lend credence to critics, usually social environmentalists who opposed drug treatment programs, who argued that mental hospital conditions were enough, in and of themselves, to induce severe psychiatric illness in otherwise healthy people.

Though it had already become clear to chemists that schizophrenia was triggered by more than bad living conditions, and though the environmental view of schizophrenia was on its way out, no one could deny that conditions in mental hospitals were atrocious.

Drug treatment, even keeping in mind the rudimentary state of the art, wasn't much better. The pay was too low to attract the best psychiatrists, and even those who served out of dedication were overwhelmed by the caseloads. Each psychiatrist was required to treat hundreds and sometimes even a thousand or more patients. Such doctors were reduced to handing out medication in unmonitored doses.

Given the realities of the madhouse, most psychiatrists succumbed to the temptation to make those doses large enough to keep the patients quiet. If tranquilization was required, other drugs would have been far better suited, not to mention safer, for the purpose—but such a strategy would have been to admit officially that society had no interest in treating the insane, only in keeping them quiet. The TD rates stayed high and the neuroleptics, with or without the conscious intent of psychiatrists, in truth became chemical strait jackets.

And so the dawn of the age of biopsychiatry was beset by irony atop irony. As the most important discoveries in the history of psychiatry were being made almost monthly in the neurochemical laboratories, the clinical world had never been . . . well, crazier. The neuroleptics were being perverted for the sake of peace in bedlam, and, outside the gates, the environmentalistic school of psychology and psychiatry was making common cause with the new-left political movement and rapidly gaining favor among laypeople.

The popular view that the human mind was shaped principally by outside forces in collision with spiritual ones, though not inherent in Freudian theory, seemed to grow from its practice. And the upper-middle-class citizen, which is to say the opinion leader, was most likely to encounter the psychiatric profession in that form. Environmentalism was something people could read about in popular magazines like *Psychology Today* and discuss at cocktail parties.

In that guise, environmentally based theories of psychology had been gaining popularity for decades, but in the 1960s it was seen as dovetailing with the social welfare movement; it was an idea whose time had come. After all, if the low literacy rates among blacks and the poor were caused by the environment, if poverty bred poverty . . . then madness must breed madness, too. In that context, schizophrenia seemed to reflect some ingrained insanity in society.

This era coincided with an increasing awareness that the neuroleptics not only did not cure schizophrenia—they actually caused damage to the brain. Suddenly, the psychiatrists who used them, already like their patients on the fringes of society, were suspected of Nazism and worse.

The laboratory scientists who knew that schizophrenia was principally a biological disease were perplexed. To them the new public attitude against the drugs and the doctors who administered them seemed like willful ignorance and political opportunism. Though it was true that Thorazine might be misused, and that patients might indeed be overdosed to achieve a tranquilizing effect, to call it a tranquilizer was to miss the whole point.

The drug had very specific effects on the perceptual functions of the mind—and *that* smacked of a biological phenomenon. To be sure, the drug was not a panacea, but it was a clue, a solid biological lead, and as such it contained a degree of promise for schizophrenia unmatched in all of psychiatry. But as the public mood swung ever further in the direction of spiritualism and away from scientific reductionism, such voices went largely unheard.

In the meantime, and despite the widespread misuse of the neuroleptics, the lot of the schizophrenic clearly was improving. But, typical of the chaotic history of schizophrenia, this improvement was destined to lead backward instead of forward.

Though the public clung to its disdain for drug treatment, politicians were recognizing that the schizophrenia problem was not as serious as it once had been. Schizophrenics, treated with neuroleptics, no longer acted so . . . so . . . crazy.

This, along with a growing distrust of psychiatrists in general and coupled with newspaper and television exposés on the hideous conditions in many mental institutions, led in the early 1970s to a reevaluation of public mental health policy. Why, people began to ask, did schizophrenics need to be imprisoned? With their hallucinations gone, couldn't they at least be cared for in the community? A decision was made to close most of the nation's mental institutions.

If arrangements had been made to care for schizophrenics in the community, such a strategy might indeed have worked. But the reason they had been committed to institutions in the first place was that the public hadn't wanted to be bothered with them, and that feeling hadn't changed a bit.

So, in one of those social policy upheavals that lays bare the stigma against mental illness, the politicians who decreed that the mental hospitals be closed on humanitarian grounds somehow neglected to budget money for the neighborhood treatment programs that were supposed to replace the hospitals.

As institution after institution closed its doors, thousands of schizophrenics were given prescriptions and freed . . . into a world that pitied them in the abstract but despised them in the flesh. Lacking supervision, many if not most schizophrenics stopped taking their drugs and were reduced to listlessly wandering the inner-city streets, lost in their recurrent hallucinations, easy prey to the winter snows and marauding bands of youths.

Inevitably, the same crusaders who had advocated the closing of mental institutions now took up the cause of the homeless ex-inmates. As the new exposés brought the dilemma to the attention of the newspaper subscriber and the television viewer, volunteers set up soup kitchens and pressure groups formed to advocate shelter programs.

The "freeing" of the schizophrenics from mental institutions, then, had simply sufficed to make their plight more obvious. Never had the problem been so acute, so visible, or, in the public mind at least, so hopeless.

Things were so bad, in fact, that if biopsychiatrists played their cards right they could emerge as conquering heroes.

If molecular psychologists could define schizophrenia chemically and produce a truly effective treatment or even a cure, they would solve an entire list of what most people thought of as insoluble problems.

Such a clinical breakthrough would restore millions of people to useful lives. It would get the schizophrenics out of the headlines and thereby help end the stigma against mental patients as a whole. It would establish once and for all the legitimacy of molecular psychology, and its ascendancy over the shrinks and the psychopoliticians. Curing schizophrenia would be a coup, a scientific coup of spectacular proportions.

As molecular psychologists like Solomon Snyder and Candace Pert watched the discoveries unfold, the possibility of such a bold breakthrough in schizophrenia research suddenly seemed very real. Given the theory of the mind-brain, coupled with the technical ability to isolate defects and develop new drugs to correct them, it might actually be something of a pushover.

The fact that schizophrenia had been the first mental illness to yield to drug treatment, for instance, was seen as a good sign. The profound nature of the symptoms seemed to indicate that the underlying chemical defect must be very basic and therefore, if one knew where to look, relatively simple to correct.

Indeed, there had been reports even before the 1950s that schizophrenics had high levels of this enzyme or low levels of that metabolite. In those days, though, the findings could never be duplicated. The brain was a seething cauldron of ever-changing biochemicals, and unless a researcher had a rationale that gave the search some direction, he might as well not bother.

The new theory of molecular psychology provided that direction, and with it the technical means. The Snyder-Pert work, and subsequent findings in other laboratories, had by the mid-1970s managed to pinpoint several chemicals and processes that might be involved.

All that was left, it seemed, was to use the new technology to seize the moment. The answer might jump right out at the shrewd scientist who did the right experiment.

And almost every molecular psychologist dreamed of being that scientist.

9

A

LESSON

IN

HUMILITY

BEFORE the Snyder-Pert breakthrough in 1973, most research on the chemical nature of schizophrenia had revolved around already-existing drugs. Pharmacologists didn't know exactly what Thorazine did, for instance, but they hoped some random tinkering with the molecule might make it do it better. So they tinkered, and then tinkered some more. They added a few atoms, subtracted a few, and generally mucked around in the hope of finding a more useful, and safer, drug.

It was slow going, though, and it was made all the slower because there was no animal model for schizophrenia. Most useful drugs are developed by giving promising compounds to rats, mice, guinea pigs, and other laboratory animals, killing them, and seeing what the drug had done to the target organ.

By this time, increasing numbers of experts were convinced that there were in fact physical differences between schizophrenics and normal people . . . but nobody knew what those differences were. Theories aside, schizophrenia could still be diagnosed only on the basis of interviews, in which the patient described a hallucinatory event or otherwise indicated that one had occurred. How would you tell if a rat was having hallucinations? How would you tell if you cured them?

Animal research, as a result, was limited to safety testing. To find out whether or not a new drug really worked, the scientists had to move directly to human trials, a slow, time-consuming, bureaucratic process. This process was rendered even touchier by ethical considerations and a social climate in which the psychiatrist's very motives were being questioned by many philosophers, artists, and politicians.

Even so, the two decades of research on neuroleptics that had preceded the Snyder-Pert breakthrough had produced a number of antihallucinogenic drugs that worked at least a little better than Thorazine. TD remained a problem, but clinical psychiatrists who had the time to pay close attention to their patients learned to moderate its severity with better drugs and more precise monitoring of dose levels.

As the new theory of the mind-brain began to coalesce, and as powerful new techniques for chemical analysis became available, scientists began the laborious task of determining which chemical changes were induced by the neuroleptics.

They assumed, as they had to, that rat brains were chemically similar to those of men and women. They administered the drugs to normal rats and other animals, killed them, ground up their brains, and painstakingly analyzed the resulting goop.

It was a tedious process that went on sporadically in a number of laboratories over a period of a decade, but by 1973 a definite pattern had emerged. Every neuroleptic that was effective in quelling human hallucinations had the quality, through one or another biochemical route, of suppressing the action of the chemical called dopamine.

Dopamine is normally found in high concentrations in several parts of the brain, but schizophrenia theoreticians focused their attention on a deep brain structure called the corpus striatum (striped body). Neuroanatomists and brain physiologists had long suspected that the corpus striatum played a central role in the processing of outside perceptions. And what was a hallucination, if not a disruption of perception?

The striatum had two projections, or nerve trunk lines, that reached up into the higher brain. One of those projections went to the limbic system, where emotion was processed; the other led to the frontal lobes of the cortex, the seat of consciousness and personality. In a lobotomy, these were the projections that were severed.

Slowly, the chemistry of schizophrenia began to come into focus.

Perhaps these projections were the conduits through which the striatum pumped powerful neurotransmitters, probably dopamine, into selected control centers higher in the brain. By spraying dopamine onto those sensitive, high-level cells, the striatum might help regulate thought and emotions.

If the dopamine system were somehow fouled up, in other words, the brain's perceptual and emotional systems might go haywire. Was that what schizophrenia was?

The question, mulled over at length and subjected to a variety of interesting but inconclusive experiments, produced a view of schizophrenia called the "dopamine hypothesis." This involved a whole string of assumptions, the first of which was that dopamine was a neurotransmitter.

Assuming dopamine to be a neurotransmitter, then the anti-hallucinatory drugs must work by blocking communication between cells that produce dopamine. Presumably this reduced the strength of impulses within the corpus striatum itself and, at the same time, muted the messages traveling from the striatum to the higher centers. The result was fewer hallucinations.

The neuroleptics, in that case, would in effect be producing a chemical lobotomy. The difference was that a true lobotomy was permanent and complete, while drug treatment could be adjusted and, if it didn't help, withdrawn.

The dopamine hypothesis was a compelling idea, neat and compact, totally consistent with the rapidly crystallizing understanding of the nature of the mind-brain. But in 1973 it was still unproved.

The first question before Snyder involved the basic assumption: Was dopamine in fact a neurotransmitter?

The only way to know for certain whether a substance found in the brain was a transmitter or not was to determine whether it had a receptor. Snyder and two postdoctoral fellows, Ian Creese and David Burt, focused on that question and, in 1974, less than a year after the discovery of the opiate receptor, they had found dopamine receptors in the brains of rats.

Following up, Kuhar applied his receptor mapping techniques to the dopamine problem, and, sure enough, the cells of the corpus striatum were richly studded with dopamine receptors. The parts of the cerebral cortex and the emotional brain served by the upward projections of the striatum also had dopamine receptors— not as many as the striatum itself, but enough to confirm its influence over the higher centers.

As the work progressed, several other pieces of the puzzle fell neatly into place. The "speed freak reaction," for instance, suddenly made infinite sense.

During the 1960s, early in the development of the drug culture, one of the more popular substances was amphetamine. Originally developed as a diet pill and for a while one of the most overprescribed drugs in the legal pharmacopoeia, amphetamine was also an "energizer" with effects similar to cocaine. "Speed," as it came to be known on the street, was an "upper" that made the user feel alert, alive, and full of both psychic and physical energy.

But some "speed freaks," after using the substance for extended periods, began to see and hear things that nobody else did. They were brought to emergency rooms by alarmed friends or, as often as not, by puzzled police officers.

At first, emergency room psychiatrists confronted with a speed freak inevitably made the obvious diagnosis: schizophrenia. The symptoms were classic and unmistakable. There was no mistaking them.

Except . . . there was.

As a rule, schizophrenics do not return to normal without treatment—but these patients did. Once the effects of the amphetamines wore off a few hours later, the "schizophrenics" magically regained their sanity and demanded to be set free. The psychiatrists, scratching their heads but conceding the obvious, complied.

As reports of such cases were published and psychiatrists began to look closely at the speed freak syndrome, they made one other interesting observation. If the user was already a diagnosed schizophrenic, it took very little amphetamine to trigger a dramatic relapse. If the user was a "schizoid personality," which was to say a borderline schizophrenic, it took a little more. If the user was normal, it took a lot of amphetamines—a whole lot, in fact—to induce the psychosis.

Once it became clear that dopamine was the messenger molecule for the deep perceptual centers, the speed freak riddle was solved. Amphetamine increases the production of dopamine, revving up the action of the corpus striatum. In a sense, speed was the mirror image of the neuroleptics.

The nature of TD also began to become clear. Dopamine was used in more than one part of the brain.

The first evidence that the brain used the same chemical transmitters in otherwise disparate centers had been contained in Kuhar's opiate receptor maps. According to those maps, rich clusters of opiate receptors were found in the centers that modulate physical pain, for instance, and also in those that process psychological pain.

This made Darwinian sense, insofar as the psychological pain circuitry presumably evolved out of the physical pain circuitry early in the course of evolution. The result was that morphine not only dulled physical pain, it also gave the user a psychological boost.

There was a similar dualism in the dopamine system. It was the principal neurotransmitter not only in the corpus striatum but also in the motor control centers higher in the brain. Dopamine mediated not only what the animal saw, in other words, but also what it did in response.

Under normal circumstances, this multiple use of transmitters posed no problems for the brain. On a microscopic scale, the striatum and the motor cortex were separated by vast distances, and there were no major nerve trunk lines between them. Wayward dopamine molecules would be chewed up by enzymes long before they diffused far enough to cause "cross talk."

But neuroleptics, given orally, penetrated equally into both parts of the brain. When they interfered with dopamine production in the corpus striatum, it was good for the patient—they corrected a metabolic imbalance and suppressed hallucinations. Conversely, in the motor centers, which had been working quite well before, the sudden drought of dopamine caused permanent damage.

Meanwhile, the scientific questions took on an ever sharper focus. Did the brains of schizophrenics have more dopamine receptors than normal brains? Or were those receptors somehow more sensitive?

As each new discovery was announced in the medical journals, the confidence in the dopamine hypothesis soared. Increasingly, scientists felt they were on the edge of a major breakthrough; rumors from the laboratory buoyed the hopes of schizophrenics and their families. But as the questions grew specific, the research began to bog down.

The stumbling block was a familiar one: the lack of an animal model. Rats couldn't be made schizophrenic and their brains analyzed; the work had to be done on human brains. And those brains had to be fresh—the neurons were more delicate than any other cell known to science, and their membranes, along with the receptors on them, began to break down almost immediately after death.

Getting normal brains was only moderately difficult. As biology in general had penetrated into the molecular level in the 1960s and 1970s, and the need for fresher and fresher specimens had increased, doctors had initiated what was sometimes called an "instant autopsy," in which dissection began seconds after death was pronounced. This was practiced only in the major medical research institutions, but even so scientists like Kuhar were able to obtain enough fresh brains to begin making dopamine receptor maps of the nonschizophrenic human brain.

It was tedious and time-consuming work, though. The radioactive tracers designed to snap into the receptors were weak, and the receptors, while critical, made up an exceedingly small portion of the brain mass. As a result, the labeled brain slices, laid against sheets of photographic film, had to be kept in dark freezers for days or even weeks to get the proper exposure.

In the meantime, obtaining the brains of schizophrenics was turning out to be a horrendous problem. Schizophrenics did not generally die in big teaching hospitals. They died in mental institutions, nursing homes, ghetto rooms, or gutters, and their bodies generally went undiscovered for hours. And once they were found, ambulance crews were in no particular hurry to get them to the morgue—and morgue pathologists weren't terribly interested in getting to them quickly, either.

Suddenly brain scientists all over the world were trying to get their hands on fresh schizophrenic brains—and there weren't any. In desperation a conference was called and, on the assumption that an occasional schizophrenic did die in teaching hospitals, a bulletin went out to research doctors explaining the urgency of the need. In addition, they established a brain bank, where the few precious specimens they hoped would be forthcoming would be frozen, stored, and parceled out for critical experiments.

Eventually a few schizophrenic brains began to trickle in, and the tedious process of mapping their dopamine receptors began. The answer, as anticipated, was that schizophrenic brains did have unusually dense dopamine receptor fields in their corpus striata.

Meanwhile, scientists had made a discovery that suggested the possibility of new drugs that would not cause TD.

The discovery was that some brain systems that were thought

113

to share the same transmitters in fact did not. The transmitters were similar, but not identical.

The best example was in the opiate systems. The natural opiates used by the physical pain system and the psychic pain system had evolved into slightly different forms. They could still cross-react, but the physical pain system's transmitters didn't get quite as good a result in the psychic centers, and vice versa.

This raised the hopes that, by studying the differences and using them in shrewd ways, chemists might be able to develop morphinelike molecules that would affect the pain control centers without doing much in the psychic pain centers. Such a drug presumably could be used to kill physical pain without the risk of psychological addiction.

If such differences could be found in the dopamine systems, new neuroleptics might be designed that would have a stronger action in the corpus striatum than in the motor control centers. With such a drug, TD might join the strait jacket and isolation cell on the ash heap of psychohistory.

Such were the hopes of the molecular psychologists. But when the results of the new round of experiments began to hit the journals, it became agonizingly clear that schizophrenia wasn't going to be the pushover that many scientists, in those heady days following the Snyder-Pert breakthrough, had hoped.

One letdown came when it was realized that Kuhar's receptor maps, showing changes in the dopamine receptor fields of schizophrenics, might not be as meaningful as they first appeared.

By this time scientists had begun to realize that, within certain limits, the normal brain was very plastic—receptor fields weren't necessarily stable. If there was too much dopamine, for instance, the cells might compensate by decreasing the density of the dopamine receptors on its surface. In fact, some experts were beginning to suspect that such changes might be involved in the processes of learning and addiction—processes that were looking increasingly similar.

If the brain's receptor fields became more or less dense in response to psychological or physiological stimuli, the differences in the dopamine fields between schizophrenics and normal people might not be significant at all. They might be caused not by the disease but the treatment.

Almost all schizophrenics, after all, were taking neuroleptics—it would probably constitute malpractice to deny them. Neuroleptics decreased the flow of dopamine. Might not the brain, responding to that decreased flow, increase the number of receptors? If so, the differences in receptor densities between normal people and schizophrenics would be meaningless.

Scientists attempting to find differences between the dopamine receptors in the corpus striatum and those in the motor cortex also came up short. If there were differences, they couldn't find them. At least for the moment, that dashed the hopes of engineering new drugs that would treat schizophrenia without causing TD.

Even more disillusioning, by 1980 scientists had begun to realize that dopamine imbalances, though obviously involved in schizophrenia, were apparently not the root cause of the disease after all. The crippling shyness, for instance, was unfortunately not mediated by dopamine. It had to do with other systems, centering perhaps in parts of the emotional brain that communicated by means of the neurotransmitter norepinephrine.

This and other information made it look more and more as though the dopamine imbalance, however disabling it might be, was probably a secondary effect of some disease process elsewhere in the brain. The dopamine imbalance, and for that matter the norepinephrine disturbance as well, might be caused by too much (or too little) stimulation from some other, still unsuspected, center.

The hallucinations, in that case, were just symptoms—and treating schizophrenia with dopamine blockers made about as much sense as treating smallpox by rubbing anti-itch cream on the skin eruptions. The misery abated somewhat, but the disease progressed all the same.

The dopamine hypothesis, in short, was wrong; the innocent

young science of molecular psychology had just learned its first lesson in humility.

The humiliation, though, stemmed more from unrealistic expectations than it did from reality. The truth was that in the seven years following the Snyder-Pert breakthrough, scientists had learned more about schizophrenia than had been discovered in all the decades before.

By 1980 there was a general agreement among molecular psychologists that schizophrenia was clearly a physical disease, and that perception was shared by an increasing number of more traditional psychiatrists. That, in itself, was a major step. And if the dopamine hypothesis had bombed out, at least the scientists were no longer wasting their time in pursuit of a wild goose.

Also there was nothing in the failure of the hypothesis to cast doubt on the basic perception of the mind as a chemical phenomenon. Each research finding seemed, in fact, a further confirmation. If the scientists were going to have to slog, at least they had a theory, and a rationale, to assure themselves that they were slogging in the right direction.

As the disappointment receded into the past, in fact, researchers quickly began to generate a blizzard of new information that served to reassure them that a cure, though it obviously wasn't coming tomorrow, was still within reach.

Since the realization that prior treatment with neuroleptics seriously marred the usefulness of Kuhar's receptor maps, for instance, scientists had been scouring the earth for the brains of dead schizophrenics who had somehow slipped through the cracks and had not received neuroleptics. A few rare specimens were eventually found, and initial reports indicated that their brains did have abnormalities in their receptor fields.

Other discoveries restored the hope that differences would be found between dopamine receptors in the corpus striatum and those in the motor cortex, thus enabling scientists to engineer neuroleptics that would not cause TD.

Other scientific teams are pursuing other ideas. At the State University of New York at Stony Brook, for instance, a group led by Dr. Fritz Henn is proceeding on the assumption that the imbalance in the dopamine system is caused by more specific defects in other systems that, in turn, trigger the abnormal dopamine reactions. Early results are promising.

In the meantime, scientists in England and at the National Institute of Mental Health have demonstrated the existence of widespread shrinkage of the cerebral cortex in schizophrenics. This shrinkage of the most "human" part of the brain could be due to a lack of chemical stimulation from deeper structures, or it could be caused by an overall dying of cells.

In either event, the shrinkage in schizophrenic patients is in some ways reminiscent of that found in people with Alzheimer's disease, or senility. And that possibility opens up a whole new set of questions and hypotheses.

As Joseph Coyle at Johns Hopkins observes, some experts have long felt that the withdrawal and other "negative" symptoms of schizophrenia were similar to some of the symptoms of senility. There is in both cases a sort of "dilapidation" of higher cortical functions and a crudening of social skills.

An increased appreciation of similarities between schizophrenia and Alzheimer's disease, which many suspect may be caused by an inherited weakness to a virus, leads to the revival of an old theory that schizophrenia may be viral in origin.

These developments, drawn almost at random from the explosion of discoveries involving schizophrenia since the demise of the dopamine hypothesis, illustrates how rapidly the information is accumulating.

Armed with the new theory of molecular psychology, scientists are literally tearing apart the corpus striatum and its associated systems, molecule by molecule. By 1986 the field was in such an uproar of discovery that senior scientists around the world held a meeting in Berlin for the purpose of integrating the new knowledge and synthesizing another working hypothesis.

In the meantime, schizophrenics and their families may not have to wait for the last piece to be fit into the puzzle before benefiting from that research. European psychiatrists are already using a new drug that is believed to have an effect on schizophrenia's "negative symptoms" as well as relieving hallucinations. The effect on the negative symptoms is believed to have something to do with the drug's ability to affect calcium metabolism.

However it works, scientists are confident that this compound is but a forerunner of a whole new class of powerful yet side effect–free antischizophrenic agents that will appear over the next decade.

But almost no insider still believes that schizophrenia will provide the new field of molecular psychology with its first spectacular clinical breakthrough. Instead, the most promising area of research now is depression.

10

THE

CHEMICALS

OF

SORROW

OF the two classic forms of mental illness, depression and schizophrenia, the latter had always seemed the one more likely to be caused by some obvious underlying organic brain disease. For one thing, schizophrenia produced thought abnormalities so bizarre that it could often be diagnosed by untrained laymen. There was also a certain stereotypical similarity about schizophrenics, which argued for a specific, more or less universal, cause.

Depression was an altogether murkier condition. It shaded almost imperceptibly from the everyday "blues" on the normal end of the spectrum to suicidal self-hatred on the other. While the symptoms could become quite strange on the extreme end, they were not totally beyond the human experience.

The clinically depressed patient usually didn't howl, hear voices, pitch into catatonia, converse with Christ or imagine himself to be Napoleon or Cleopatra. As a result, even many biopsychiatrists suspected that depression, unlike schizophrenia, was probably an environmentally induced "psychological" disease.

The differences between normal and "clinical" depression seemed primarily to be those of degree. A normal person, focusing his mind on the dark side of reality, could easily think himself into depression.

In fact, if you're not depressed by the inevitability of pain and death, the fleeting nature of love, man's celebrated inhumanity to man . . . then you're probably just not paying attention. Most people don't, most of the time. That's how we cope: we ignore the things we can't change and focus, instead, on those we can.

But even the most well-balanced person sometimes must confront the grim realities of life. The death of a loved one, the loss of a job, a watershed birthday, and a whole list of more minor setbacks are universal "downers." When we confront them, we get down in the dumps.

What's more, a perfectly normal person, when depressed, may often become self-destructive. Studies have shown that depressing situations or times dramatically increase the risk that you'll cut your finger while chopping vegetables, break your leg in the bathtub, or lose control of your car and slam into a bridge abutment.

But normal depression generally has an identifiable cause, and sooner or later it runs its course. Then the dark clouds lift, attention shifts to the positive things in life, and normality returns.

Clinical depression can also be triggered by a serious and devastating event, such as the death of a family member. But it's more likely to have no obvious cause at all, or, if it does, the depth of the depression is all out of proportion to the problem. And however appropriate the depression is or isn't, clinical depression doesn't go away by itself.

As month follows month, year follows year, the victim is overcome by a deep malaise and loses all interest in the outside world. Sex ceases to be interesting. Food loses its taste, and eating habits drift to one extreme or the other. A feeling of impending tragedy sets in along with an overwhelming sense of helplessness, a conviction that nothing will make any difference. The depressed person feels incompetent, and from that grows self-hatred.

Such feelings, as they sift through the complex passageways of the human mind, are often translated into acute physical symptoms, most notably "ghost pains." The depressed person may have headaches, backaches, or stomach pains. Some even feel as though their intestines are rotting.

But the symptoms aren't always strictly psychological—as the disease runs its course, the patient often fails to practice good hygiene. He may eat spoiled food, not noticing. His teeth rot, and, as malnourishment or obesity takes its toll, his immune response dwindles, and he becomes subject to infection, heart disease, and other frankly physical ailments.

As the disease progresses, common self-destructiveness intensifies into suicide fantasies and from fantasy to reality. Sometimes the suicidal urge plays itself out in the context of alcohol and drugs, but it's often less subtle. Depressed people regularly throw themselves out of windows, cut their wrists, or swallow poisons.

Until early in this century, the victim of depression was rarely distinguished from the schizophrenic or, for that matter, patients in the final throes of syphilis. Some therapists, spotting a glimmer of the true problem, tried to combat the disease with "logical" therapies like light music, tickling with feathers, and jokes. It didn't work, of course, and for the most part the melancholics were treated pretty much like everyone else in the asylum. They were chanted at, they were scolded, they were whipped, they were immersed in ice-water baths and wrapped in wet sheets. Subject as they were to suicide, they also felt the confinement of boxes, padded cells, and strait jackets.

Like the schizophrenic, the melancholic also underwent shock treatments, but here at least there was a discernible difference. Shock treatments, in the cases of at least some depressed people, seemed to provide a long-term remission of symptoms. Lobotomy, on the other hand, didn't seem to help as much as it did with schizophrenics.

But these differences, by any measure, were as crude as the treatments. The most dramatic split between the two groups, in terms of the effectiveness of therapy, came with the advent of the neuroleptics. Thorazine worked dramatically for schizophrenics, but all it did for depressed patients was make them a little drowsy.

Even so, Thorazine at least tipped off scientists that a chemical treatment might be possible. And depression, so much more common than schizophrenia, attracted a lot of attention—and the psychiatric community, once alerted to the possibilities, began to find clues.

The first solid indication that depression might be chemical in nature emerged from the study of high blood pressure, which in the early 1950s was beginning to be recognized as a major health problem.

One of the most effective drugs for lowering blood pressure was reserpine, but it had a strange side effect: patients taking it often began to exhibit all the signs of severe depression, including loss of appetite, insomnia, flagging sexual interest, and psychosomatic pains.

The second lead came from studies of the then-new anti-tuberculosis drug, iproniazid. The drug did wonders for tuberculosis, which was then a disease at least as dreaded as cancer is today. In the sanitariums, the patients began dancing in the halls.

That was natural enough, of course. But healthy jubilation is like normal depression: in due course, it subsides. But in the sanitariums the patients danced, and danced, and danced, and danced, until their doctors finally began to get suspicious. Iproniazid apparently did more than just cure tuberculosis.

Scientists, tipped off to the mood-altering characteristics of reserpine and iproniazid, gave them to rats. The rats who got the reserpine lost their appetites and their interest in sex; they spent their days in what appeared to be a blue funk, cowering in the corners of their cages. The rats that got iproniazid, on the other hand, became the friendliest and best-humored rats the scientists had ever seen.

The brains of the depressed, reserpine-drugged rats turned out to have a notable lack of two chemicals: norepinephrine and serotonin. The brains of the iproniazid-treated rats had more of both.

As the biochemists refined their experiments, they discovered the mechanism behind the difference.

A law of biology holds that the abundance of any substance in any organ at any given moment is a function of how fast it is being manufactured, how much is stored, and how quickly it is being used up or destroyed. Reserpine, the scientists finally figured out, worked by depleting the stores of norepinephrine and serotonin.

Iproniazid operated a little differently. Norepinephrine and serotonin are normally broken down by the enzyme monoamine oxidase, or MAO. Iproniazid depleted the levels of MAO, which meant that norepinephrine and serotonin couldn't be broken down as fast. As a result, their overall levels increased.

The experiments were published, replicated, and finally accepted. As a result, scientists who were most intimately involved in this new field of neurochemistry concluded that depression, whatever it was, had something to do with levels of norepinephrine and serotonin in the brain.

They didn't know what those chemicals did, of course. But that didn't stop them, any more than the mystery surrounding Thorazine stopped scientists from developing better versions of it. So while basic scientists concentrated on discovering the importance of serotonin and norepinephrine to the operation of the human mind, clinical pharmacologists set up trial-and-error drug screening programs that, they hoped, would yield compounds effective against depression.

The earlier neuropharmacologists were hampered by the same problems that plagued their colleagues who studied schizophrenia. The most serious of these problems was a lack of animal models. That meant doctors had to choose candidate compounds by hunch and guesswork and then screen those promising drugs by administering them, with crossed fingers, to mental patients.

Even so, by the 1970s several antidepressant drugs had been developed—most notably a class of drugs called the tricyclic antidepressants, like imipramine. But these drugs were discovered by accident, and, since they couldn't be improved through animal tests, they retained serious, unpredictable, and sometimes deadly side effects. Imipramine, for instance, could (and often did) cause irregularities in the heartbeat that, if not detected by the psychiatrist, resulted in sudden, massive, and fatal heart attacks.

Further, no compound worked well on all depressed patients, which meant the psychiatrist had to "shop around" through his pharmacopoeia, trying first this drug and then that one, adjusting the dosage according to instinct and symptoms until he got a result he could be satisfied with.

Such case-by-case experimentation took time, of course, and patience. In the mental hospitals, where there were few doctors to go around, the results were less satisfying than in private practice. But even in private practice, and even when the psychiatrist was very good, the depressed patient often lacked the patience to stick with it. Failure after failure led to further depression, playing as it did into the preexisting conviction that nothing was going to work anyway.

As a result, many if not most people who might have benefited from the therapy dropped out of treatment. Many found their final solution, instead, in the form of suicide.

Even under the best of conditions antidepressants didn't work for everyone, but as the treatment became more sophisticated, and the response rate grew, psychiatrists began to notice that there was one group in which the drugs almost never worked. These patients suffered by a peculiar form of depression called manic-depressive disease or bipolar depression, a peculiar ailment characterized by alternating ups and downs.

The bipolar patient would experience a period of mania, in which he almost seemed to be under the influence of some strange—and desirable—stimulant. He was happy, happy beyond all reason. His mind worked incessantly, churning out creative and grandiose ideas, and while those ideas might seem strange to an outsider, the patient liked them a lot; he was possessed by an elated feeling that he could do no wrong.

But the cardinal principle of bipolar depression was that what went up must come down . . . with a resounding thud. The mania was typically followed by a depression as debilitating as the high had been desirable. Some patients cycled rapidly, going from mania to depression in hours; some followed a pattern that carried them from peak to valley over a period of weeks.

The disease wasn't very common, compared with regular or "unipolar" depression, involving only about 15 percent of all depressed patients. But because the disease was so disabling, and the victims had such a high suicide risk, bipolar depression constituted a disproportionately large problem. A drug therapy was needed, and needed badly.

The answer in fact had been around since 1949, when a psychiatrist by the name of John Cade accidentally discovered the ability of lithium salts to prevent mood swings. But for a variety of reasons, his discovery was not put to immediate use.

One reason was probably medical-nationalistic chauvinism: Cade was an Australian, and his nation was not known for producing psychiatric breakthroughs. Another was that lithium salts had at one time been tried as a substitute for table salt, and several deaths had been attributed to it. Finally, until the late 1960s manic-depressive patients were generally lumped with depressed patients by statisticians, and the scale of the problem wasn't fully realized.

But the possibilities of lithium treatment began to become apparent in the 1960s, and by the early 1970s lithium was recognized as one of the great leaps forward in chemical psychiatry.

The drug was administered as lithium sulfide or lithium carbonate (eventually shortened to just plain "lithium"). Nobody knew how it worked, but what mattered was that it did. It worked, and it worked dramatically, for about 85 percent of all victims of bipolar depression.

Oddly enough, though, its efficacy was not confined to patients with bipolar depression. Some unipolar patients who hadn't gotten any relief from the tricyclics turned out to respond to lithium as dramatically as the bipolars did. This made scientists scratch their heads. Reports appeared in the literature that such patients often had relatives who suffered, or had suffered, from manic-depressive disease. But other reports contradicted them.

The question of whether manic-depression was fundamentally different from unipolar depression, and if so how, had implications far wider than they first appeared. The question of taxonomy, of sorting out the various mental diseases from one another, had by the 1970s become one of the cutting edges of psychiatry.

The hope was that by dividing the various forms of mental diseases, they could be conquered. Those with obvious physical causes might be isolated, their mechanisms understood, and effective new treatments devised. Since depression included the easily identifiable subgroup of manic-depression, scientists who studied the relationship between the two diseases were on the forefront of this divide-and-conquer movement.

If depression could be divided into subtypes, and particularly if those subtypes could be identified by some physical test, on the basis of some "marker," it could be of immense benefit.

For one thing, the various drugs would probably work better on some subtypes than others—already it was known that lithium, for instance, was more likely to work on bipolar disease and that the tricyclics were generally preferred for unipolar depression.

If that sort of distinction could be made on a finer scale, it would be of great practical value. If a psychiatrist knew what type of depression he was treating, and which drugs usually worked on that type, he would probably have to do less tinkering with each patient's prescription. If nothing else, he would have a place to begin.

And, if it could be done with depression, there was a hope that it might be done with other diseases as well.

At first the idea of a physical marker for depression seemed like a pipe dream, particularly for those who doubted that depression had any organic cause in the first place. But as time went on, there were increasing indications that depression, whatever its cause, sometimes did produce measurable physical changes.

One intriguing piece of evidence came from the National Institute of Mental Health, where scientists reported finding abnormally high levels of a metabolite of norepinephrine in the spinal fluid samples taken from suicide victims. Since most suicide victims were presumably victims of depression, and depression was thought to have something to do with norepinephrine metabolism, the discovery seemed suggestive.

It wasn't very clinically useful, though. Drawing samples of spinal fluid is an awkward, somewhat painful process accompanied by low-level but very real risks of spinal cord damage. It would hardly serve as a method of screening people for depression.

A better measure would be a blood, skin, or urine test—something easy, safe, and inexpensive.

Scientists pursuing that course discovered that distinctive chemical abnormalities in fact could be found in the blood and urine of some depressed patients. There was, for instance, a set of blood proteins that occurred more frequently in depressed people than in normal ones—and those proteins were suggestively related to the MAO enzyme that, in the brain, was involved in the metabolism of serotonin and norepinephrine.

Unfortunately, such markers weren't always found in depressed patients, and they were often present in normal people, so the evidence was contradictory and confusing. But the work went on.

In the strictest scientific terms, the search for a marker was calculated to produce clinical tools, not at finding the root causes of the diseases in question. After all, any such marker, however distinctive it might be, might represent not cause but effect.

Psychological states are quite capable of changing metabolic processes, increasing heart rate, and suppressing the production of immune system cells. State of mind, or the stress associated with being depressed, or even the experience of being hospitalized, might well be capable of altering proteins in the blood.

But science proceeds not on proofs but on hypotheses, and the mere hint of a physical connection tended to heighten the enthusiasm of a growing number of experts who suspected that some physical process lay at the root of depression. And that physical process, many hoped, might well be laid bare by the discovery of a marker. So there was more at stake than just a clinical tool.

The Snyder-Pert breakthrough in 1973 poured gasoline on the fire, and scientists rushed back to their laboratories to see whether the new information could lead to some pattern that made sense.

Norepinephrine and serotonin had been repeatedly implicated in depression. Serotonin in particular made sense, since it was apparently critical in sleep, and sleep disorders were common among depressives.

The question, now, was obvious: were the two chemicals neurotransmitters? If they were, there ought to be receptors. Armed with the Snyder-Pert techniques, researchers went looking, and, sure enough, they found the receptors.

Meanwhile, other scientists set their sights on finding out how imipramine and the other tricyclic antidepressants worked.

The imipramine story, it turned out, was reminiscent of that of morphine: imipramine had molecular properties similar to a natural neurotransmitter. When taken in pill form, it entered the patient's blood, circulated to the brain, and snapped into a previously unknown receptor in the emotional part of the brain.

Morphine, of course, directly interferes with a major neurotransmitter system, the normal function of which is to establish a pain threshold. As that threshold rises, the morphine user gets a "high."

Imipramine exerted a much more subtle and specific modulating effect. The receptor it activated apparently controlled fine-tuning in the serotonin system, which is responsible in part for the maintenance of mood equilibrium.

Under normal circumstances, the natural form of imipramine triggered a metabolic chain reaction that resulted in the brain becoming more sensitive to its own serotonin—the brain, in becoming more sensitive to serotonin, became more easily elated. If the natural form of imipramine diminished, depression resulted. Thus, the brain controlled mood.

This suggested that depression, or at least some form of it, might be characterized either by the production of too little imipramine or too few imipramine receptors. The result in either case would be depression—and it could be overcome, as depression often was, by the administration of imipramine.

Another wrinkle to the imipramine story illustrates how scientists, as they become more facile at finding, analyzing, and otherwise experimenting with receptors, began to develop innovative ways of solving old problems.

Scientific work with mental illness, for instance, had always been hobbled by the dilemma of trying to study an organ the scientists couldn't even touch—the human brain. Scientists studying the skin, the kidneys, or even the heart could biopsy the organs they were interested in, removing bits of diseased tissue to study in the laboratory. A biopsy of the brain, though, would almost inevitably cause serious damage. Ethically, the human brain was out of reach.

But as laboratory scientists began to fully appreciate the role of the receptors, and with the explosive growth of biochemical technology for detecting them, a whole series of new possibilities presented themselves.

The key was that all cells in a given individual have the same genetic information in their nuclei, be they cells of the brain or of the skin. The thing that makes cells different is that in each case different genes express themselves. Dopamine receptors, for instance, are found on the surfaces of neurons in the corpus striatum, but not on skin cells. But that doesn't mean the skin cell lacks the genetic ability to manufacture dopamine receptors. That ability is just suppressed.

It turned out, though, that in practice the "gene switch" was not always entirely off or on. Sometimes a little bit of information sort of leaked out. Blood platelets, for instance, were found to have a few imipramine receptors on their surfaces. Even more exciting, such platelets from depressed people often had fewer of those receptors on their skin cells than normal people did—and the number of receptors returned to normal once the patient recovered!

As with other markers, the differences weren't clear-cut enough, or reliable enough, to be of much clinical use. But such experiments led to the realization that scientists might be able to study the brain receptors of depressed people through the roundabout route of skin cells.

The variation in the numbers of imipramine receptors on depressed people's platelets, and the way those receptors varied with the progress of the disease, probably reflected a process going on in the brain as well. Clearly, scientists needed to look at cells from accessible parts of the body for metabolic defects that they thought might exist in the brain.

In theory this was simple, but in practice it was complicated almost beyond belief. For one thing, such natural genetic "leakages" as those involving the imipramine receptors were rare. If this technology were to become truly important, scientists would need to figure out how to manipulate the environments of cell cultures in such a way as to trick cells into expressing receptors that normally would lie dormant.

As delicate as this task might be, it was deemed worth the effort and a number of laboratories began trying. By the early 1980s, there had been several reports that skin cells had in fact been induced to express brain receptors, and that such receptors on the skin cells of mentally ill patients were indeed different from those of normal people.

Such reports, however, represented but momentary glimmerings of possibilities. In no case were scientists from other laboratories able to duplicate the complex experiments; more often than not, even the original scientists had difficulty doing it again.

There were just too many factors to control, and too little was known about precisely what made specific receptors express at some times and not at others.

In the meantime, scientists first at the University of Pennsylvania and then at other research institutions produced a breakthrough that, with a single stroke, put the field of depression leagues ahead of that of schizophrenia: an animal model was developed.

The method was simple, involving what psychologists euphemistically term "exposure to adverse stimuli." A rat, for instance, might be put in a cage with a metal floor and exposed to occasional, unpredictable electrical shocks to its feet.

But it wasn't the shock itself that induced depression. If there was a ledge the rat could jump onto after each jolt, the animal could endure the shock cage for extended periods of time while remaining psychologically normal.

But if the shelf or other escape route was removed, and the rat was totally helpless, the effect was dramatically different. When the rat couldn't predict when the shocks were going to come and had no means of escape . . . when it was waiting all the time to get hit, never knowing when the jolt would come . . . something very human seemed to happen to it.

These rats seemed to just give up. They stopped trying to get away and, for that matter, stopped trying to do much of anything.

Like depressed humans, the rats developed eating disorders and lost interest in mating. They had trouble sleeping, and, when scientists attempted to teach them to run mazes, they seemed downright stupid.

Depressed people often told psychiatrists that they felt helpless, without any ability to influence what happened to them. The rats acted, at least, as though they felt the same way.

What's more, once enough stress had been administered, the rats didn't get over their depression. If they were put back in the shock cage but were now provided with an escape route, they didn't use it. They didn't even seem to have the will to try; instead, they hunkered down and accepted the shocks almost as though they deserved them.

The scientists tried other animals, from mice to monkeys, and got the same results.

Similar work had been done before by psychologists but had always encountered the fatal criticism that depression was a psychological phenomenon—and no matter how the rats acted, nobody could say how they felt. But now there were more objective measures of depression.

For one, there were the tricyclic antidepressants. The scientists treated the rats with the same drugs effective in humans and, sure enough, they returned to normal. Once again they were interested in sex, they ate normally, and when put in the shock cage they tried to escape.

Once an animal model was available, work spread to other centers. At the State University of New York at Stony Brook, for instance, a group led by Fritz Henn killed rats at various stages of the stressing process and analyzed their brains for chemical changes.

The group reported that, as the rats became depressed, predictable changes occurred in their brain receptors—the receptors became more dense in some areas, less so in others. The changes occurred at the same time the behavioral alterations were taking place and centered in the areas believed responsible for depression in humans.

The principal changes were concentrated in a subtype of norepinephrine receptors in one area and serotonin receptors in another, again corresponding to the suspected defect in human depression.

This was the first animal model of depression, but it was not the last. Several other models are now being used in molecular psychology laboratories, and there is the promise of more to follow.

The development of these models for a mental illness that affects humans is a historic breakthrough. As a result, drugs can be engineered specifically to activate or suppress the affected parts of the brain and can then be tested and improved on live animals.

"I'm very excited about this," said Henn. "It shows us that the brain changes with experience . . . and that it stays changed. And with animal models we can really take apart the neurochemical systems and see what's changing, and what's changing in conjunction with the behavioral changes.

"And we can then treat the animal with medications and we can reverse the behaviors. We can look and see what's changing."

Although the rat experiments proved beyond the shadow of a doubt that depression could be induced by strictly environmental means, many scientists believe the experiments ultimately cast doubt on the theory that it happened that way in people.

"The first thing that strikes you as you look at those experiments," mused one scientist, "is that environment could cause depression. In a way, though, that wasn't surprising. After all, we've all been depressed, though transiently, by things that happen to us. What really surprises you is how very, very much stress it takes.

"You put rats in a cage, and you shock them. It takes a long time. Hours, days of conditioning, before their minds close down. To depress a monkey you have to put him in an isolation cage for weeks. Humans, in the normal course of events, are rarely subjected to that kind of pressure. So either we're very sensitive . . . or there's some other very important factor."

What that other factor might be was hinted at by a difficulty experienced by Henn's group as it moved its laboratory from Iowa, where the original work was done, to Stony Brook, where it is now in progress. Henn, using the same equipment and procedures but a different strain of rats, for a while couldn't duplicate his own experiments. Once he went back to the original strain of rats, however, the experiments worked fine.

Some rats, in other words, were genetically more depressive than others. The idea that the same might be true of humans brings us to what is probably the single most explosive issue in all of biology: psychogenetics.

TWISTED

MOLECULES

THE idea that human personality, character, and intelligence are inherited is one of the most persistent, and at the same time one of the most abused, concepts in all of human history.

Until this century, though, it was more than merely acceptable—it supplied the philosophical underpinnings of the social order. How, otherwise, could some men be born kings and others serfs? How else could one race justify the bondage of another?

If the strengths of character that lay behind the claim to title, land, and peasantry could be passed from parent to child, it made equal sense that weaknesses such as madness were also a result of breeding. So this, too, was assumed.

Ironically, the most striking example of hereditary mental frailty in the eighteenth and nineteenth centuries was found not in the low born but at the pinnacle of the aristocracy itself, in the insanity that frequently accompanied the hemophilia, jutting jaws, and other infirmities of the inbred royal families of Europe.

Human nature being what it is, of course, the aristocracy ignored this all-too-close example and pointed instead, as proof of hereditary weaknesses of character, to the coarse ways of the common people. The fact that the average citizen for the most part acquiesced in this view is a further irony, testifying as it does to the strength of social environment and the power of a prevailing idea.

In the mid-1800s, Charles Darwin's theory of evolution, while unacceptable to many on a variety of grounds, could nonetheless be seen as providing support for the existence of a privileged class. Darwin and his supporters believed that behavioral as well as physical attributes of animals were products of evolution, and if one had the stomach to make the leap from animals to human beings, why . . . there you had it.

Inevitably, as the industrial revolution picked up speed, the inheritability of the mind was applied to explain and validate the rise of the commercially monied class. Packaged as "social Darwinism" by philosopher Herbert Spencer, it held that some people were naturally better than others, and, that being the case, the devil *should* take the hindmost. Thus it served to justify the actions of generations of robber barons.

All this rested on a philosophical house of cards, of course, and had little if anything to do with science. In fact it wasn't until the early twentieth century that researchers documented the existence of what in hindsight might be called the first example of genetically caused insanity: Huntington's chorea.

Huntington's chorea struck its victims in their middle years, drove them mad, and then killed them. It was indisputably genetic; if one parent died of it, an average of half the victim's progeny would die of it as well.

In terms of genetically induced madness, though, the disease was not a very satisfying example. Then as now, most people, doctors included, made a sharp distinction between the physical substance of the brain and its more "spiritual" characteristics. Disease was one thing, madness quite another.

Huntington's chorea confused the dichotomy, but its first symptoms were physical, most notably disabling muscular spasms —the word *chorea* has the same root as "choreograph," and implies a dance. Victims of Huntington's chorea didn't lose their senses until late in the disease, often just before they died. So most physicians thought of it, without really thinking about it at all, as physical.

Still, the discovery that Huntington's chorea was purely and classically a genetic disease, and that insanity was one manifestation, was thought provoking. Might there be other physical ailments that attacked only the brain, producing madness but leaving the rest of the body unaffected?

The first to test that hypothesis scientifically was Ernst Rudin, a German scientist. In his view, schizophrenia, the most obvious and devastating of all the insanities, was probably the one most likely to be proved genetic. So he conducted a statistical study of its victims and their relatives and, in a 1916 scientific paper, concluded that it did indeed run in families. In fact, the sibling of a schizophrenic was far more likely to become a schizophrenic than was the average person.

Looked at another way, though, Rudin's statistics weren't nearly as clear-cut as those, say, for Huntington's chorea. The brother or sister of a Huntington's patient faced even odds of also becoming a victim, but the sibling of a schizophrenic had a nineteen in twenty chance of being normal.

On the one hand, Rudin clearly had a point. There was definitely something going on in schizophrenia, some risk factor of some sort that ran in families. But, to the geneticists of the time, one-in-twenty odds just didn't make sense.

The rediscovery of Mendelian principles of genetics was still less than two decades old, and geneticists were still dealing in the simplistic terms of dominant and recessive genes. If a bad gene was dominant, as the Huntington's chorea gene clearly was, then the chances of passing it along were fifty-fifty. If it was recessive, as it was for blue eyes, the chances of passing it along were 25 percent. The idea of a gene that expressed only one time in twenty was alien to the point of being inexplicable.

Besides, by the time Rudin's paper was printed, there had arisen a perfectly satisfactory nongenetic explanation for his findings. Brothers and sisters shared more than genes. They shared environment.

The rise of environmentalism among psychologists and intellectuals early in the twentieth century was based on solid scientific evidence that environment could in fact bear heavily on human personality. In one sense that was a strictly psychological fact; in another, it was the key to political revolution.

Most of the environmentalists in fact were intellectual insurgents whose professed purpose was to strip the aristocracy of its legitimacy and destroy the foundations of social Darwinism. Environmentalism, regardless of its scientific legitimacy, was psychology in support of political ideals. At bottom the issue didn't have anything to do with mental illness. It had to do with whether the human mind was shaped primarily by parentage, as the aristocracy and the very rich maintained, or was instead a product of environment.

This set the stage for what is euphemistically termed the "nature-nurture debate," one of the most acrimonious ideological struggles in all of history. It was intellectual trench warfare of the ugliest sort, and the fact that the battlefield was the psychological sciences was destined to confound and confuse research efforts into mental illness throughout most of the rest of the twentieth century.

As the combatants staked out their turf, the view that there was an inbred human nature was inextricably linked to conservative forces and the political right. The opposite argument, that environment determined human behavior, provided a platform for liberals to assert that the poor were poor only because they were cursed from childhood with the disadvantages of their parents' poverty.

The combatants were quickly forced into extreme positions.

Even as Rudin was calculating the excess risk to the sisters and brothers of schizophrenics, John B. Watson, already a looming giant in psychology, was staking out the claim that genes played no role at all in personality.

"Give me a dozen healthy infants, well-formed, and my own specified world to bring them up in," Watson wrote, "and I'll guarantee to take any one at random and train him to become any kind of specialist I might select—doctor, lawyer, artist, merchant-chief and, yes, even beggar-man and thief, regardless of the talents, penchants, tendencies, abilities, vocations, and race of his ancestors."

Such a philosophy contained the germs of many ideas, such as racial equality, that modern societies hold dear. But at the same time it left no room for the hypothesis that mental strengths or weaknesses, or even diseases, could be inherited.

The ideological turf on the other end of the spectrum was occupied by a group of gentleman scientists and parlor philosophers, including the novelist H. G. Wells and the playwright George Bernard Shaw.

The "eugenicists," as they called themselves, had taken the gospel of Darwin quite literally and convinced themselves that all human strengths and weaknesses, including the psychological ones, were a product of breeding.

One of their conclusions was that a population, such as that of the United States, could be improved through the sterilization of criminals, alcoholics, syphilitics, prostitutes, "moral degenerates," and mental patients.

They also advocated the imposition of immigration quotas on peoples of "inferior" blood, including those of southern Europe and Africa.

The eugenicists weren't much impressed by Rudin's studies of schizophrenics, either. Such a minor increase in risk was, by eugenics standards, pretty anemic stuff.

Though Watson held his ground among psychologists, the eugenics movement quickly won the hearts and minds of the very same common people whom the environmentalists, by their arguments, were trying to free. Eugenic thought swept the country during the first third of the century, pushing the Congress before it and resulting in the sterilization of perhaps 60,000 Americans and severe restrictions on immigration from "non-white" cultures.

Although sterilization laws were on rare occasion enforced in Virginia as late as 1972, the eugenics movement lost most of its credibility during the late 1930s when its premises were seen to be similar, philosophically if not in method, to those adopted by Adolf Hitler. The result was a backlash of revulsion in the United States; the eugenics movement, as a result, began to crumble.

As the magnitude of the German atrocities became clear after the war, the pendulum of public opinion in the United States swung even more dramatically to what might be called the psychological left. American public opinion now embraced environmentalistic principles as completely as it had accepted eugenics just a decade earlier.

The role of psychogeneticists in this convoluted tale was for the most part minor, but some scientists forever tarnished their names by their association with right-wing ideas and ideals. Rudin, for instance, the scientist who originally launched the notion that schizophrenia might be genetic, in 1935 coauthored the official Nazi book on the implementation of sterilization regulations.

Most scientists who jumped on the eugenics bandwagon early on, though, jumped right back off again when it became clear that their science was being grossly distorted for political ends. As one scientist charged, eugenics was to science what pornography was to art.

Still . . . the eugenicists had claimed to base their philosophy on genetics, and, true or not, the perception stuck and the psychogeneticists paid a bitter price for it.

The nurture advocates held almost total sway throughout the 1940s, 1950s, and 1960s, with most behavior research money going into studies of interactions between behavior and environment. During those decades, massive amounts of evidence were produced showing that the human personality could indeed be dramatically influenced by socioeconomic conditions and by family and peer relationships.

The politics of science, like that of any other field, made for strange bedfellows. One of the strangest was the alliance of the environmentalists and the Freudians.

Sigmund Freud had been convinced that the human mind was fundamentally mechanistic, which is to say genetic, but in the postwar years that was forgiven and forgotten by laymen because Freudian pathology was also heavily laced with the idea of childhood trauma—an environmentalist idea. Besides, Freudian therapy relied on human interchange, human understanding, and human introspection, which seemed to the layman to be warmly humanistic.

Freudian therapy, though, was known to be of little help when applied to serious mental illnesses like schizophrenia. So it was by a strange logic that the Freudian cause was nonetheless ascribed: it was the mother's fault.

The science of psychogenetics, in the meantime, cursed by a perceived association with the Nazis, was in almost total eclipse. Nevertheless, a few psychogeneticists quietly persisted in their efforts.

They received occasional encouragement. When it was discovered in the 1950s that various drugs could relieve schizophrenic hallucinations, for instance, geneticists could assume that the drugs were correcting some as-yet-unknown genetic defect.

But the most optimistic set of events was the development of a genetic understanding of a disease called phenylketonuria, or PKU.

PKU was a form of severe mental retardation, and as early as 1934 it was noted that its victims could be identified by an excess of phenylalanine in their urine. In the late 1940s, it was revealed that the excess was due to an inability to metabolize that chemical—an inability that could be laid at the feet of a single defective gene.

By the 1960s, it was possible to identify such infants at birth and, by restricting their diets during the critical period of brain growth, prevent most of the mental damage.

The PKU story was a model of what psychogeneticists hoped would happen in other, more subtle, mental and emotional diseases. If genetically based mental illnesses could be identified, and their metabolic processes understood, they, like PKU, might be prevented from manifesting themselves.

But in the public mind of the 1960s, the PKU breakthrough indicated no such thing. In a loop-around logic that makes psychogenetists grind their teeth, the mere fact that PKU was physical in nature removed it from the category of mental illness.

Mental illnesses weren't physical—by definition. In the public's perception, there were even grave doubts that they were illnesses at all. They were psychological, which was to say unquantifiable, which was to say spiritual . . . even moral. Certainly there was something vaguely shameful about them and the victims—if they could be called victims—were not referred to in polite company.

With the liberal swing in the 1960s, though, came a philosophical dilemma. The social climate was at odds with the stigma that attached to the mentally ill and their families—the mentally ill were victims, and it wasn't right to blame them. At the same time, the movement was nothing if not moralistic, and blame had to be placed somewhere.

And so there arose, particularly on the revolutionary left, the romantic idea that schizophrenia was a healthy manifestation of social rebellion: the hallucinations constituted a sane response to an insane society.

Meanwhile, the psychogeneticists, what few of them there were, put together small sums of money for studies designed to probe the possible genetic background of several mental illnesses.

One of the objects of their study was the old psychogenetic

standby, schizophrenia, and another was manic-depressive disease. Both diseases seemed to run in families and the psychogeneticists, using various statistical manipulations, convinced themselves that such family patterns could not be explained away by environment.

In the meantime, clinical psychiatrists, pressing forward with the discovery of new psychoactive drugs to mitigate their patients' delusions and hallucinations, were raising a related question: How could chemicals be effective against psychological ills unless those ills were, themselves, somehow chemical as well?

The question played right into psychobiological thinking. Of course madness was biochemically caused! And what was the underlying determinate of biochemistry? What else but genetics?

Cursed by a perceived association with right-wing politics, shunned for a quarter century by all right-thinking people, psychogeneticists could not have picked a less opportune moment in history to reemerge than the radical, environmentalistic 1960s. The nature-nurture controversy was more politicized than ever, and scientists who voiced genetic theories of behavior could expect to be jeered at and even attacked by placard-carrying young people.

The situation was made worse by the fact that, even in the private opinions of many psychogeneticists, the demonstrators were in some instances right on target: some of those who grabbed headlines from the fringes of behavioral psychology probably were fascists and racists whose purpose, like that of the eugenicists before them, was to twist genetics to conform to their ideas. They served to cloud the issues even further and make life even more difficult for legitimate psychogeneticists.

But according to some who lived through that era, such as the National Institute of Mental Health's chief scientist Fred Goodwin, the adversity this time proved to be a positive force.

The psychogeneticists now had the techniques and the confidence required to prove their case; the critics forced them to polish their work to perfection. The result was a series of carefully designed studies that rammed their point home to all but the most vociferous opponents.

The painstaking nature of the psychogenetic research that was brought to bear on the subject is typified by a study of schizophrenic twins undertaken by the late Dr. James Shields and his younger colleague, Dr. Irving Gottesman.

Their hypothesis focused on twins, of which there are two types. One type, identical twins, grow from the same egg and therefore share all their genes. The other type, fraternal twins, come from separate eggs and are no more alike than other brothers and sisters, sharing an average of half their genes.

If there was anything to the genetic theory of schizophrenia, then, the sibling of an identical twin who was schizophrenic should be highly likely to go mad himself; the fraternal twin of a schizophrenic should be less likely to.

Gottesman, now a professor of psychiatric genetics at Washington University in St. Louis, recalls that his part of the study began in 1962 with a survey of 45,000 psychiatric patients admitted to Maudsley Hospital in London between 1948 and 1964.

He and Shields sorted through the records and found sixty schizophrenics who had a twin brother or sister.

Twenty-six of those sets of twins were identical, and thirty-four were fraternal. Gottesman, armed with a battery of psychological tests and a tape recorder, set about tracking down those twins and determining whether or not they, too, were schizophrenic.

The scientists knew their results, if positive, were going to attract intense scrutiny. So they took special care to anticipate criticism. Their exhaustive detective work took years and today stands as a model for clinical genetic studies involving other mental diseases.

For instance, they did not make the diagnosis of the twins themselves; they merely administered the tests and interviewed the patients and their twin brothers and sisters on tape. The

143

test results, patient histories, and excerpts from the tapes were sent to a panel of six independent psychiatrists who made the judgments.

The first results of the study were published in 1966, and they were nothing short of dramatic. When one identical twin became schizophrenic, the odds were 58 percent that the other twin would become schizophrenic as well.

If borderline cases of schizophrenia ("schizoid" and "schizotypal" personalities) were included in the figures, the concordance rate went up to 67 percent.

As expected, the concordance rate between nonidentical twins was notably lower. If one such twin became schizophrenic, the odds that the second one would do so too were only 12 percent, compared with 0.5 percent° for the general population.

But for all of the scientists' careful planning, the critics still found a loophole.

Identical twins, because they look exactly alike, are treated differently than fraternal twins, who have more individualistic features. Identical twins often wear identical clothing. Their friends can't tell them apart. They develop an ego identification with one another.

If one twin became schizophrenic, the critics argued, the other might also—for reasons that had nothing to do with genetics.

Gottesman and Shields maintained that statistical manipulations rendered this interpretation absurd, but the most suspicious critics considered such manipulations to be just that—manipulation. This final objection was put to rest in another study, this one of the biological relatives of schizophrenics who had been adopted as children, conducted by a team led by Dr. Seymour Kety.

Then at the National Institute of Mental Health and later at the Harvard School of Medicine, Kety and his colleagues set the pattern for later studies by tapping the massive banks of

---

° Some researchers, seeking to focus in on the most seriously ill schizophrenics, use the 0.5 percent figure, as opposed to the generally cited 1 percent.

health and population data maintained by the Scandinavian countries.

The Kety group focused on Denmark. Records there, the scientists found, made it possible to track down the health records of the relatives of adoptees who had become schizophrenics.

The first results of the Kety adoption survey, published just two years after the Shields-Gottesman twin study, confirmed the point. A biological child of a schizophrenic ran a significantly elevated risk of becoming schizophrenic, even if the infant was adopted into a healthy family.

That study, coupled with a definitive study of schizophrenic mothers and their adopted-away offspring done by Leonard Hess, clinched the matter.

Clearly, however, the disease wasn't passed on according to the neat, dominant or recessive pattern of classic Mendelian genetics that describes how a child inherits, say, blue eyes.

It was more subtle than that, almost as if what was being inherited wasn't schizophrenia itself but rather some weakness for it—a propensity, as the scientists said, for becoming schizophrenic. This propensity probably involved some chemical imbalance in the brain. Whether or not that imbalance expressed itself as full-blown mental disease was, presumably, a question of environmental stress.

It was still too early for such a hypothesis to make much specific sense, or to be tested; the theory of molecular psychology would not arrive on the scene for ten years.

But, though a few critics remained—and remain today—the work of scientists like Shields, Gottesman, Kety, and Hess convinced most scientists that while environment might still be important as a stress-triggering mechanism, schizophrenia was in large measure a genetic disease. As the 1970s opened, the larger psychogenetics question had thus been shaped and formed.

How, specifically, might a disease of the mind be inherited? How could a luckless schizophrenic, for instance, inherit a tendency to hallucinate?

It wasn't long before the answer was forthcoming—along with

a flood tide of other answers to questions that no one had yet thought to ask.

The source of almost bewildering enlightenment was the Snyder-Pert breakthrough and the cascade of secondary discoveries that followed. For the first time, scientists had achieved the ability to watch the large-scale functioning of the mind at work.

The brain, scientists were discovering, was every bit as complex and delicate as poets had surmised. It was a churning cauldron of fluctuating metabolic rates, squirting neurotransmitters, oscillating receptor sensitivities. . . .

As the first few of those processes became increasingly understood, it was easy to see how a genetic defect could throw a monkey wrench into the works.

The logic was straightforward.

Behind every thought or feeling, there was a molecular reaction in the brain. Behind every molecule in the reaction, there was an enzyme that created that molecule; behind every enzyme was a gene.

If the gene was defective, the enzyme would be defective; if the enzyme was defective, so would be the molecule; if the molecule was defective, so would be the chemical reaction and so, inevitably, would be the thought the reaction produced.

Or, as one scientist simplified it, in a few words with many levels of meaning, "Twisted molecules lead to twisted thoughts."

12

THE

BAD

SEEDS

THOUGH critics of psychogenetics feared that the idea behind that science would in and of itself give aid and comfort to racists, sexists, and reactionaries of all ilk, the psychogeneticists themselves saw it in a positive light.

In the first place, the truth was the truth whatever its political and philosophical implications. In the second place, the 1980s were fundamentally different from the 1920s; ideas that might have been oversimplified and misinterpreted early in this century would probably be handled quite differently by the present generation. The idea that we were all fundamentally different from the very beginning, in fact, might sharpen our appreciation for human diversity.

Closer to the issue at hand, proof that at least some mental conditions were genetic might trigger the long-needed rethinking about our attitudes toward the mentally ill. Everyone knew, after all, that genes were physical things, beyond the control of the individual—in the genetic model of mental illness, the victim could not be blamed.

What's more, if genes could be shown to cause some forms of insanity, that should open minds to the possibility that other purely physical factors, such as viruses and poisons, might also play a role. If that could be documented, the public might have a lot more sympathy for the victims of mental illness.

On another level, the discovery that a mental illness had a specific genetic cause would trigger a chain of scientific events that might well lead, ultimately, to new treatments and even cures.

If scientists could unequivocally identify a behavioral problem that had a genetic base, then molecular geneticists would inevitably become interested in the problem. That should eventually lead to the discovery of the specific gene involved, and that, in turn, should allow chemists to work out the nature of the faulty metabolism.

Once the metabolic error was pinpointed, it should be relatively straightforward, as such things go, to find corrective treatment. Ultimately, genetic engineers might be able to replace the faulty gene itself, thus effecting a complete cure.

Thus, the studies that firmly linked schizophrenia to genetic defects opened the floodgates of similar research into other diseases. Soon a new generation of psychogeneticists were seeking to drive home the lesson in as many categories of mental illness as possible.

The second and third wave of psychogenetic studies in Sweden and Denmark were more sophisticated and broader in scope than the first. The focuses now ranged from the old standby schizophrenia through alcoholism and hypochondria to sociopathology and criminality.

One of the most recent studies, parts of which are still being published, was conducted by C. Robert Cloninger, a scientist at the Jewish Hospital of St. Louis and also, like Gottesman, a professor at Washington University. Cloninger teamed up with a scientist in Sweden to collect adoption data as they relate to mental illness.

One of the conditions on which Cloninger focused was alcoholism. To do this, he traced the genetic, environmental, and behavioral history of more than 3,000 adoptees, their adoptive parents, and their natural parents.

The overall result was that the children of alcoholics were highly likely to be alcoholics themselves, even when they were reared by adoptive parents and never saw their natural mothers and fathers.

This result in itself wasn't surprising. Alcoholism experts had long argued that alcohol addiction was a metabolic disease and that it ran in families. But the scientists were astonished to discover that the Swedish alcoholics divided neatly into two major and statistically distinct subtypes.

The largest group of alcoholic adoptees, accounting for about three-quarters of the total, began using alcohol while they were young, but their consumption, at first, was moderate. It was only later in life that they became frankly alcoholic.

And while these people might be alcoholics, they were not destructive ones. Even though they often drank enough to destroy their health, they continued to function as marginally normal parents and employees; only rarely were they involved in violence or other obvious antisocial behaviors. Cloninger labeled this group "sick" alcoholics.

Investigation revealed that the natural parents of "sick" alcoholics tended to be alcoholics of the same type—there was definitely a genetic connection.

But as the numbers were examined more closely, it became apparent that genes themselves weren't enough to do the trick. There was another factor at play: childhood socioeconomic conditions.

If a child had had a "sick" alcoholic for a natural parent but had been adopted in infancy by a middle-class family, the child's chances of growing up to be a "sick" alcoholic were no greater than average. It was almost as though there was something in the middle-class environment that seemed to protect the adoptee against an inborn susceptibility to alcoholism.

The story was dramatically different, though, when the child who carried the "sick" alcoholism gene was adopted into a poor family. Then, with both genetics and environment going against him, the child ran a dramatically elevated risk of growing up to become a "sick" alcoholic himself.

The second group of alcoholics identified by the Cloninger team was smaller than the first, comprising only about 25 percent of the total number of alcoholics studied. But they were far, far more disturbed.

As was the case with the "sick" alcoholics, they began drinking as teenagers. But in these people the addiction didn't steadily worsen; it exploded into obvious, full-blown alcoholism in a matter of months. By the time these people were married and trying to hold down jobs, they had progressed so deeply into addiction that they almost invariably failed miserably at both.

But two factors made these alcoholics stand apart from the others. One was that they were all males. The other was that they were usually very violent and often ended up in jail for crimes involving injury to others. As a result, Cloninger labeled them "violent" alcoholics.

The statistics indicated that the genetic component of "violent" alcoholism was much stronger than with "sick" alcoholics. Whereas the adopted-away children of the sick alcoholics seemed to need both genes and environment going against them before they suffered an increased risk of alcoholism themselves, environment didn't seem to play any role at all in "violent" alcoholism.

A male child born to a "violent" alcoholic ran an 18 percent chance of developing alcoholism himself, and it didn't seem to matter at all whether he was adopted by a rich family or a poor one.

This is a striking statistic. Eighteen percent is the highest risk ever documented for a genetic mental illness, and approaches the classic 25 percent risk prescribed by Mendel's law for recessive genes.

The tempting conclusion was that three out of four of the boys born to "violent" alcoholic fathers didn't get the gene and weren't at risk. But the luckless fourth boy was almost doomed from the start.

The big puzzler, of course, was . . . why only boys? Why did girls escape?

The obvious conclusion was that the gene was sex-linked, like hemophilia. In that well-known genetic bleeding disorder, women are carriers but generally only boys get the disease.

This was not to be the case however, with the "violent" alcoholics. Further research was to lead scientists to a conclusion that, at least to outsiders, would seem even stranger than the existence of the alcoholism gene.

Years earlier, while doing research in the United States, Cloninger had noticed something rather strange about many female relatives of alcoholics. Many of them, it seemed to him, had undergone an unusually large number of operations.

When he questioned them about it, they told him the problem had all started when, as teenagers, they'd begun to experience severe pain. Usually, that pain came from above the waist.

They'd gone to their doctors, of course, but their doctors hadn't been able to isolate the problem. Still, the pain persisted. Finally, in their misery, the women had resorted to surgeons; the surgeons had operated, as surgeons are wont to do. But they found nothing.

Still, there was pain. So the women had gone surgeon-shopping, trying first one and then another in a desperate quest to end the pain. By the time Cloninger met them, many of the women had been crippled by multiple exploratory operations, none of which had been able to end the pain.

They were, in a word, hypochondriacs—hypochondriacs of a very self-destructive kind.

Cloninger was sure he had a hint of something . . . something strange . . . but what?

Why did these women feel pain that their doctors couldn't isolate? Was the anguish in their minds, perhaps caused by a defect in the part of the brain that processes pain? And, if so, was it put there by the environment . . . or by their genes?

The question stuck in Cloninger's mind and nagged at him for years. Finally, when he commenced his work with the Swedish health records, he cast his statistical net to include psychosomatic pain.

That net pulled in the sisters of the "violent" alcoholics.

The women who should have been at risk for "violent" alcoholism, but who were not because they were female, ran an 18 percent risk of phantom pain that no physician could ever find and no surgeon could ever cut out. That was the female version of the "violent" alcoholism gene.

Why the genetic defect should express itself so differently in men and women left scientists scratching their heads. It might be hormonal, of course—hormones are known to be a factor in the development of the fetal brain. But it might also be an environmental effect.

In Sweden, as in the United States, alcoholism is more tolerated in males than in females. Perhaps the men who became "violent" alcoholics felt the same pain their sisters did, but found in alcohol a socially acceptable way of treating it. Perhaps the women with the same painful genetic defect, denied the succor of the bottle by social pressure, went to doctors instead.

Whatever the answer, the male-female difference in the expression of faulty genes may not be unusual. The Cloninger study, in any event, found at least one other case.

This group, too, involved female hypochondriacs—but of a different sort than the sisters of the "violent" alcoholics.

One difference was that this group of hypochondriacs, while predominantly female, did include a few men. Another was that the pain, in this case, usually came not from above the waist as in the first group but from the abdomen and lower back. And in this group the pain seemed even worse than in the first group.

Having earlier discovered the sex difference in the "violent" alcoholism gene, scientists were prepared now with the next question: What happened to the men who corresponded to this second group of hereditary hypochondriacs? Were they, too, alcoholics?

The answer popped out of the statistics: No.

In fact, as it turned out on closer examination, the men were hypochondriacs too. But their complaints were almost totally eclipsed by another behavioral propensity that was guaranteed to raise eyebrows.

They tended to be violent criminals.

Criminality, whatever that may be, has long been known to run in families. But outside the close-knit circle of psychobiology, the tendency in this century at least has been laid to environmental factors. For a scientist to even hint otherwise, in fact, has been to embroil himself in violent ideological argument.

One report in the early 1970s, for instance, held that many prison inmates who had been incarcerated for repeated minor crimes, usually nonviolent in nature, had an extra male chromosome in their cells.

This study, implying that potential perpetrators of at least some crimes might be identifiable on a physical basis, created an uproar that raged for months on the front pages of newspapers. The controversy eventually died down, leaving most observers with the impression that the work was completely discredited.

But most psychobiologists, while not wanting to exhume the controversy, believe otherwise.

"That work had some problems," explained one molecular psychologist on the stipulation he would remain anonymous. "I'll grant that it had problems. But follow-up work was done, and in my mind it's very clear that men with that extra chromosome are much more likely to end up in jail than the average male. They're not violent, you understand. But they're prone to burglary, shoplifting—that sort of thing.

"The difficulty is that people leap to conclusions. What the critics worry about, and I sympathize with this, is that unthinking people will leap to the conclusion that people with this extra chromosome are all criminals. That would lead to gross discrimination, which would of course be a shame and probably a crime.

"In the first place, we're not talking about 'criminality' genes. This extra chromosome probably doesn't make the victim a criminal—assuming you can define what 'criminal' is. From my reading of that work, that extra chromosome probably makes the person impulsive—and impulsive people are inclined to take what they want, right now, rather than wait for it. Impulsive people shoplift, for instance.

"But at the same time, a lot of people learn to control their impulsiveness, and when they do, they make good citizens, just like you and me.

"And frankly, I think most of the critics of work like this in fact do recognize its validity. They're not really criticizing it as bad science so much as bad politics. They're afraid people will jump to simplistic conclusions. I share that fear. So it's best, for the moment, to let sleeping dogs lie."

The dog, however, doesn't sleep very soundly. Even before the 1973 Snyder-Pert breakthrough, many scientists had come to the conclusion that at least some forms of criminal behavior stemmed from wholly physical phenomena in the brain.

A form of violence particularly suspect, in the eyes of biologically oriented psychiatrists, involves explosive outbursts of temper. Study of explosive temper disorders produced a hypothesis that likened such behavior to epileptic seizures.

The difference is that classic epilepsy begins in the motor areas of the brain and precipitates physical convulsions. Temper outbursts, on the other hand, are believed to begin as electrical storms in the emotional brain. Instead of physical convulsions, the victim experiences overpowering rushes of emotion. While seized by such emotions, a person may commit all sorts of behaviors, some of them violent, that he would ordinarily be temperamentally incapable of.

In the 1970s, this theory led to some experimental attempts to treat episodic violence by means of electrodes planted in the criminal's brain. But public opinion in this country is traditionally opposed to experimentation on prisoners, and the work was halted after it became a subject of controversy.

But work elsewhere, based on a similar philosophy but using antiseizure drugs instead of electrodes, continued. These experimental programs at least partly avoided controversy by treating mainly volunteers whose violent outbursts were destroying their personal lives, but who had not yet been convicted of crime.

The upshot was that anticonvulsive drugs, combined with other forms of therapy designed to help the patient control his emotional storms, indeed did work wonders on some patients. Today such therapy, while denied to prisoners, is quietly available at a number of medical schools and is even being offered by some psychiatrists in private practice.

The Snyder-Pert breakthrough, combined with preliminary hints that certain forms of criminality might indeed be inheritable, sparked increased interest in the subject.

Given the new theory of molecular psychology, it was easy to see how a person might be born with weaknesses, say, in the brain systems that inhibit violence. Certainly levels of aggressiveness in animals are genetically controlled—which is why, for instance, the most aggressive sheep isn't nearly as aggressive as the shyest wolf.

Though public opinion has hobbled violence research in the United States, the same political realities do not apply in many European countries. In Western Europe, where prisoners are routinely offered psychiatric care and physical measures such as castration for rape are considered acceptable, scientists are considerably freer. They have, therefore, taken the lead.

One of the best-known of those scientists is Paul Mandel, a biochemist with the Center for Neurochemistry in Strasbourg, France. Working with rats, mice, and other animals bred for a variety of violent and passive tendencies, the Mandel group has focused on two major neurochemical systems.

One of those systems involves the neurotransmitter serotonin, which has also been implicated in depression. The other is called GABA.

The basic action of GABA, worked out in the 1970s, makes it one of the most fascinating neurotransmitters in the human skull. Unlike most other neurotransmitters, it works almost exclusively as an inhibitor. Along with serotonin it composes, in effect, the reins that keep the mind in check.

Also unlike most other transmitters, it's found in copious quantities throughout the brain. It is at work everywhere, holding back the various centers, preventing action, censoring thoughts, and generally keeping the machinery from running away from itself. Through studies of GABA, scientists have come to the sobering realization that perhaps as much as 90 percent of the brain is devoted not to action, but to preventing action.

So it made sense, infinite sense, when the Mandel team in France showed that strains of rats that were aggressively violent had lower levels of GABA in their brains than did passive strains.

In Mandel's original series of experiments, the aggressive and passive rats were produced by breeding—evidence that genetic predisposition can play a role in serotonin and GABA levels and, thereby, in aggression. But levels of GABA and serotonin can also be changed, and behavior altered, by manipulation.

Drugs, for instance, worked well to alter aggressive-passive behaviors. Aggressive rats became markedly less so when they were given substances that raised serotonin and GABA levels; passive rats were made aggressive when they received chemicals that lowered those levels.

Environment could also do the trick. One classic experiment involved isolation, which is known to produce aggressive behavior in both animals and humans. Studying several groups of rats, the French scientists found that isolation lowered GABA and serotonin levels for all the animals.

The most interesting experiments, however, involved the interplay between environment and genetics. When isolated, rats that had a genetic disposition to violence (as measured by low GABA and serotonin levels) became much more violent than the others—and tended to do so with less isolation stress.

When subjected to overcrowding, the opposite effect occurred. GABA and serotonin levels went up, and the normal animals became abnormally passive and lethargic. But the violence-prone animals, whose brains were genetically low in GABA and serotonin, merely became more normal.

In another, highly suggestive, set of experiments, Mandel demonstrated that rats became more violent, and that their brain inhibitor levels dropped, by merely seeing other animals being aggressive. Watching a rat kill a mouse, for instance, made GABA levels drop in bystander rats.

Mandel, less cautious than many of his colleagues about extrapolating to the human condition, says that the experiments indicate that human children do become more violence-prone when they watch violence on television. Likewise, publicizing crimes—and capital punishment—presumably begets still more violence.

Extrapolating further, Mandel believes that emotional self-stimulation can also change serotonin levels and trigger changes in the tendency to solve problems by violent means. Religious fanaticism, he predicts, will one day prove to be linked to lowered levels of brain inhibitors.

"Take the Ayatollah Khomeini, for instance," says Mandel. "He's suppressed his GABA and serotinin levels through religious excitation . . . and now there's no inhibition."

Like an increasing number of his colleagues, Mandel believes that violent behavior is sometimes a result of environmental processes that damage the mind and that it sometimes stems from genetic defects. Perhaps most often, the culprit is a mix of the two.

But even with that background, it still came as a surprise, even a shock, when Cloninger's study of Swedish adoptees showed that the brothers of the second group of female hypochondriacs tended to have records of violent crime.

The idea that human violence may have a genetic component

is perhaps one of the most sobering concepts to emerge from psychogenetics to date. But the meaning and implications of such data are not yet clear.

A second statistical cluster in the criminality statistics involved petty crime and came as less of a shock—at least to those who still took the old extra-chromosome study seriously. Children born to fathers and mothers with records of shoplifting, theft, and vandalism tended to pursue careers of petty crimes themselves, even when they were adopted away at birth and raised apart.

The statistics indicated that both environmental and genetic factors seemed to play strong roles. In this instance, the environmental variable seemed to be not socioeconomic class but rather the emotional stability of the adopted home.

Boys born to fathers not implicated in petty crime, and raised in stable adopted homes, ended up on police blotters for property crimes only about 3 percent of the time. When boys born to law-abiding fathers were raised in unstable homes, however, 7 percent of them got involved in petty crimes.

In contrast, 12 percent of boys born to fathers with records of petty criminality but raised in stable homes went on to commit property crimes. When boys had both factors going against them, the likelihood of becoming petty criminals rose steeply, to 40 percent.

When girls were studied, the results were similar except that the numbers were dramatically lower. The percentage of petty criminals was 0.5 percent in those who had neither genetic nor environmental predisposition, 3 percent if they had environmental only, the same if they had genetic only, and 11 percent if they had both genetic and environmental factors going against them.

"Essentially what we found was that in order for the daughters to become criminal, they had to have a more severe form of genetic predisposition," Cloninger mused. "It looked like the girls almost needed a double dose before they could become criminal."

Research on the genetics of the mind, as it continues to accelerate and to spill out of traditional mental diseases and into the realms of such things as criminality and even intelligence, raises both hopes and fears. Diseases, once properly identified and understood, may be treated and even cured.

In the meantime, the questions they raise touch on powerful ideological issues involving our view of mankind. On the right there will be a predictable urge to seize these answers, unexamined and oversimplified, and convert them into social policy. On the left the knee-jerk response is anger and denial.

But what we are really seeing in Cloninger's numbers, and in the brain juices of Mandel's rats, vindicates neither position. What we're seeing instead is a new kind of truth, a truth that after seventy-five years finally settles, once and for all, the nature-nurture controversy.

Both sides were correct. But, in denying the equal validity of the opposition, each was utterly and disastrously wrong.

THE
NATURE-NURTURE
THEORY

A S the results of the genetics studies sank in and were factored into the emerging theory of molecular psychology, the fallacy at the heart of the nature-nurture debate became abundantly clear. It had been a classic case of blind men trying to discern the nature of an elephant, one grabbing a ropelike tail, one a snakelike trunk, and one a treelike leg. Practically everyone had been right, in a way—but not nearly right enough to justify the righteousness that characterized, and polarized, the controversy.

The human mind-brain, whatever it might be, was as complex and as contradictory as the behavior it secreted; it would not be simplified to satisfy philosophers or justify the neat theories of ideologues. If it yielded to description at all, it, like the universe itself, would do so only in the cold and unsatisfying equations of the mathematician, the physicist, or the chemist.

For those who would in the meantime apply the crude tools

of human language to the problem, the mind-brain was simply a product of all of its ever-changing ingredients. It was a dollop of heredity, mixed well with a mother's smile, blended with a virus or two, and leavened with a kick in the tail, two jiggers of brandy, and a lottery ticket just one number off the money.

The set, genetically determined architecture of the brain, for instance, did in fact exist—though in practice it was somewhat theoretical. The brain, by the moment of birth, had already been significantly altered by the environment of the womb.

As the child grew, its brain would be changed further as each thought, observation, and experience etched its reality into the substance of enzyme, lipid, transmitter, and receptor. The human mind, as a concept to be applied by other human minds in a confusing, all-too-human world, arose neither from nature nor from nurture. It was a product, instead, of the interactions between the two.

From the point of view of the molecular psychologists, this reduced the problem of mental illness to specifics. Different diseases of the mind would be like different diseases of the body, which was to say . . . well, different.

Some of them, such as the retardation that accompanied PKU and the dementia that characterized the last stages of Huntington's disease would be purely genetic. In such cases, the substance of the brain was so disrupted by underlying metabolic defects that the hammer of the environment in effect struck a cracked bell and could not ring true.

Other diseases, if one could believe the lesson of the rats driven to depressive madness by isolation or electric shocks, were the result of physical damage caused by purely psychoenvironmental forces. The late-stage dementia of AIDS, the work of a virus, was due to strictly physical causes.

But the statistics produced by scientists like Kety and Cloninger just weren't that elegant. Even in the case of "violent" alcoholism, they weren't strictly Mendelian. Clearly some people got the "bad" gene but went on to lead more or less normal lives despite it.

That seemed to argue not for direct causation but for genetic propensities, subtle genetic defects or weaknesses that didn't cause insanity directly, but that made the victim vulnerable to environmental stresses that could cause mental illness.

Those environmental stresses might be classically "psychological" in nature, in which the brain damage was caused by a depriving socioeconomic environment or unloving parents.

But the precipitating stress might also be more physical in nature. By means of a genetic defect, for instance, some key cells at some critical crossroads of the mind might be rendered exquisitely sensitive to some environmental chemical. Exposure to that chemical would destroy the cells and trigger madness in vulnerable individuals, while leaving most people unaffected. The environmental factor, for that matter, might as well be a virus as a chemical—virus sensitivities were known to be genetic.

How these possibilities played themselves out in the scientific mind is illustrated by the "polygenic, multifactoral theory of schizophrenia" developed by Gottesman as he sought to make sense of his twin studies.

Gottesman's view focuses on the central fact of the human brain: its complexity. Though the brain comprises only about 2 percent of the body's weight, for instance, it requires more than half of the 100,000 or so human genes to code for it. The blueprint for major systems like the dopamine or the norepinephrine system, which are implicated in schizophrenia, may involve thousands of genes.

Although a genetic defect in any particular gene is rare, the odds are that we all have a few "abnormal" genes tucked away somewhere in our chromosomes. This being the case, the brain probably has built-in redundancy and extensive secondary systems, so that if a chemical reaction can't proceed in one direction it can go, instead, in another.

With this in mind, Gottesman interprets his statistics as indicating that schizophrenia probably results from an extremely complex interplay of genes and environment. In this view, the underlying predisposition for the disease might reflect not one but several genetic defects that, taken together, serve to weaken the brain's ability to process chemicals and hence thoughts.

Even so, the schizophrenia-prone individual, given fortunate environmental circumstances, might be able to learn to compensate and lead a normal life. But under stress of some unknown type, he or she would be much more likely than another individual to develop the disabling symptoms of schizophrenia.

Schizophrenia, in this case, might be a very individual disease. The stress would have to match the defect—a person who might become schizophrenic if infected by a particular virus, for instance, would be capable of dealing with a normal amount of psychological pressure. In this case, the virus, and only the virus, would produce madness.

Also, in this scenario, some brains would be more susceptible than others. Some people might have a low dose of defective genes, in which case it would take considerable environmental stress to push them to the threshold of schizophrenia. Others, with many defective genes, wouldn't require much stress to push them over the edge. Even "normal" people, subjected to intense stress of the right sort, might become schizophrenic.

Another view comes from Kety of the National Institute of Mental Health. He points out that the tendency of the disease to run in family trees is only an average tendency. It may turn out that the numbers only seem soft because schizophrenia, like alcoholism or heart disease, isn't a single condition but rather various different diseases with similar manifestations. Some of them may be purely genetic and some of them, as Gottesman suggests, may involve genetic propensities coupled with environmental factors.

Of the suspected environmental triggers or causes, the mind automatically leaps to thoughts of psychological pressures, including indifferent mothering, bad neighborhoods, and dehumanizing social systems. But brain damage during the birth process is known to cause schizophrenia, and, in recent years, other possible physical causes have attracted increasing interest.

Certain chemicals, for instance, are known to be capable of

causing brain damage. This lesson has been driven home with horrible consequences in recent years by the appearance of "designer drug" substitutes for heroin and other illegal drugs. Some such substitutes contain, as a by-product, a substance that inflicts deadly and irreversible damage to the dopamine system.

Many theoreticians have also given a lot of thought, in recent years, to the virus theory. Viruses often kill certain cells in an organ, while leaving others intact. That this happens in brain cells as well has been shown, with grim drama, in the case of polio.

In addition, in recent years it has been discovered that at least one type of virus can in fact produce what might be called a temporary mental illness. Certain strains of the influenza virus leave their victims profoundly depressed for months.

No virus is known to produce comparable schizophrenialike symptoms, but some scientists believe there are epidemiological patterns suggesting that schizophrenia may be at least as communicable as, say, AIDS. In this scenario, the virus passes from person to person, generally causing a subclinical infection that goes unnoticed. The only people who get sick are the occasional susceptible individuals.

As research goes on, a majority of scientists are concluding that many if not all of the above possible causes of schizophrenia may turn out to be true. Schizophrenia, as Kety suspects, is probably a number of quite different diseases that affect the same brain systems and produce superficially similar symptoms.

This reclassification already appears under way in at least one major mental illness: alcoholism. And in the process of arriving at specific explanations, scientists are homing in on metabolic defects that hint at possible new treatments and cures.

The Cloninger study, for instance, in pinpointing a specific type of strongly genetic "violent" alcoholism in the Swedish population, has already led to the tentative identification of the underlying problem. The victims, far from being weak or immoral as legend suggests, may have inherited a defect in the mind gene that codes for an enzyme called monoamine oxidase, or MAO.

In recent years, MAO has earned the keen interest of many

molecular psychologists. It is involved in the metabolism of nor-epinephrine, which is implicated in both schizophrenia and depression, and defective MAO-related substances have been found in the blood of some depressed patients.

More germane to the disease of "violent" alcoholism, similar defective MAO-related chemicals have also been found in some people who have a cluster of hyperactivity symptoms, including short attention span, impulsiveness, and uncontrollable pleasure-seeking behavior. These symptoms were also found frequently in Cloninger's "violent" alcoholics.

Cloninger believes that the critical point may involve pain thresholds. This idea is supported by experiments indicating that the brains of individuals with low MAO levels have a peculiar way of processing pain.

The normal person thinks of pain as an unusual phenomenon, but in fact the body is constantly sending pain messages to the brain. We don't feel them, however, because the brain automatically dampens such signals when they are below a predetermined threshold. This threshold varies from individual to individual, with some people more sensitive than others.

But instruments that measure flow of impulses through nerves indicate that the brains of people with low MAO levels are very peculiar in this respect. Instead of suppressing pain, they seem to be amplifying it.

The patients being tested aren't aware of any difference, of course. For one thing, if they're in more pain than most of us, they've been that way all their lives—they simply don't know any other way.

For another, the pain processing centers are deep within the brain, far below the levels of consciousness. Experience with depression proves that deep pain can be shuttled aside, and turned into other symptoms, at midbrain levels.

Assuming the instruments aren't lying, brain anatomy as well as psychiatric experience leads one to suspect that this enhanced sensitivity to pain probably extends to psychological as well as physical pain.

That might explain the short attention span and pleasure-seeking tendencies of the victims of low MAO levels. People in pain naturally tend to have difficulty focusing their minds on other things, and they do seek pleasure to counteract the pain.

Might the low-MAO alcoholics be drinking alcohol to anesthetize their pain? The idea, in the minds of Cloninger and others, makes perfect sense.

Why their hypochondriac sisters don't reach for the same bottled-in-bond crutch, Cloninger admits, is a real puzzler.

Because drinking and violence are more tolerated in males than in females, one explanation is sociological. Another explanation, which Cloninger considers equally viable, is that the difference is caused by variations in hormone balances and their effects on the brain. Maybe alcohol doesn't work for females.

Either way, the females tend not to use alcohol. That being the case, they might feel the pain more directly . . . and the fact that it comes from their brains, and not their bodies, would make the agony no less real. The result might well be the type of female hypochondria that the Swedish study linked with male "violent" alcoholism.

The MAO-defect hypothesis fits this category of alcoholism-hypochondria so neatly that studies are now being conducted to find out whether the "violent" alcoholics and their affected sisters in fact do have abnormal MAO activities. Early results, says Cloninger, tend to confirm the hypothesis.

Is there a similar mechanism at work in the other and more common type of alcoholism identified by the Cloninger study—the one that seemed to require a "double hit" of both genetics and environment before it expressed itself as "sick" alcoholism?

Nobody knows, but there is no shortage of possible explanations. One comes from Japan, where scientists have zeroed in on a specific metabolic trait that seems, at least in that population, to predispose people to alcoholism. The trait, oddly enough, is not a weakness but a strength.

The work focuses on an enzyme that helps the body break down and eliminate alcohol from the body. The enzyme appears to come in two forms: some people inherit a slow-acting enzyme, and some a fast-acting one. Among Japanese, the inheritance odds for each type are about fifty-fifty.

If a person inherits the slow-acting enzyme, he will be unable to hold his liquor and will get very sick if he drinks large quantities of alcohol. If the drinker belongs to the 50 percent of the population that has the fast-acting form of the enzyme, on the other hand, he will be able to hold his liquor well and drink large quantities of alcohol with relative impunity—at least in the short term.

But there is more risk to alcohol than just vomiting and hangovers. Large quantities of it, imbibed over extended periods, can lead to changes in the brain and consequent addiction.

And that, apparently, is what happens. Screening tests in Japan reveal that while half the population has the slow-acting enzyme, only 2 percent of the alcoholics have it. Men and women who are "blessed" with the biochemical ability to hold their liquor make up 98 percent of the alcoholic population.

And so, ironically, the ability to "hold your liquor," an attribute that has been praised and prized since time immemorial, may in fact be a genetic defect that makes the inheritor a sitting duck for alcoholism.

The frequency of these genes in other populations is as yet unknown, though scientists are working on relevant studies. Meanwhile, other possible factors are cropping up rapidly.

Researchers in Indianapolis and Denver, for instance, have been able to breed rodents with a set of specific neurochemical abnormalities that seem to lead directly to a willingness, even a compulsion, to consume alcohol. And recent reports indicate that at least some alcoholics have brain wave abnormalities—abnormalities that are restored to normal through the ingestion of alcohol.

Such research comes down heavily in favor of the theory that alcoholics are "self-treating" an underlying disease. This again brings to the fore the possibility that if those underlying diseases can be pinpointed and diagnosed, they can be treated directly.

Clinically this idea has been bolstered in recent years by reports that, in at least a few chronic alcoholics, drinking masks a severe underlying depression. Identifying those individuals is currently a difficult, time-consuming, and not very accurate process. But if they are identified and treated with antidepressants, their whole psyche seems to change. Though past attempts to quit drinking may have been notably unsuccessful, they now achieve long-term sobriety with relative ease.

Nevertheless, most alcoholics do not respond at all to antidepressant therapy, and thus there is apparently some other specific disease involved.

The upshot is that alcoholism is clearly not a single disease but several—and perhaps many. Cloninger and others believe that in the coming years those diseases will begin to separate out, and that their victims will prove to have only one thing in common: their symptoms can be assuaged by alcohol.

This breaking up of a major mental illness into individual diseases with specific underlying pathologies of the physical brain marks a historic moment in psychology. In more traditional "physical" medicine, a similar breakup of catchall categories earlier in this century foreshadowed the explosion of modern medicine.

"Heart failure," for instance, was once a vague and essentially untreatable condition. But as scientists pinpointed specific pathologies like rheumatic heart disease, hypertensive heart disease, coronary heart disease, bacterial endocarditis and syphilitic heart disease, treatments became specific. Some people got antibiotics, some got surgery, some got blood pressure medication—and many began living longer and more normal lives. A similar breakup, followed by effective and specific treatments and cures, is now occurring in the field of cancer.

That a similar pattern of events is unfolding in the diseases of the mind is perhaps the single greatest testimony to the power of the new science of molecular psychology.

Though the advances are still tentative and confusing, the insights become firmer with each passing year. Today scientists are almost unanimous in their expectations that, as the twentieth century wanes, we can expect to see this process of divide and conquer play itself out across the entire spectrum of mental illnesses.

No one can predict, of course, what the precise answers will be—any more than penicillin could be foreseen in Louis Pasteur's cloudy flasks of moldy broth. Yet . . . already there are flashes of insight.

One of the most spectacular of those insights, as well as one of the most exciting stories from the gray frontier, came recently in a series of experiments at the National Institute of Mental Health in Bethesda, Maryland, outside Washington.

There, for a fleeting moment at least, scientists held in their test tubes the definitive answer to one of the worst of all mental illnesses.

14

A

TANTALIZING

CLUE

A GENETIC defect, by definition, is present in every cell in the victim's body. Though it may do its most visible damage in a single organ, it usually interferes, to some degree, with the metabolism in other cells as well. That's why PKU, for instance, affects mainly the brain but can be detected at birth by high levels of phenylalanine in the urine.

Realizing this, early psychobiologists dreamed of finding some test, some urine assay or blood analysis, that would reveal physical differences between normal people and those with specific mental illnesses.

The payoff for the discovery of such a "marker," as it was called, would be dramatic. For one thing, it would once and for all make the link between the mental and the physical. For another, on a more practical level, it would be of immediate value in the clinical diagnosis of the specific mental illnesses being isolated by researchers.

In those days the broad spectrum of mental impairments was still a rat's nest of categories, subcategories, and subsubcategories, subject to vociferous disagreement among experts and viewed differently by each practicing psychiatrist. Diagnoses were so subjective, in fact, that five different psychiatrists might assign a different patient to as many different subcategories of, say, schizophrenia.

One thing the experts could agree on was that the disagreements, which often occurred in public arenas such as courtrooms, seriously damaged the credibility of psychiatry as a whole. It was one of the things that made the whole field such a laughingstock.

Worse, as long as psychiatrists couldn't define the various forms of mental illnesses, they would not be able to devise and test specific therapies for specific types of illness.

In an effort to correct this situation, psychiatrists met regularly in attempts to define the various categories and reach general agreement. But the attempts almost invariably broke down into bitter arguments between experts and ideological partisans who viewed this and that disease as being the same or different.

Such controversy often attracted the interest of the popular press, which gleefully made matters worse by hanging out the psychiatric community's dirty laundry on the front pages of newspapers.

The diagnostic categories that emerged from the various conferences were helpful, in the absence of anything better, but psychiatrists were painfully aware that they were as reflective of political compromise as they were of the underlying similarities and differences of the various diseases.

In this embarrassing and frustrating climate, the possibility that some diseases might have physical markers assumed the importance, among psychobiologists, of a holy grail. A physical marker, unlike a behavior, was something everybody could agree on. It was either there, damn it, or it wasn't. Period.

There was nothing superficial about the ambition to find

markers, and at least for the psychobiologists it had few if any political overtones. It was a very practical thing. A reaction in a test tube, say, that distinguished one type of schizophrenic from another, could lead to consensus, and that, given the proper funding and the scientific expertise that funding would attract, might well lead to a cure.

As always, schizophrenia was the index disease. During the 1940s and 1950s, hundreds of scientists occupied themselves at one time and another with testing samples of schizophrenics' bodily reactions and fluids. They tested skin conductivity, cultured skin cells, analyzed blood, saliva, and sweat, and stared reflectively into test tubes of schizophrenic urine.

The result of all this was a continuing series of announcements that this or that difference had been found. One early researcher, for instance, claimed to have isolated a substance from the urine of schizophrenics that made spiders weave cockeyed webs. Another group thought that the blood of schizophrenics contained a faulty metabolite of adrenaline that caused hallucinations. Still another proposed that the disease was caused by a vitamin deficiency.

Such developments made great newspaper stories, which generally hinted, or predicted outright, that the enigma of schizophrenia had finally been solved. Unfortunately, in the light of close scrutiny none of the discoveries held water. Kety himself, who was to become a dominant figure in psychogenetics, finally wrote a survey paper in 1959 in which he sadly concluded that none of the "breakthroughs" was of any value whatsoever.

The result, from the public's point of view, was the impression that psychobiologists were forever announcing the discovery of the cause of schizophrenia . . . and yet nothing ever seemed to happen. Eventually, such research, like the rest of psychiatry, ceased to be taken seriously by the layman.

Today, with the advantages of a generation of hindsight, Kety says that early attempts to find markers failed because scientists of that era lacked several important tools. For one thing, they didn't have access to modern analytical instruments that allow today's scientists to field-strip living cells into their component molecules.

Even if they'd had the instruments, though, they would probably have failed anyway, simply because they had no theoretical framework for their search. Not knowing the critical role of receptors in the thought process, their experiments were little more than shots in the dark.

But as the theory of molecular psychology developed in the 1970s and early 1980s, the vision of the clinical researchers began to pay off. As statistical studies authored by scientists like Kety, Shields, Gottesman, and Cloninger established the importance of genes in mental illnesses beyond a shadow of a doubt, more and more bench scientists turned their efforts toward finding the specific molecule or molecules that could be used to diagnose specific mental illnesses.

The research, now, was guided by the theory of molecular psychology. If thoughts and emotions were modulated by transmitters and receptors, then the key genetic defects would logically be expected to involve them, as well as the enzymes and other molecules involved in their manufacture and breakdown.

The guiding rationale was the old concept that while the defective molecules did the most damage in the brain, where their function was of primary importance, the code for them existed in all cells. Therefore subtle defects, if one knew where to look, should be found in skin and blood cells as well in those of the brain.

The key, of course, was knowing where to look.

The enzyme MAO, for instance, with its known connection to depression, became a key focus of scientific interest. By the 1980s, scientists had found that abnormalities of MAO metabolism could indeed be found in the blood and that the presence of those abnormalities, along with other criteria, could be helpful in diagnosis. But that marker, as well as others, had the disadvantage of being rather nonspecific—many people, in addition to psychiatric patients, had it.

Another line of thought focused on the receptor. As its key role in psychology became apparent during the 1970s, scientists began to realize that serious mental illnesses might well be caused by defects in specific receptor systems.

By 1980 researchers knew that receptors were subject to the same manufacture-and-breakdown process as all other living molecules. Receptors were assembled deep in the cell, floated to the surface of the oily membrane, functioned for a while, and then were chewed up and disposed of by other enzymes. In the meantime, other receptors floated up to take their place.

The sensitivity of the cell to chemical messages depended on the density of receptors on its surface, and this density might change from time to time. It was thought, for instance, that if neurotransmitter levels fell, brain cells might be able to compensate by increasing their receptor densities—the effect would be the same as a person cupping his hand behind his ear to better hear soft sounds.

That such changes could indeed take place, and that they could in turn alter behavior, was demonstrated by animals that had been depressed by isolation or shock cages. They definitely exhibited changes in the densities of receptor fields, particularly those receptors designed to "hear" messages transmitted via norepinephrine and serotonin.

This mechanism, triggered by purely psychoenvironmental forces, might cause receptor field changes in humans as well. Yet people were rarely subjected to the same levels of stress as the experimental animals. So why would such changes occur?

As scientists mulled this over, and sorted through the evidence, a tantalizing hypothesis arose. Might a genetic defect result in a tendency to over- or underproduce a certain type of receptor? And might that tendency, when coupled with "normal" stress, cause its victims to pitch into madness?

The question could be answered readily through examining the brain tissue of depressed patients and their nearest relatives. But that, obviously, was impossible.

The other option was to attempt to trick cells from other parts of the body into expressing the receptor-producing genes. The receptors could then be tested to see whether they were normal; if they were not, the same abnormality presumably existed as well in the subject's brain.

In theory, this was a straightforward task, but in practice the science of cell culture is at least as much art as science.

Even at the cellular level life is a very complex process, entailing constant nourishment and excretion, and the requirements for most types of cells are not completely worked out.

Cell culture experts get around this by feeding their cells on natural products, such as serum from the blood of fetal calves. This works well enough, in a rough sort of everyday way, but calf serum consists of thousands of unknown and unsuspected chemicals.

That makes it a little difficult, in a fussy experiment, to find out what's happening. Worse, since a calf's serum may change from day to day, and since the companies that sell the stuff use serum from different calves, every shipment is a bit different. This is only a minor problem in most cell culture experiments, in which the phenomena being studied are natural and obvious ones.

But tricking cells into expressing "dormant" genetic information that would normally be expressed only by cells in other organs is a subtle, subtle business, and scientists trying to tease out receptor markers by tricking skin and blood cells into making brain receptors immediately ran into trouble. Though several scientific teams reported successfully teasing out abnormal responses from various nonbrain cells, their work couldn't be duplicated by other scientists.

Meanwhile, just outside Washington, D.C., a National Institute of Mental Health (NIMH) research team directed by Elliot Gershon was zeroing in on the one form of depression thought most likely to have a genetic component: manic-depressive disease.

On the whole, there was broad disagreement about whether or not depression had a genetic component. For years many psychiatrists had had the distinct impression that depression sometimes ran in families, but the idea was difficult to nail down. Psychogeneticists studying the problem obtained dramatically conflicting results. There seemed to be some correlation, but it appeared and disappeared—and the statistical results often couldn't be duplicated.

The clinical picture was equally confusing. For one thing, a given drug might work beautifully on one patient, so-so on another, and not at all on a third.

A unipolar depressive patient might respond to one anti-depressant and not another, for instance, and very few of them responded to lithium at all. There seemed to be no statement that could make for depression for which there weren't abundant exceptions.

The least confusing group seemed to involve manic-depressive disease. For one thing, 85 percent of the manic-depressive patients responded to a single drug, lithium—a statistic almost unheard of in clinical psychiatry.

For another, the genetic studies, when focused strictly on manic-depressive disease, indicated that there was at least some genetic basis for it. So manic-depressive disease made some sense, at least when compared with other forms of depression.

That didn't mean there were no contradictions. When manic-depression was separated out from unipolar depression, for instance, it often refused to stay separated. The relatives of manic-depressive patients seemed to have a lot of unipolar disease as well, which muddied the water considerably. Even so, the theo-retical basis for a manic-depressive gene was stronger than for any other form of depression.

The first sweet whiff of that success came in 1980, when Natraj Sitaram, then a member of an NIMH group allied with the Gershon team, made a historic observation about rapid-eye movement sleep.

REM sleep, as it's called, refers to a phase of deep sleep, often correlated with dreaming, in which the eyes move back and forth.

Because it is an obvious phenomenon (the movement can be observed even through the closed eyelids), it had been well studied.

Sitaram was working with a chemical called acetylcholine, a neurotransmitter related to norepinephrine. He discovered that when he injected a sleeping patient with a drug that stimulated the production of acetylcholine, REM sleep was triggered. Conversely, he could halt REM sleep with the injection of an acetylcholine-blocking drug.

That meant two things. Obviously, the acetylcholine system, whatever it had to do with depression, was a key factor in REM sleep. Second, now that the fact was known, scientists could directly probe the acetylcholine system in the brains of living human beings—REM sleep, in a sense, was a "marker" for acetylcholine activity.

There followed a period of intense research in the NIMH sleep labs. Volunteers slept with catheters in their arms; at various times during the night, scientists injected acetylcholine-affecting drugs and recorded the results.

They quickly discovered that people who had suffered from severe depression, and therefore theoretically had something wrong with their acetylcholine systems, responded much more quickly to the REM sleep–producing drugs than did normal subjects. The depressive patients seemed especially, almost exquisitely, sensitive to the action of the acetylcholine stimulators.

Equally important, the scientists discovered, it didn't seem to matter whether the patient was currently depressed or not. If he had experienced clinical depression in the past, but was now normal, he was nevertheless supersensitive to acetylcholine. This meant that *at least some depressive patients had an underlying defect in their acetylcholine systems.*

The most straightforward explanation for the acetylcholine sensitivity was that, deep in these patients' brains, the cells that handled acetylcholine messages had too many receptors on their surfaces. And, since the sensitivity existed whether or not the

177

patient was depressed at the time, that overabundance of acetylcholine receptors must represent an underlying, predisposing factor.

It looked, in a word, genetic.

The way to find out for certain would be to find some other cell, outside the brain, that could be induced to produce acetylcholine receptors. If the genetic hypothesis was correct, such cells taken from depression-prone people would have more acetylcholine receptors than normal people.

The Gershon group eventually settled on a type of primitive skin cell called a fibroblast.

Fibroblasts were already known to have receptors for norepinephrine on their surfaces, and norepinephrine was a neurotransmitter very similar to acetylcholine. If receptors for one were there, receptors for the other might be easily produced. Cell samples were taken, grown, and manipulated.

In October 1980, N. Suzan Nadi, a neuroscientist who was expert in the new technology of receptor "counting," joined the Gershon group and went to work trying to discover whether there were acetylcholine receptors on the cultured fibroblasts.

By midsummer of 1981, she had the answer. The receptors were there, all right, she told Gershon. And she could measure them, very precisely.

The scene was now set. All that remained to be done was to decide which patients to test.

The REM sleep studies had been performed on seriously ill depressed patients with unipolar disease, but the Gershon group decided to run their first series of fibroblast tests on skin cells taken from eighteen manic-depressive patients.

Gershon, thinking that manic-depression was probably more than one disease, assumed that most of the eighteen would test negative. With luck, he thought, perhaps two or three would have abnormally high receptor densities.

The results, however, were much more dramatic than that. Two-thirds of the manic-depressive patients proved to have dramatically higher levels of acetylcholine receptors than did normal people.

Surprised, the scientists tracked down the families of those manic-depressives and found that, indeed, many of them had experienced clinical depression at some point in their lives; some were sick at the time.

The illnesses in the families of the test subjects weren't all manic-depression, though. Most of them suffered, instead, from especially severe depression.

The tests were run on the family members who agreed to donate skin cells, and again the results were spectacular. Most of those who were ill, or who had been ill in the past but were not ill now, had extra-dense acetylcholine receptor fields.

The NIMH group had discovered a specific genetic weakness that was handed down from generation to generation.

Sometimes it expressed as severe depression, sometimes it was manifested as manic-depressive disease, and sometimes—presumably as a result of fortunate environmental circumstances—it didn't express at all.

In some families, though, it almost always expressed.

One clinically depressed mother and father, for instance, produced five daughters. Two of the daughters had very high acetylcholine receptor densities and were manic-depressives. A third daughter, who had committed suicide before the time of the Gershon experiment, had been diagnosed as a unipolar depressive. A fourth daughter, from whom no skin sample was taken, was moderately depressed. The fifth daughter tested out to have moderately dense acetylcholine receptors and had a variety of minor psychological disorders.

In hindsight, scientists realized that earlier researchers were probably thrown off the track by the assumption that manic-depression was a specific disease in and of itself. In fact, two-thirds of manic-depression apparently is nothing more than a usual yet particularly severe manifestation of depression caused by acetylcholine sensitivity.

This explained why certain unipolar patients responded to lithium salts, which were normally thought to affect only manic-depression. It also meshed with the impression, long held by clinical psychiatrists, that those depressives who responded to lithium were those who had manic-depressive relatives.

The NIMH data indicated that acetylcholine-sensitive depression affected 2 to 3 percent of the population.

As the picture coalesced, Nadi at NIMH had a brainstorm. She added lithium to a culture of fibroblasts with high-density acetylcholine receptors.

The density of the receptors promptly decreased.

That, then, was apparently why lithium changed the minds of manic-depressive patients: it reduced their sensitivity to their own acetylcholine.

Because the work was so delicate, the phenomena so subtle, and the conclusions so earthshaking, the Gershon group did not immediately release its data. The experiments were repeated, the calculations were checked and rechecked, and other scientists were consulted. Still, the results held.

When the work was finally published in 1984, there was the predictable fire storm of publicity. Lengthy articles were run in the *Washington Post* and the *New York Times*. They went out over the wires and were eventually printed all over the country.

It was the most optimistic story to come out of the mental health field in decades. The skin test, if it could be simplified so that it could be done in local or even regional centers, could accurately predict which patients would respond to lithium and which would not. Further, it would provide solid clues that should lead, in straightforward fashion, to the invention of new and better drugs.

And then what the Gershon group had feared most happened. Suddenly and without warning their experiments stopped working. The skin fibroblasts in the culture dishes quit expressing acetylcholine receptors.

The scientists worked frantically to discover what was wrong with their experiments. They repeated them, exactly the way they had done them the first time . . . and nothing happened. In the Gershon laboratory, there was consternation bordering on hysteria. The scientists tried, and tried again. A month passed, and then another.

Nothing.

Slowly, reports began to filter in from other laboratories, where scientists had attempted to duplicate the NIMH experiments. They, too, got negative results.

By 1985 the Gershon group, methodically checking and cross-checking their procedures, had arrived at several possible answers. The most obvious possibility was suggested by the fact that, shortly before the experiment stopped working, the culture technicians had started feeding the cells from a second batch of fetal calf serum.

Perhaps the first batch of serum had come from one fetal calf, and the second batch from a different one.

Whatever the reason, the sudden collapse of the experiments was a crushing setback; until the problem is solved, and the missing (or extra) ingredient in the culture medium is discovered and dealt with, there can be no useful outcome.

Even in the face of difficulties, however, the experiments worked long enough to part the curtain of mystery that had so long obscured the nature of at least one of the worst forms of depression. And it was a landmark victory for psychogeneticists, who had long believed there were important connections between genes and human behavior.

At Johns Hopkins, in Baltimore, a jubilant Susan Folstein, a medical expert on Huntington's chorea, expressed the sentiments of the entire neurochemical community. "We've just been waiting for this to happen," she said. "It's exciting because it says, 'Ha! You see! I told you!'"

Psychogenetics had finally and irrevocably joined the revolution in molecular psychology.

At the same time, however, the ultimate collapse of the NIMH experiments demonstrated the limitations inherent in trying to dope out chemical events in the brain by indirect means. What was needed was some direct method of analyzing chemical events as they occurred in the living, thinking, feeling organ of personality.

What was needed was a mind-scanner.

15

THE

SCANNERS

A s ever, scientists who sought to make connections between the human brain and human behavior were held back, and often thwarted, by the delicate and fundamentally human nature of the organ they studied.

The study of other organs was much easier. Biopsies could be taken, and, if the whole organ was needed, it could be removed in "instant autopsies" performed within seconds after death.

But the brain was different. Biopsies were unthinkable, and the brain, by definition, must be dead before the most prompt autopsy can begin. Brain death is the very essence of human mortality, and until the delicate neurons cease to squirt transmitters, and the volatile receptor fields begin to dissolve, the brain—and the person it encodes—lives on. By the time it lies on the marble table, ready for slicing, it is by definition a fossil.

Some things could be done with animals, of course. Rat, cat, and dog brains could be explored with probes and chemicals. Their functioning brains could be removed and quick-frozen, to be sliced and scrutinized later in essentially lifelike condition. But who knew what the results might mean? While rat hearts and kidneys may be comparable to human ones, to say the same thing about the brain is to stretch credibility.

As a result, brain scientists are unique among human biologists; they, and they alone, are forced to view the object of their studies from a distance. Scientists like Elliot Gershon, if they are to experiment with the chemical properties of the living human brain, are reduced to convoluted extrapolations from cultured skin cells to neurons embedded in the organ of personality.

At best such experiments are expensive, tedious, and difficult to interpret. At worst they are so delicate and complex that even the scientists themselves cannot reliably duplicate their own work.

The obvious solution was to devise instruments capable of watching the brain function from beyond the boundaries of the skull.

The history of such attempts goes back to the beginning of this century. It met its most useful early success in the electroencephalograph, or EEG machine, which is designed to monitor electrical activity. But until recently, only those "brain waves" generated at the surface of the brain could be detected; thus, activity in the important deep structures involved in mental illness remained a mystery.

Even with modern, computer-analyzed data, such machines are subject to the fundamental limitation that electricity is electricity is electricity. Recording brain waves tells scientists little or nothing about the flux of neurotransmitters that mediate the flow of personality.

Instruments capable of imaging the physical substance of the brain met with similar limitations. X-ray shadows could sometimes be of value to clinicians, and the circulatory system within it could be outlined by means of injecting x-ray opaque dyes into the blood. In more recent decades, computer-assisted instruments like the CAT scanner have made it possible to reconstruct brain shadows as precise, three-dimensional images. But even the CAT scanner, for all its value in finding tumors and diagnosing brain swelling, fails to show chemical processes.

Scientists trying to correlate brain activity with thoughts and actions have always dreamed of similar machines that could zero in on chemical activity. Such a machine would drive the mind-brain connection home in dramatic fashion and have a thousand technical and clinical uses besides.

Attempts to build chemically based scanners date back to the early 1960s. By the middle of that decade, in fact, scientists had managed to build a machine capable of at least hinting at metabolic activity in the living brain.

The first such scanners were based on the idea that neurons are voracious consumers of oxygen—and the faster they're making and squirting neurotransmitters, the more oxygen-carrying blood they need. Nature has met this variable need by designing the vessels of the brain so that they operate as valves as well as conduits, dilating when the centers they serve are working hard and oxygen demand is high, while at the same time clamping down, and restricting flow, to the centers that are at rest.

In other words, if blood flow could be monitored, the changes would reveal which centers were working hardest at any given moment—they would be the ones that got the most blood. If the subject was reading, for example, the vision centers should light up. If the person was moving his arm, the relevant part of the motor cortex should light up.

In practice, monitoring blood flow meant injecting a radioactive dye into the bloodstreams of first animals and then humans and watching the flow of that material by means of sensitive radiation-detection devices arranged around the head.

The first machines were relatively crude. For one thing, exposures were long, which meant the images were blurred. There was no way, with such images, to trace the sequential action of the various centers as they kicked in and then turned off in fractions of a second. The second major drawback was that the blood flow, like the EEG, could be shown only for the surface of the brain.

Even so, the results were dramatic in their confirmation of ideas painstakingly worked out by brain scientists over the decades. The areas that lit up under various circumstances were exactly those that neuroanatomists and physiologists would have predicted.

The left hemisphere of the brain, for instance, long thought to be involved in the processing of language, got the lion's share of blood when the patient was talking. When the subject was concentrating on a picture, the visual cortex at the rear of the brain lit up like a neon light. And, most intriguing of all, when the subject was meditating with eyes closed, blood flow concentrated in the prefrontal lobes of the cortex, the seat of personality.

This strongly hinted that one day such scanners could, in fact as well as in theory, make the connection between mind and brain. But precisely how that might be done was not clear until the Snyder-Pert receptor-labeling breakthrough in 1973.

The explosion of information that followed that work generally was not available to scientists outside the disciplines directly involved. The information was highly technical, involving as it did invisible chemical reactions between receptors and neurotransmitters, spectroscopic analyses of the molecular topology of enzymes, graphs, formulas, and arcane reasoning—and worst of all it was couched in terms that only another neurochemist could truly understand.

At best there was always something abstract about that kind of data, which made it difficult to relate the scientific papers to the real world where human behavior is measured in action, emotion, and motivation. When the molecular psychologists began producing information with implications for value-laden subjects like mental illnesses, addiction, violence, and criminality, the neuroscientists themselves were hard-pressed not to lose the threads of their arguments.

A picture is worth a thousand words, and when those words are multisyllabic science-ese, only a picture will really do at all.

The first advance came soon after the 1973 breakthrough, when, as mentioned earlier, Kuhar at Johns Hopkins began producing photographs of receptor fields by freezing rat brains, labeling their receptors with tracers, and exposing the slices to film.

But there had been serious drawbacks to the Kuhar technique. It often took weeks to get pictures and those pictures, once obtained, were static. The brain, having been sliced and frozen, was beyond thinking even rat thoughts. Finally, the technique could be used in humans only in the rare instance in which a more or less undamaged brain could be obtained immediately after death.

What was needed was a scanner that could label and eventually trace the activity of the mind chemicals in the living, thinking, feeling human brain. And, unlike the early scanners, it had to do so not just on the surface of the brain but also in the all-important emotional and pain-processing areas deep within.

The challenge was taken up by several scientists, most notably by Michel Ter-Pogossian and his associates at Washington University in St. Louis. By the late 1970s, he had built a prototype of what would be called the PET scanner. It was, hands down, the single most complex and expensive instrument ever to serve medical science.

Like the blood flow scanners before it, it featured a doughnut-shaped array of radiation detectors—in this case designed to monitor positron emissions—in which the subject placed his head. Adjacent to the doughnut was the ubiquitous computer, programmed to reduce the data to picture form. But the heart of the process, and the thing that made the PET scanner so complex and expensive, wasn't the scanner itself. It was the associated equipment, and the small army of experts needed to make it all work.

If the chemistry of thought was to be traced, for instance, then exotic tracer molecules had to be devised that would mimic the

187

natural molecules so closely that they would be mistaken in the brain for the real thing and thus get caught up in the chemical process. Radioactive chemicals of that sort, if they were to be safe, had to be very short-lived, which meant they had to be manufactured on the spot. That meant a cyclotron was required, with an additional echelon of nuclear chemists, radiation specialists, and technicians.

How the process works is demonstrated by one of the simpler experimental processes, designed in the mid- to late 1970s. In this experiment, the scientists traced the metabolism of glucose.

In some respects, glucose-tracing experiments are similar in concept to the early blood flow scans. Glucose is the fuel of the living cell, and the harder the cell works the more it needs. In other words, the cells that are firing the fastest and manufacturing the most neurotransmitters at any given moment are the cells that will take up the most glucose. Tracing the movements of radioactive glucose through the brain reveals which centers turn on and off during a specific mental task.

A radioactive glucose experiment, for instance, can "light up" the visual centers in the brain as the subject examines a picture or a test pattern. Radioactive glucose tracers can also show which parts of the brain are involved in such tasks as emotional memory, movement coordination, or even meditation.

The process begins as the subject is positioned with his head inside the doughnut. Then, when all is ready, nuclear engineers use the cyclotron to produce a vial of the appropriate, short-lived radioactive atoms. The vial is then transferred to a chemist who, working quickly before the radiation dies down, incorporates the radioactive atoms into the biological molecules that will mimic the real thing. This substance is then handed to the physician, who administers it to the patient. Then, as the tracers flow through the patient's brain, the detectors in the doughnut record exactly where they go.

"It takes a lot of people," explains NIMH neuroscientist Candace Pert. "It's a team effort. . . . It's ten people sitting around the table. It's organizational, high-tech, lots of steps, hard to do . . . like putting a man on the moon."

As a result, a PET scan facility approaches the cost of a small astronomical observatory. Johns Hopkins scientists, for instance, estimate they have $2 million invested in their PET scanner—and that doesn't include the operating budget for the team of specialists required to operate it.

At the same time, it was immediately apparent that the PET scanner, and the more sophisticated scanners that were certain to follow, would be well worth the time, effort, and money it would take to build and operate them. By allowing scientists to peer for the first time into the working mechanism of the brain, the scanners were obviously destined to do for human psychology what the telescope did for astronomy.

In the beginning, the scientists were confined to simple experiments like those with glucose. But by the time those experiments had confirmed the basic operations in the deep brain, tracers had been developed to allow more complex probes.

Enthusiasm for the scanners was so great that by the mid-1980s perhaps fifteen scientific institutions around the world had found the money to build them. And in the meantime at least one other type of chemical-tracing scanner, using a totally different principle, was being developed.

The NMR scanners (NMR stands for "nuclear magnetic resonance") are based on the principle that the nuclei of normal, unradioactive atoms have north and south poles—just like the earth. And, like the earth, the nucleus of the atom occasionally reverses its polarity. As it does so, it emits a tiny burst of radiation. Each atomic element has its own "signature" type of emission.

An NMR scanner consists of a huge magnet that flips all the atoms in the patient's body into the same polarity. Once that is done, detectors monitor the atoms as they flip back. By identifying the location of "marker" atoms in specific molecules, the scanners can trace those molecules as they make their way through the metabolism of the brain.

189

As the NMR scanners capable of monitoring the human brain were being developed, the PET scanners, which were already in use, multiplied. As they did, scientists developed an agreement to avoid duplication of effort. As a result, each installation focuses on a different aspect of molecular psychology.

Scientists at Johns Hopkins, for instance, installed a second-generation PET scan facility dedicated to answering the all-important questions involving receptor field changes in diseases like drug addiction and schizophrenia.

To this end, scientists plan to first create receptor maps of the normal human brain. This is being done by using radioactive chemicals that attach themselves firmly to the receptors.

Once scientists know what "normal" is, they'll scan drug addicts and mental patients in various stages of their diseases and treatments to see whether, as expected, changes in personality and mental processes are matched by changes in the receptor fields.

Kuhar, the Johns Hopkins pioneer who produced the first receptor maps of dead brains by means of the laborious slice-and-expose process, articulates the enthusiasm the PET scan facilities have generated among neuroscientists everywhere.

"That thing's incredible," he says. "It used to take us weeks to produce a study. Now a subject lies down on the table, you inject him [with radioactive tracers], you turn on the scanner . . . and there's his receptor map! And he gets up off the table and walks away!

"And you can do him again if he gets well, or gets sick, or whatever, and you can compare the two studies. To go that distance in ten years absolutely blows my mind, just blows my mind. I just can't tell you. It's amazing!"

Another scientist, at another center, picked up the theme. "I feel like Galileo," he said. "It's like pointing a telescope at the heavens for the first time. Everywhere we look, we see something new and unexpected. We can't lose. It almost doesn't matter what we do.

"And every time we see something, even if that something is

normal, in principle we've discovered two more diseases. For every normal reaction we find, for every necessary chemical state, you can bet there's someone, somewhere, who has an underreaction . . . and someone else who has an overreaction. The trick is going to be linking what we're seeing to known mental diseases."

In the meantime, the old dream of a scanner that could finally link the physical and the mental is being dramatically fulfilled. With the passage of time, it becomes increasingly clear that the images being produced with the new scanners pertain not just to the brain but to the mind as well.

Increasingly, the scanner laboratories are producing a cascade of discoveries that illuminate the physical basis of thought and emotion. Even the "normal studies," preliminary to the study of disease states, are producing startling conclusions.

At the University of Texas Health Science Center in Dallas, for instance, scientists using a scanner similar to the PET scanner have discovered that each normal person has a characteristic way of using the brain. This is reflected in highly individualistic scanner patterns.

"We call it a 'fingerprint,'" says A. John Rush, a research psychiatrist at the Dallas facility. "What we've found is that there's a great range of normal people. They have no brain disease, no psychiatric disease, but they all have a distinctive [scanner] pattern.

"If you ask the same . . . normal person to come back three times . . . say, separated by a week . . . [he or she has] basically the same [scan] pattern. But that pattern could be quite different from that of other very normal people."

Initial studies have generated a strong sense that the patterns found by the Dallas scientists reflect individual personalities. Presumably they change over time as the person experiences new situations, learns new things, and matures. At one point, the Dallas team used its scanner on a patient with multiple personalities . . . and were able to observe a personality switch.

As the patient's personality changed, so did his scanner "fingerprint." Though the follow-up research is far from complete, the irresistible implication is that "mindprints" do in fact represent personalities.

Meanwhile, Johns Hopkins scientists led by Henry Wagner, chief of nuclear medicine, have discovered what may be an important peculiarity of the dopamine receptor fields in the normal brain.

Dopamine receptors in primitive structures at the base of the brain usually serve in part to modulate alertness and as a processing center for perception. They are high on the list of receptors to map because of their presumed involvement in schizophrenic hallucinations.

But in examining dopamine receptor densities in normal brains, the Wagner group discovered that the sexes differ dramatically. In females, the densities of dopamine receptor fields remain stable for life, but in males the fields thin out with increasing age.

Do these changes correlate with the increasing calmness observed in the aging male? Might they have to do with the observed tendency in male drug addicts to "mature out" of their addiction in their thirties? Might they reveal something about differences in male and female behavior?

No one knows, but such questions, being generated faster than answers at PET scan facilities all over the world, testify to the fertility of the field. And already, even before the studies of the normal mind-brain are complete, discoveries involving mental illness are beginning to emerge.

And the list goes on. At UCLA, scientists have photographed epileptic seizures as they explode in the living brain.

At Washington University, researchers discovered that activity varied in the speech centers of right- and left-handed people, with speech functions of right-handers concentrated on the left side and vice versa.

At NIH, one team has been able to use a PET scanner to separate out four visual processing stations in which objects are classed for size, color, shape, and texture. They have even been able to figure out how visual images become associated with emotions such as fear and pleasure deep in the brain.

At Brookhaven, audio hallucinations in a schizophrenic child were linked, through the use of a PET scanner, with metabolic changes in the section of the forebrain thought to be critical in emotional control.

Similar preliminary work at other centers has scientists hopeful that the mind-scanners will soon produce characteristic patterns for schizophrenia and depression. Initial findings indicate that receptor field changes may also play a role in addiction.

The first solid cause-and-effect link between a specific mental illness and a PET scan–detected physical abnormality of the brain, however, has already been forged.

The mental illness is a distinctive panic-anxiety syndrome characterized by sudden, inexplicable attacks of raw fear. It affects between 1 and 2 percent of the population.

Because patients who suffer from this syndrome also have an exercise intolerance, and because panic is characterized by changes in heart function, victims often end up in emergency rooms with what seem like heart attacks. As a result, the syndrome was long thought to be a form of heart disease. But in recent years the panic attacks were found to be triggered by elevations in blood lactate levels. That explained the exercise intolerance, since lactate is normally produced by exercise.

This served to deepen the mystery, though, not solve it. Normal people have elevated blood lactate levels when they exercise, too, but the lactate doesn't cause panic attacks. Presumably the high lactate levels triggered some otherwise benign defect in the brain. But what defect? And where?

Pathologists, dissecting the brains of dead panic-syndrome patients, could find no visible gross abnormalities. Likewise, nothing unusual appeared under the microscope. So a group of Washington University scientists, including neurologist and PET scan expert Marcus Raichle, decided to probe the brains of living patients with a mind-scanner.

The defect leaped right out at them: emotional centers in the left mesial temporal lobe, a part of the emotional brain, were not "kicking in" when they should. The companion centers on the opposite side of the brain were functioning normally.

"These people are different," Raichle explained. "The brain, if you will, is kind of unbalanced."

One of the most striking results of the experiment is that there were no exceptions; every patient with the syndrome had precisely the same defect. For the first time in history, a discrete brain abnormality had been identified in patients with a primary psychiatric disorder.

These discoveries were made with scanners that, according to experts, are relatively primitive. The current generation of machines have a resolution only between a quarter- and a half-inch, and, like the earlier machines, they require exposures measured in minutes. As a result, the pictures they produce are far too blurry for scientists to be able to pinpoint the actual flow of thought from one tiny brain center to another.

Those limitations are, to a certain extent, already being overcome by refinements in the machines and in the ways in which the information is processed through the computer. But PET machines, the most popular version of the modern mind-scanners, have theoretical resolution limits that will forever bar them from producing really precise, moving pictures of the thought process.

"We haven't figured out yet how to do that," remarked one brain scientist. "And frankly, I don't have any clear picture of how we can.

"On the other hand, we're just getting started with this, and I have even more difficulty imagining that these problems won't be overcome. I don't think Galileo could have foreseen Mount Palomar and the Orbiting Astronomical Observatory, either. But they were inevitable."

As new scanners come along, as scientists grow ever more proficient in their use, and as their findings dovetail with those of brain chemists, psychogeneticists, neurophysiologists, and experts from other interlinked fields, the pace of discovery is sure to increase exponentially. As it does, we should develop an ever more precise picture of how human thoughts, emotions, and behavior arise from the dynamic chemistry of the brain.

The usefulness of this knowledge will be first to pinpoint the physical causes of the different forms of mental illness. This, in turn, should suggest what sort of drug therapy should be designed to overcome the physical defects. Such knowledge, coupled with the new chemical techniques that allow rapid development of new psychoactive compounds, should dramatically accelerate the rate at which new drugs become available.

The scanners should also shorten the time it takes to get experimental drugs out of the laboratory and into the pharmacy. Today the testing of new compounds proceeds largely on hunch and guesswork. It requires years of animal testing, in which scientists deduce the effects of drugs by observing behavior and dissecting dead brains, and then more years of cautious and extremely expensive clinical trials on humans.

Such caution is necessary because of the lack of precision involved—the scientists really don't know what the drug is doing, dynamically, inside the brain. But as the brain is mapped and scanners become available to watch the action of new drugs inside the mind-brains of animals and people, the developmental process should become much more deliberate. The scanners, in fact, represent the final development necessary for the emergence of true "mind engineering."

But while drugs are the most obvious outgrowth of the new technology, they are not the only one—and they may not even be the most powerful. The mind can be changed in many ways, and the most precise and natural of these is by the process of experience. The psychologist, by talking with the patient, and the Freudian analyst just by listening, can also change the mind.

The existence of unique "mindprints" indicates that our brains are as plastic as the personalities they exude. Chemicals flow with every word and thought, and as we achieve understanding and our minds change, our brains undergo physical changes as well. The fact that rats' brains can be damaged by isolation and enforced helplessness leaves little doubt that some human pathologies result from experience-mediated changes in our brains.

It seems equally clear that traditional psychotherapy, despite its imprecision, can often be useful. Such usefulness must also be mediated by changes in the mind-brain induced by the experience of "talk therapy." But what are the nature of such pathologies? What are the changes? How are they corrected by psychotherapy? And why is psychotherapy so often ineffective?

Initial experience with the mind-scanners, coupled with the overall theory of molecular psychology, may offer specific answers. If the physical damage that lies behind what used to be called the "neuroses" can be identified by mind-scanners, then specific diagnoses can be achieved. With specific diagnoses, treatment can be better prescribed—analysis, say, for the phobic workaholic with forebrain malfunction and psychodrama for a similar patient with a limbic system disorder.

The result could be a division of the "minor mental illnesses," which in aggregate are in fact very major, into separate diseases with specific "talk therapies" for each. How well each therapy worked could be determined, scientifically, by monitoring selected patients during the process of treatment.

All patients would not, of course, need to be scanned in order for the defects to be sorted out and linked with diseases. That might be done, using mind-scanners, by medical school research laboratories assigned to work out the nature of the various diseases. In clinical practice, the type of disorder might well be determined by behavior, physical reactions, or perhaps even chemical tests of blood or urine.

In fact this use of scanners, confined to research only, is just what many experts foresee.

For one thing, the scanners may simply be too expensive to ever proliferate into small hospitals. Their multimillion-dollar price tags, particularly in a climate of growing alarm over escalating health care costs, may at least for the moment bar the instruments from routine clinical use.

A growing number of experts, however, disagree. The high

costs, they say, may be offset by dramatically improved therapy for patients. Misdiagnosis and ineffective treatment, they point out, can also be very costly—both in terms of money and human suffering. If a scan cost $10,000, say, but led to a series of therapeutic events that restored a worker to productivity, it might be cheap at the price. The cost would be more than offset by savings in long-term hospitalization, welfare, and the social costs of mental illness.

And the optimists do not automatically concede that the scanners will remain as expensive as they presently are. The history of technology, after all, is that expensive innovations eventually become less so—and why should the scanners be any different?

Recent improvements in scanner technology, coupled with the successful development of NMR scanners and hints that new generations of PET scanners can use longer-lived tracers and so won't need cyclotrons, are prompting an increasing number of skeptics to soften their predictions that the equipment will never be used clinically. If the optimists are correct, the day may come when mind-scanners are commonplace in hospitals.

There are also possibilities outside medicine. Mind-scanners might be useful, for instance, in diagnosing accused criminals who plead insanity. Since "mindprints" probably can't be faked or altered, they could serve to identify people who are, say, involved in security operations. They might be useful in conjunction with aptitude tests. They could also be used to screen students or job applicants, and they might even be used, somehow, to monitor the progress of students and suggest to professors which points should be covered next.

These, of course, are speculations; we will have to wait and see what the future brings. But in the meantime it's become increasingly obvious that mind-scanning technology is destined to be the catalyst that unifies the various disciplines of molecular psychology.

And so, before we move on, let's stop and contemplate, for a moment, what our technology has wrought.

As we focus our eyes on the first blurry pictures of the human mind, pictures still wet from the fixer of history, we are sure to be overcome by a certain awe of the moment.

Here, etched on the film, is something never before seen. And though we see it only darkly, through a distorted mirror of assumption and oversimplification, we nonetheless see it. And for the first time in all of the long human trek from the steamy jungles of East Africa, the human enigma takes on a shape.

The shape is fuzzy yet. It wavers and dances with this interpretation and that, yet even so . . . even so, it slowly begins to coalesce before our very eyes into something that's just . . . about . . . to make sense.

16

THE

MECHANISM

AND

THE

MECHANICS

PSYCHOLOGY is not a science like other sciences, directed outward. It has nothing to do with building bridges, or designing microscopes, or programming computers, or arriving at the relative positions of various objects in n-dimensional space. Instead, it examines the more personal universe, the warm one, the one inside. Psychology is in fact a mirror.

This cuts both ways, of course. Mirrors bring out our vanity, and we love to stand in front of them and primp. At the same time, mirrors sometimes show us things we'd just as soon not see. So psychology is also the uncomfortable science.

The smug truth, though, is that the mirror has always been mercifully blurry. We could see in it stimuli and response. We could perceive our own knee-jerk reactions to the world. We could recognize our basic programmed needs and their overlays of neurosis. We could admit to our cravings for Mama's love and

Papa's approval. But for the most part psychology was simplistic and unsubtle, suited more for white rats than for men and women. For most of us this reduced psychology to the status of a fascinating intellectual toy.

But the new mirror is different. Molecular psychology reflects reality far better than what's come before.

We are at first caught up with this new image of our inner selves. We ooh and ahh over what we see, endlessly vain, endlessly captivated by our own reflections.

We are curious, too, of course, and we admire the correlation between PET scan picture and personality, the correspondence of molecule and emotion. We are taken by the logical tidiness of it all. Yes, yes, yes . . . certainly, it makes good sense.

But eventually the newness wears off, and it dawns on us that this new image of man is no mere toy. What we see is heavy with implications for the future.

Many of those implications are optimistic ones, full of hope for the mentally ill and maybe even for the rest of us as well. That much is easy enough to take. But what catches our attention is something less digestible.

What we see in the mirror, the grand chemical symphony that seems to explain us so well, is wholly materialistic.

This view of ourselves as gizmos is sobering. It clashes, and clashes violently, with the idea that we are fundamentally spiritual creatures.

This perception that we are more than the sum of our parts isn't just an idea, it's a rock-solid belief. It's part of being human— it comes with the territory. And while in our thoughtful moments we may have had an intellectual doubt or two along the way, we've always known emotionally that we were more than matter, and that that "moreness," which the religious call a soul, is somehow related to our value as individuals.

Our parents had the same faith. So did their parents, and theirs, and theirs, back through the ages until history fades into legend and legend dissolves into screams, giggles, and grunts in the night. It's a truth, that's all, a truth so compelling and seductive that it's understood intuitively by Australian aborigine, Manhattan accountant, and UCLA philosopher alike.

This spiritual view of ourselves seems to be at or near the center of our philosophical guidance system. When it's challenged by the molecular psychologists, we experience a sort of philosophical and perhaps even moral vertigo. How could a creature as warm and human as I be a mere mechanism?

The human response is a sudden revulsion, and an urge to turn away from the mirror.

We don't, of course—or, if we do, we then return. Ever since Copernicus yanked man out of his comfortable nest at the center of the universe, scientific revolutions have always challenged what seemed to be true. This, too, comes with the human territory.

So we look again at the PET scanner photos, reconsider the statistics gathered by the psychogeneticists, rethink the results of the neurochemical experiments. They all point in the same direction: materialism.

It's more a matter of pattern than of proof. Molecular psychologists haven't disproved the existence of the soul, or the primacy of God, or the ephemeral nature of art. They haven't even tried, and won't. What they've done is surge out ahead of those beliefs, leaving them behind.

The situation is reminiscent of Darwin and the uproar his theory caused in the 1850s. In those days, there was no proof that the theory of evolution was valid, and you could argue if you liked—and you still can—that the old man proved nothing. You would even be correct. But the argument turns shrill and defensive, like the verbal maneuvering of a defense attorney who demands absolute proof in the face of overwhelming circumstantial evidence.

Darwin had put his finger squarely on a pattern, a pattern that was internally consistent, a pattern that explained with elegant simplicity the existence of improbable creatures like men and women, a pattern that simply was too useful not to adopt—and a pattern that, by shaping the thoughts of biologists, created the proper environment for what would become modern medicine.

The theory of molecular psychology is likewise a fabric, a patterned web spun of a single theme. And that theme is that mind and matter are the same.

Like the theory of evolution, it is internally consistent and at the same time all-inclusive. With it, scientists in Dallas can link a physical defect of the brain with the ancient, clawing panic of a psychological syndrome; with it Elliot Gershon at NIMH can equate depression with abnormal acetylcholine receptors. With it we can define a mechanism behind the human craving for drugs and alcohol, and understand the dopaminergic nature of hallucinations.

As the neuroscience journal articles arrive each month with their fresh crop of discoveries, and are Xeroxed and passed from hand to hand, and filed under eureka! and farout! we come slowly to understand that the enigma of the mind is perfectly capable of solution.

What's more, we are in fact solving it, minute by minute and month by month, molecule by molecule. And in every piece of the puzzle we see reflected the same theme, that mind and brain are one—for every thought there is a molecular reaction, and for every molecular reaction there is a thought.

Once we are primed for it, we see mechanism wherever we look. The smile of the baby that warms the mother's heart and solidifies her love is reducible to chemical equations, and to mechanism. The brain has mechanisms with which to hear, mechanisms to convert the output of the eyes into meaningful images, more mechanisms with which to clothe those images in emotional connotations, mechanisms that regulate the fragile balance between mania and depression, mechanisms that let us distinguish the outside world of rocks, buildings, and books from the inside world of imagined angels and dragons, mechanisms to change the other mechanisms as we experience and learn . . . mechanisms within mechanisms within mechanisms.

There will of course be a certain sadness as the "human spirit" joins the flat earth, papal infallibility, and creationism on the list of widely held but obviously erroneous convictions. And we can't

help but be at least a little disturbed by the materialism of molecular psychology. It does seem at first to be cold and forbiddingly
amoral.

But have we really lost anything? Did it really matter, once
the shouting was over, that the earth wasn't the center of the
universe? Did it matter that humans were descended from
animals? Didn't we remain the same in any case, for better or
for worse?

And, once we consider it, has human spirituality really been
the font of whatever goodness we can claim to possess? Hasn't it
been capable, on occasion, of unspeakable cruelty?

Being moral, we slip easily into righteousness; believing, we
grow judgmental. Spiritualism embraces pogroms and inquisi-
tions and provides the justification for holy wars against infidels.

More to the point, it is precisely our spiritual view of ourselves that has always cast mental illness in a moralistic, super-
stitious light.

We're all guilty of that, though we routinely deny that we are.
We say, as we're supposed to say, that mental illness is a disease.
So is alcoholism. The victims of behavioral disorders are luckless
creatures, the litany goes, and there but for the grace of God
go you and I.

The phrases come easy to our tongues. We have been trained
to them. Our lips move, and the correct, socially acceptable words
come out. Mental illness is a disease. Mental illness is a disease.
Mental illness is a disease.

But our actions speak far louder than our words.

"There'll by God be no halfway house in my neighborhood!"
we say. *"Put it somewhere else!"*

We cross the street to avoid contact with a bag lady or a
derelict alcoholic. We whisper about Uncle Fred, and his bottle,
and try to keep both hidden away lest they embarrass the family.

We say that we feel compassion for the mentally ill, but somehow when it's time to put together state budgets we always end
up allotting more for housing criminals and building sports
arenas than for sheltering the insane. We spend millions on

science aimed at curing physical diseases and then, almost as a guilty afterthought, toss a few pennies into the cup for the study of madness.

We assign one psychiatrist to attend a thousand schizophrenics, and then point gleefully to his failure; it proves, we say, that psychiatrists are incompetent. That being the case, we might as well close the mental institutions and house all schizophrenics elsewhere.

So we close the institutions . . . and then, by some oversight, forget to put aside money for the "elsewhere." Then we complain, bitterly, that the downtown is full of creeps and sleazeballs sleeping on gratings and defecating on the sidewalk.

It's not that we, as a culture, lack generosity. Our minds and wallets are open to the disadvantaged. Think of the poster children who are selected and used with good effect by those who collect money to combat cystic fibrosis, cerebral palsy, and muscular dystrophy. Our hearts go out to those children, and it provokes our generosity. It is a good gimmick, for a good cause, and we respond with compassion.

Of course, the National Mental Health Association has no poster child. It would be . . . well, inappropriate. A picture of a schizophrenic adolescent, grinning desperately at us from a placard in a window, would not make us dig into our pockets for loose change. No, we would turn away in revulsion.

Such actions speak eloquently to the belief that man is spiritual and that behavior is therefore a moral matter. Misbehavior, whether labeled "mental illness" or somethings else, is at bottom a deficiency—especially if it involves drugs, alcohol, or violent or sexual behavior.

Thus our spiritualism justifies our belief that the mentally ill are not like you and me, that they did something wrong. Perhaps they let their thoughts run in forbidden channels. Or they're weak. Or there's some other black mark on their souls.

And as for science . . . well, the acceptable position is that sure, we should study mental illness. But we know, as a corollary of the spiritual nature of man, that the human mind is beyond the purview of science. Science, at least the science of the psyche, is a laughingstock.

Unfortunately, we sigh, that means we can't do anything about mental illness. So, except for the pennies, just enough to keep up appearances, there's no real use trying.

This in the final analysis is the ugly fruit of the spiritualism to which we have clung so tightly. From the human spirit, if such spirit is to be believed, there grows an inability to identify with the mentally ill—and from that inability there flows a meanness that ultimately manifests itself as pennies in the bottom of a cup.

But the pennies have inexorably added up, as has the knowledge of the human mind. And if our immediate response to the materialism is to turn away in revulsion, a closer examination reveals that molecular psychology is anything but cold or cruel.

The new synthesis, after all, had its roots in the desire to cure the mentally ill—a humane goal if ever there was one. And it teaches us that if the mind is mechanism then so is madness; insanity, in the gospel of the new psychiatry, is no more a matter of fault than varicose veins.

Molecular psychology tells us that mental illness is as real, and as physical, as cancer. It is as specific as juvenile diabetes, as understandable as influenza, as curable as pneumonia. Like the classic diseases of the other bodily organs, it is sometimes caused by genetic forces, sometimes by environmental ones, and most often by the two working in tandem. But whatever the cause, the effect is always physical damage to the gray organ in question.

Just how important a concept this is is illustrated by the current revolution in psychological categorization, in which the major mental illnesses are breaking up into specific diseases, each with its own underlying physical cause. The parallels between this and the similar breakup of physical diseases earlier in the twentieth century, just prior to the blossoming of modern medicine, is striking.

One obvious example of how molecular psychology is reshaping the clinical view of madness can be found in the work of Gershon and his group at NIMH.

Their finding, as you may remember from an earlier chapter, was that serious depression is often caused by a genetically determined overabundance of acetylcholine receptors on the surfaces of the victim's brain cells. As a result, those cells—and the personalities they produce—tend to overact to their own acetylcholine.

On a practical level, the Gershon research implies that one day soon psychiatrists who treat such patients will no longer have to "shop around," trying first one drug and then another before finding one that works. Instead, laboratory tests will lead them directly to the drug of choice.

This should dramatically shorten the lag time between the first treatment and the time when the depression begins to lift. That, in turn, should significantly reduce the nation's suicide rate.

Though the new knowledge can obviously lead to broad advances in the treatment of mentally ill people, experts believe that it will have much greater impact when applied to early diagnosis and prevention. Here again, the revolution in molecular psychology parallels the explosion in physical medicine earlier in this century.

Rheumatic heart disease is an obvious example. Once it strikes, treatment involves the replacement of the damaged valves—a painful, dangerous, expensive, and ultimately unsatisfactory therapy.

A far better solution became possible with the discovery that the valve damage resulted from a runaway streptococcus infection. Once pediatricians recognized the danger and began aggressively diagnosing and treating strep throats, rheumatic heart disease all but disappeared.

Could the early diagnosis of mental illness, by means of various markers, lead to similar success in the field of mental illness? In a word, yes.

In recent years, scientists have found considerable evidence that mental illnesses may actually make themselves worse, as epilepsy does, with each recurrent crisis. In effect the "spells" of madness, caused by metabolic problems in the brain, make that damage worse—and set the stage for recurrent crises. The more often one has an attack of clinical depression, for instance, the more susceptible one becomes to another attack.

Pursuing this line of research, scientists at the NIMH have come to recognize a phenomenon called "kindling"—as in kindling a fire. In this scenario, the first crisis is the critical one; it is the first domino that, when knocked over, starts a process of crisis and brain damage that leads to a life of chronic mental illness.

The implication is obvious: if victims could be identified and treated before that first crisis, kindling might be prevented and lifelong disease might never develop.

Psychiatrists who would like to identify and treat such patients early can narrow the search for potential patients by examining the children of parents who have experienced some mental illness. The child of a manic-depressive, for instance, has a 25 to 30 percent chance of developing the disease himself. The first attack will usually come during the teenage years.

But lithium, though one of the safest of the antipsychotic drugs, is too powerful to give to a child on a 30 percent chance it will be needed.

In theory, doctors could watch carefully for the first signs of depression to appear, and then jump right on the case and treat it aggressively. But theory, in this case, runs headlong into a brick wall of reality.

The problem is that manic-depressive disease, like many other forms of mental illness, usually erupts first in the teenage years. And how does one tell a mentally ill teenager from a normal one? What teenager isn't at least a little bit mad?

We may chuckle at that, but it's not funny when a seriously depressed child gets lost in the almost universal craziness of adolescence. And that, more often than not, is precisely what happens.

Such children go through an entire adolescence of tremendous turmoil and upheaval. In their anguish they are likely to become involved with drugs and alcohol, and they may begin a pattern of violence and lawbreaking. They'll do poorly in school, and they'll destroy the relationships that might give them strength.

When their peers grow out of such behavior but they don't, they become easy to identify. Then, in hindsight, parents and others recognize that such children's teenage traumas were in truth a little worse than usual, a little more damaging . . . a little less normal.

But that's in hindsight. And as Fred Goodwin at NIMH puts it, "By then the disease is on top of us."

By then the mental illness has already kindled and flared into serious disease—disease usually complicated by drug use, behavior problems, low self-esteem, an inability to form relationships, and the patient's distrust of his or her own feelings. By that time, treatment is complex and, more often than not, doomed to failure.

But the appearance of a reliable physical test for the acetylcholine supersensitivity that underlies this type of depression could yield startling results.

Many scientists, including Goodwin, believe that if children at risk could be positively identified by physical tests, and drugs administered before the first attack, kindling could be prevented altogether. Once the might-have-been victims emerge from the adolescent crisis, the drugs might no longer be necessary.

It's still too early to tell whether Gershon's work will yield a diagnostic test in the near future. But even if it doesn't, so many other groups are looking for markers that one seems bound to succeed soon. At Harvard University, for instance, a number of blood tests are already in experimental use.

According to Joseph Schildkraut, a prominent Harvard neuroscientist, the age of psychiatric chemistry does not lie in the future —in truth, it's already begun. As the century plays itself out, he and other experts say, routine physical tests will be developed for an increasingly wide variety of mental illnesses.

With them will come many futuristic-sounding prevention

strategies, from vaccination programs for virus-caused insanity to more socially oriented mental health programs for environmentally caused or triggered madness.

Ultimately these and related tactics, coupled with the development of new therapies, should produce cures for many forms of mental disease that are now considered chronic and incurable.

Most scientists expect the first wave of the new therapies to come in the form of drugs that, like Thorazine and the tricyclic antidepressants, exert their influence by changing the sensitivity of receptors or the abundance of transmitters. The effect is to turn the target brain subsystem up or down.

The difference between the new drugs and the old ones is that the old ones were discovered almost by accident and, because scientists couldn't really tell for sure what they were doing in the human brain, they could never be made very specific. Thus the neuroleptics suppress the dopamine system in the corpus striatum, stopping hallucinations, but also wreak havoc in the motor system and often produce TD. The tricyclic antidepressants influence the heart as well as the brain; if not handled properly, they can kill.

The confidence that the next generations of drugs will represent a quantum leap in neuropharmacology is based on two technologies.

One is the advent of the scanners, and their growing ability to identify molecular-level defects in the brains of the mentally ill. The other involves a whole series of engineering techniques, developed by scientists like Snyder at Johns Hopkins, that will allow scientists to confirm PET scan discoveries and tailor-make drugs to correct metabolic imbalances.

The promise of these technologies, as well as the economic incentive to develop them, is illustrated by two drugs that have already hit the market. Called the "beta blockers," they act on the peripheral nervous system—one of them calms the nerves of the heart and the other prevents the secretion of acids in the stomach.

The drugs were discovered before the nature of the revolution in receptor-transmitter interactions became clear, so they weren't designed rationally. But, because each acts on its target organ with almost no side effects on the rest of the body, they illustrate the remarkable specificity that's possible. These receptor-active drugs almost certainly foreshadow the development of other drugs that will be engineered from conception to influence specific receptors.

In a world in which economic forces always play a role in research and development, though, it's also important to note that the beta blockers have become two of the best-selling, most profitable drugs of the 1980s.

As the new techniques are applied to the chemistry of the brain, scientists are actively searching for new antischizophrenic drugs that, perhaps by taking advantage of differences between the receptors in the corpus striatum and the motor system, will quell hallucinations without causing TD.

There are also reports from Europe of a new compound that, at least according to preliminary tests, may improve schizophrenic withdrawal as well as control hallucinations. Research is proceeding as well in the search for side effect–free new drugs for the several forms of depression.

Genetic engineering techniques that replace the defective mind-gene with a healthy one would, of course, be the best therapy for inherited mental illnesses like acetylcholine depression. Pending that, however, drugs aimed at correcting the problem are the most obvious hope.

Even when the metabolic damage to the brain is caused by strictly psychological stresses, as is the case with animals kept in solitary confinement, drugs can provide a direct means of restoring chemical balance.

New drugs are also being sought to settle the brains of hyperactive children, to increase the memory capacity of senile patients, to make prisoners more tractable, to correct the pain-buffer problem that seems to underlie chronic addiction, and even to enhance the learning capacity of dull students.

Scientists taking still another tack are hoping to help prevent morphine addiction among patients and medical personnel by designing compounds that will dull pain without affecting the psychological pain system and producing a "high."

But as our ability to tease out genetic, infectious, and psychological factors in mental illness improves, awkward questions are sure to arise.

To what degree, for instance, does our society wish to ensure mental health by chemical means? If severe depressives are to be maintained on drugs, what about people who are moderately depressed? And what about people who are depressed, perhaps, for good reason? Isn't there a danger, in the end, of coming to rely on pills as an easy answer to our problems?

After all, even acetylcholine depression has a strictly psychological component—otherwise, all people with acetylcholine supersensitivity would become profoundly depressed. Unless the environmental factor is physical, such as a virus or a chemical, at least some potential victims must be either escaping the stress or devising coping mechanisms to deal with it.

These questions become all the more acute as experts, reflecting on the development of molecular psychology over the past few years and remembering the many failures of Great Society programs, for example, begin to see slums in a new light.

Slum dwellers have a much higher incidence not only of classic mental illness but also of drug addiction and criminal behavior. The environmental explanation for this, while probably valid enough, represents only one facet of the reality. In addition, there is probably a tendency for victims of genetic forms of mental illness to sink into poverty, and hence into the slums— where the stressful environment exacerbates the problem.

Research on the brain, and the physical causes and effects of stress and mental illness, should help us understand how the various genetic, environmental, economic, and social factors play into one another. And the answers, as they come, should guide us to more workable social policies.

"It's going to be sticky, though," admitted one neurochemist, musing over a beer after a conference on the possibility of anti-violence drugs. "We're getting into something that's very complex.

"On the one hand, slums and poor parenting are definitely risk factors for mental disease. Slums are problems that need to be solved, and no responsible neurochemist advocates the use of drugs in lieu of addressing those problems.

"But don't forget that while drug use and mental illness are epidemic in the slums, they aren't pandemic. Everyone in the inner city isn't crazy or on drugs, not by a long shot.

"Some people probably do end up in the ghetto because their family has a genetic susceptibility to schizophrenia. But people also live there because Daddy got killed in an industrial accident, and Mommy is prevented by sexism from making decent wages—and now she's clinically depressed. I would be, too, in her fix. It's a complicated mix, and it's going to take us a long time to sort it all out.

"And yes, some of the scenarios give me the creeps, too. I'd hate for us to just give everyone who's unhappy a happy pill. Unhappiness can be healthy, and it drives us to accomplish things.

"All the same, if we can find drugs that will cure mental illness, or alcoholism, or criminality . . . then we're going to use those drugs. We've got to. To refuse to treat people while we sit here and argue over ideological or philosophical objections, to let people lose their hope and perhaps their lives while we equivocate . . . that would be unconscionable.

"If a person is disabled by depression caused by the fact that his surroundings are damned depressing, that doesn't make him or her any less depressed. And in the end it's depression that makes it impossible for that person to get the hell out of the mess he's in.

"So if we have drugs that work, then that person has the right to them. To say otherwise is to say that people in New Delhi don't have the right to cholera treatment because they have such a lousy sanitation system—it's to say that we shouldn't treat the casualties of war, because what we really ought to be doing is understanding the causes of violence. It's nice logic, and it even sounds moral, but you don't have to carry it very far before it gets cold as ice. And my distinct impression is that the goal of medical science is to help people."

But are drugs the only therapeutic answer, short of a model society?

That's certainly the sense that one brings away from the neuroscientific conventions and meetings. This revolution is, after all, being conducted by neuropharmacologists—many of whom have lucrative consulting contracts with drug companies. One would also get that impression by talking to Freudian psychiatrists and other "talk therapists," many of whom tend to feel extremely threatened by the breath-taking advances in neurochemistry.

But to focus entirely on drugs is to forget the most obvious truth about the chemistry of the psyche: it evolved to change with the environment.

The most specific way to affect the brain's molecular processes is not to use drugs. Drugs, however specific, are a meat ax compared with the scalpel of thinking, talking, seeing, feeling, or experiencing.

Certain diseases like schizophrenia probably involve such dramatic damage to the chemical substrates of the mind that only a compensating drug will make normality possible.

But even acetylcholine depression, as strongly genetic and as profoundly physical as it is, is apparently countered by some people through the development of strictly psychological coping mechanisms. If we knew what those coping mechanisms were, it might be easier and safer to instill them with traditional psychotherapy rather than give the patients drugs.

The problem with traditional talk therapies, in fact, isn't that they aren't effective. Although some brain scientists have nothing but disdain for the "shrinks," most of the more reflective ones believe that psychotherapy does in fact work, at least for some illnesses, and in some cases. The problem is that it doesn't work predictably.

At least part of the reason for that is that the process of psychological diagnosis remains a dark art. If what works for one patient fails to benefit another, the patients may not be comparable. Their symptoms may be similar, but the underlying disease, as in the case of manic-depressives, may be quite different.

A good case in point involves alcoholism. Some alcoholics, though not very many, achieve and maintain sobriety with Alcoholics Anonymous. A larger percentage achieve the same effect with non-AA group therapy programs. This disparity has sparked a bitter feud between group therapists and AA partisans as to which program is preferable.

As research continues to show that there are apparently a large number of diseases that go under the rubric of "alcoholism," however, there is a good chance that the arguments miss the whole point. Some forms of the disease may respond best to AA methods, and others to group therapy. Still others may respond only to treatment with drugs that have not yet been devised.

If that's the answer, it should become apparent as we learn to diagnose the various types of alcoholism more specifically. It might well turn out that the proper diagnosis, and the referral of each alcoholic to the best program for him as an individual, would raise the success rates of both forms of therapy.

In a larger sense, our ever-increasing understanding of the mind-brain should eventually lead us to more precise models of what the mind is and does on all its many levels. That, in turn, should provide better rationales for all the talk therapies.

Sigmund Freud never, in sober moments at least, claimed that his introspective model of the mind, with its triad of ego, super-ego, and id, was meant to be the final and definitive word. And in fact in recent times it has been modified so many times and shown to have so many exceptions that it's become reminiscent of the eventual fate of Ptolemy's originally simple earth-centered model of the solar system.

By the fifteenth century, attempts to make that model account for all the observed movements of the planets in the sky had turned it into a nightmarishly complex system of wheels within wheels within wheels. Copernicus, by moving the sun to the center with the planets revolving in orderly fashion, simplified it all once again.

A similar overhaul of Freud's concepts may be due. If so, the shape of the new model will be at least partly determined by a subculture of brain scientists whose interest it is to search for the physical sites of psychological phenomena.

The search has gone on for some decades and has been fraught with all manner of complexities. Things happen so fast in the brain that they almost seem to be happening everywhere at once. And a dream that one is running away from a dragon may involve not just the dreaming center but also those involving leg movements, vision, and balance. As a result, answers have been elusive and subject to ferocious argument among experts.

Now that scientists are gaining access to sophisticated modern technology such as PET scanners, however, the tide may be turning. There are indications, yet unconfirmed, that the nature of memory may be about to unravel. A Rockefeller University scientist, Jonathan Winson, claims in a new book[*] to have pinpointed the physical location of the unconscious mind and, along the way, unraveled the nature of dreams.

As continuing research clarifies the nature of psychological processes, it's difficult to believe that new psychotherapeutic methods won't be devised to take advantage of them. In the process, the art of psychotherapy may finally take its place among the respected—which is to say documentable—medical sciences.

As with so many aspects of the brain science revolution, however, the psychotherapy of the future may not occur often in its pure form. Chances are that the talk therapies will, instead, merge with the chemical ones into combination therapies that will be more effective than either chemicals or talk alone. In fact, this has already begun to happen. Therapists are increasingly using drugs in combination with talk sessions, and reports from California indicate that such a strategy may even be helpful in that most intractable form of madness, schizophrenia.

Though psychotherapy has long been known to be ineffective

[*] *Brain and Psyche: The Biology of the Unconscious* (Garden City, N.Y.: Anchor Press/Doubleday, 1985).

in treating schizophrenia, a recent experiment has shown it to be remarkably successful as an adjunct therapy.

The talk therapy was provided both to the schizophrenic and his family and was aimed at helping them understand and cope with the problems of living with schizophrenia. As a result, the family was less disrupted, and the patient, now living in a more supportive environment, tended to take his drugs more regularly and to suffer fewer schizophrenic episodes.

As more diagnostic tests are devised, and patients are sorted into more orderly categories, and the best therapies for each category are determined, such combination programs will probably become increasingly important. Technology may one day even invade the sanctity of the Freudian psychiatrist's office.

One is tempted to imagine, for instance, the neurotic of the future lying on a couch with a helmet on his head, talking about his relationship with his mother. The goateed psychiatrist, cloaked in traditional knowledgeable silence, watches his patient's personality as it flickers across a monitor screen.

In the meantime, as scientists proceed to examine the molecular reactions that correspond to thought and feeling, their work has inevitably begun to encroach on what we call the "normal."

Out of this has grown various schemes to improve the lot of man by improving his mind. One especially hot area involves the development of memory enhancers.

"That's not just pie in the sky," says Goodwin at NIMH. "We're doing work on that right now. We know we can enhance memory in normal individuals. There's an IV infusion [required], so right now there's the question of whether we can do it under practical conditions . . . but that's an engineering problem.

"So we know that there are drugs that do correct memory deficits of certain sorts, and that will enhance memory even in normal people.

"Another thing is creativity enhancers. Candace Pert is working on the phencycladine (PCP) receptors—PCP is a hallucinogen. She's found a place in the brain that binds quite specifically to PCP, and others have replicated it now, and she and a couple of other groups are madly racing to find the [natural analog for PCP]. What the hell is normally in the brain that binds to that place?

"Whatever it is, the question is . . . what does it do? One speculation is that it is a part of the brain's normal mechanism for the capacity to experience imagination, reverie, creative experiences . . . milder forms of hallucination.

"It's sort of a neuroscientist's way of conceptualizing the relationship between creativity and craziness . . . which of course has been noticed in many artists and highly creative people, who seem to be just on the edge of being crazy.

"So such a peptide might turn out, when administered in small amounts to certain people, to make it easier for them to imagine, or to fantasize, or to connect disparate thoughts together. In other words, we could conceivably make some people more creative."

Again, many scientists feel that these hoped-for or predicted advances point the way toward an increasingly drug-modulated society. Given time, researchers believe they can develop very specific drugs to reduce appetite, enhance learning . . . even, one top scientist speculates, reduce shyness.

But Pert, despite her central role in the neurochemical revolution, rejects the notion that drugs are destined to be the only outcome—or even the most important one. She sees the millennium differently. She says . . . but no, Candace Pert speaks best for herself:

"A drug for shyness?" she asks. "Yeah, I can see that. Drugs to alleviate shyness, drugs to make us get along better. Those are all theoretically possible—I can conceive of them, easily.

"I can conceive of a drug, or a battery of drugs, that make some cortical connections . . . *zzzt! zzzt!* . . . and you will fall passionately in love for life with the face that you're presented with during the next sixty seconds. I can see that.

"But that's a narrow way to look at it, because I can also see somebody who's shy getting transformed by self-awareness training and by making up for missed cuddling. We may just learn to understand ourselves well enough that we won't need drugs.

"There are true diseases that will actually be helped by drugs, but . . . scientists who consult for drug companies think [drugs are] the first thing that's going to come out of all this. I don't know about that.

"We talk about neurochemistry and we think about drugs, but that's because drugs are obviously something we can make. And sell. We like to have things we can sell. But I think that's a very narrow view. There's more to it than that, a whole lot more.

"Sure, our minds are chemicals. Everything is chemistry. But I think it's a big, big mistake to say that leads to drugs, and more drugs, and still more drugs. It leads in a lot of directions.

"And, you know, I don't think it's limited to what we call 'medicine,' either. I think what we're talking about is understanding ourselves. Understanding who we are. Why we feel the way we do. How we can be better people.

"What I would like to see this science do is bring us peace with ourselves and bring us a new vision of how to take care of ourselves—a new concept of mental hygiene, that we can practice on a daily basis, that will keep us from going crazy in the first place."

And with that, she points her finger at a central truth. Even if molecular psychology cured all the depression in the world, and made all the schizophrenics normal, and mellowed out the criminals, and sobered up the alcoholics, and straightened out all the drug addicts . . . there would still be a lot of craziness in the world.

17

THE

DEVIL

BELOW

I T was the dream of a cure for pathological madness, a desire to ease the pain of schizophrenics, depressives, and phobics, that led molecular psychologists to the threshold of revolution. It was the study of addiction that gave substance and meaning to the receptor. It was the investigation of depression that showed us how mental propensities could be passed from parent to child. It was the examination of multiple personality and panic reactions that demonstrated the capability of the PET scanner. It is in the service of medicine that new drugs are now being sought.

It's only right that the new science should be driven by pathology. Disease, after all, must be the immediate focus of medical science. It is the first task of the neurochemists to search out and develop the new penicillins of the mind, and they are clearly embarked toward that end.

But while we watch their progress, fascinated, the woman whose hands touched the first match to the revolution in 1973 tugs at our sleeves. We are in grave danger, Pert warns us, of missing the point.

It doesn't demean hard science to observe that it's a narrowly focused discipline, and that the search for reductionistic truth is by necessity sharply confined. Neurochemists are superspecialists, and it would be naïve for us to expect them to create not only the revolution but also the context in which it can flower.

Pert reminds us that disease, while intriguing, is at most one small facet of the human condition. New drugs for schizophrenia and depression will surely change many lives, and there will be economic benefits—spectacular economic benefits, if the numbers are to be believed—for all. But the new knowledge that flows from the scientific presses, while directed at the aberrations of the psyche, speaks between the lines to a broader truth about the normal mind, and the nature of the human dilemma.

This revolution will not be confined to the test tube or the mental institution. If it says something about madness it says even more about what is normal. It is a mirror, and if we will but use it as such it will show us a truth that will make us free.

The first question is: Who are we?

On this, the mirror is quick and precise: We are mechanisms. Whence, then, did we come?

The answer, this time, is more enigmatic: We came out of time.

To grasp the meaning of this answer, we must now turn away from the precise paradigms of neurochemistry and travel to Poolesville, Maryland. There, just north of the nation's capital, we find a large, sprawling facility that houses NIMH's Laboratory of Brain Evolution and Behavior.

Inside, in a cluttered office that smells faintly of monkey urine, we find one of the world's leading experts on man's travels through the eons: Paul MacLean.

MacLean, who is now more than seventy, is arguably the nation's best-known neuroanatomist. He has spent a lifetime teasing apart the brains of living lizards and monkeys in a quest to understand the evolutionary roots of the human brain and, by that means, to grasp the nature of human behavior.

More than a quarter of a century ago, long before the explosion in molecular psychology, MacLean was one of the scientists who was engaged in the effort to localize the sources, in the brain, of specific behaviors.

But as he looked at his findings, and at those published by his colleagues, he realized that he was seeing more than mere anatomy. He was seeing, in the architecture of the primate brain, the indelible footprints of several hundred million years of evolution.

Nature, when constructing the brain, had (as always) been thrifty; she had thrown nothing away. At each great leap of evolution, from reptile to mammal and again from mammal to primate, she had built on what had come before.

As a result, the human animal did not have a brain.

It had three!

And—at best—only one of the three was his own!

Once MacLean knew what to look for, the "triune brain" theory fell quickly into place. As it did, so did a broad new understanding of what a complex thing it is to be human.

The first brain to evolve was the reptilian one, a nub of tangled gray tissue that sat atop the spinal cord and persists, basically unchanged, in modern reptiles.

The reptilian brain, though primitive, already contained all the familiar neurotransmitter systems. It used GABA, norepinephrine, serotonin, endorphin, dopamine, and all the rest.

Using those chemicals to communicate, nature had endowed the reptile with all the structures necessary for life. There was, for instance, the clock that must be included in any computer. There were discrete clumps of cells dedicated to regulate breathing, temperature control, pain perception, and alertness. There

221

was even a perceptual processor, the corpus striatum—which has already been mentioned here in reference to its role in schizophrenic hallucinations.

From the perspective of 250 million years of hindsight, the lizard brain seems fairly primitive. Though there is obviously a method to its wiring scheme, the cells appear under a microscope to have been laid down in a random tangle. And it's clear from the limited behavioral repertoire of modern lizards that the chemical tides and the connecting axons are very specifically programmed in the genes.

This deprived the dinosaurs, as well as the modern gila monsters and kimodo dragons, of much element of choice. Such a creature is essentially a puppet on an evolutionary string, compelled to march to the orders of its ancestors. Lizards are, in a phrase, breath-takingly dumb.

The first major improvement on the lizard brain was the development of an extrusion of tissue that MacLean calls the "mammalian brain." The mammalian brain first appeared in the skulls of tiny, warm-blooded creatures that scampered beneath the thundering feet of the dinosaurs; with the passage of time and the disappearance of the thunder lizard, the mammalian brain grew large. And when it was finished, the new brain had wrapped around and all but enclosed the old one.

This is not to say, however, that the new brain took control. It didn't. It was tightly connected to the old one, and most of the data that flowed from one part of the mammalian brain to the other had to be relayed through the reptilian circuits underneath. Thus the reptile kept its scaly thumb on the mammal. The new brain was, to borrow the terminology sometimes used by computer experts, a "slave unit."

The new circuits incorporated in the mammalian brain used the same transmitters as did the reptilian brain, but the structure of the cells was notably neater. The wiring pattern of the reptilian brain had apparently just grown, like Topsy, but the mammalian brain seemed to be patterned on some, well . . . master scheme.

A human computer designer wouldn't hesitate to call it more advanced.

The evolution of the mammalian brain also introduced a new bioprogramming language called "emotion." Affection, for instance, was superimposed over the lizard's sexual drive; fear was superimposed over the programs that instructed the lizard to stay away from bigger creatures.

The result was that while the tiny, rodentlike mammals that scurried between the legs of the ponderous dinosaur shared the thunder lizard's basic programming, there was a difference. The dinosaur had to follow that programming. The mammal might want to follow its genetic programming, might in fact yearn to do so, but in the end didn't actually have to.

In short, the mammal was a slave, but not a puppet. This dramatically increased its ability to respond in unique ways to changes in the environment.

Eventually, almost yesterday as evolution is measured, still another "slave unit" evolved from the outer substance of the emotional brain.

Once again history repeated itself and the "primate brain" grew larger by far than the one it had evolved from. And once again there was a major design improvement. The primate brain consisted of a cap of specialized cells, highly organized into tiny, cylinder-shaped arrays that make modern computer experts think automatically of parallel processing systems.

Again, a new processing capability appeared. The underlying mammalian brain spoke emotion, a genetically programmed language with comparatively few nuances. But the primate brain was the first more or less fully programmable biocomputer. It could speak English, Spanish, German . . . even, with some effort, music and mathematics.

The upshot of all this was that a small dinosaur ran from the large one because . . . well, because it ran, because it had to run, because it had no choice. The mammal ran, too, but it ran not because it had to but because it was scared out of its wits. And so one day an advanced primate could read a science fiction book about dinosaurs and experience fear, even though the object of that fear hadn't walked the earth for 150 million years.

Or, looked at another way, a male lizard took a female lizard, did his thing, and that was the beginning and the end of it. A male mammal did the same and sometimes in the process something more subtle happened along the way and he fell in love. But it took millions more years of evolution, and a third brain of amazing and convoluted complexity, to allow the human male to turn on to black fishnet stockings and a pair of high-heeled shoes.

And so it is that each of us today, be we garbage collector, teacher, police officer, preacher, or president, must march to the tune of three different drummers. And so each of our thoughts, before we are allowed to think it, must meet the approval of a cold-blooded, scaly thing that nestles at the psychic crossroads in the center of our brains.

If the awesome power of the reptilian brain over our thoughts was ever in doubt, those doubts were dispelled a few years ago when two Johns Hopkins brain scientists made a discovery with chilling implications.

The scientists involved were Joseph Coyle, a psychiatrist, and Mark Molliver, a neuroanatomist. They had been studying the development of the embryonic brain. In the process, they found out how the higher cortex, which includes the "human" part of our brains, organizes itself.

The first part of the brain to develop, early in pregnancy, is the lizard brain.

Then, when the lizard brain is practically complete—when the biological clock has started its ticking and the breathing and pain centers are wired into place—a few gray cells undergo a dramatic change.

These cells sprout axons that grow upward, arching into the empty space that will one day contain the fully formed brain. The axons are thinner by far than the human hair, and the distances they grow, in the microscopic world, are equivalent to human miles. They arch upward, ever upward, following a preprogrammed course that ultimately sketches the outline of what will, one day, be a human cortex.

Then, the outline completed, the axons cease to grow. On their ends, boutons develop.

Meanwhile the cell bodies, still imbedded in the lizard brain and doing its bidding, begin to produce norepinephrine—a chemical so prehistoric that it can be found in the nervelike cells of the worm, the spider, and the crab.

The cells pump this transmitter up their hollow axons until the boutons, far above, are filled. Then, stimulated by electrical charges that propagate along the axons, the boutons begin spraying norepinephrine out into the cavity that is not yet a brain.

As the norepinephrine diffuses through the empty space, finally reaching the lizard brain below, a portentous thing happens. Embryonic cells, a few at first and then many more, respond by detaching themselves and rising—migrating like so many moths up the gradient of the neurotransmitter.

Slowly, like so many automatons, the immature cells align themselves in the empty space. And there, still under the command of the norepinephrine pumped up from below, they organize themselves into hierarchies and ranks. Then, each having taken its assigned place, they settle down to produce axons themselves and, with them, to weave the miraculous thing that will one day process the electrochemical messages that correspond to language and mathematics.

And so it is that the very architecture of the human cerebral cortex, our finest and most human organ, does not stem from logic or reason. These qualities, though they may be exercised by the higher brain, are not an end in themselves but only a means.

We can study. We can go to college. We can read books. We can peer through electron microscopes and stare at photographs of faraway galaxies, we can concoct theories and invent equations, engorging our minds with truth and convincing ourselves that we are masters of the universe.

But when we follow Pert's advice and direct our gaze inward, using what molecular psychology has taught us so that we might better understand ourselves, we see reflected in the new truths an old one, ancient even when mankind was still young.

We are children of time and darkness, and there is indeed a devil. He is a prehistoric master that dwells at the center of each of us, communicating his overriding commands in the whiplash imperatives of pleasure or pain.

Denied even the solace of awareness, we obey. Like moths to a flame, we play, and mate, and procreate, and obey, and obey, and obey, and obey, abjectly and hopelessly obey, even when we see clearly that the result of our obedience is racism, or nationalism . . . even when we see children starving, and highway fatalities mounting, and ghettos boiling, and factories churning out world-killing missiles called "Peacekeeper." Even when we see our own love turning slowly to lonely hatred, we obey, we obey, we obey.

This, then, is what we call normal. Another word, of course, might be slavery.

It is a terrible realization, and it's only human that we would turn our heads away, look at something else, think other thoughts, go about our daily business as we always have.

But the message from Pert, on the frontier of the human psyche, is that we must not. It is only by accepting the nature of our slavery that we can begin the long trek toward freedom.

18

OF

ANCIENT

YEARNINGS

MOLECULAR psychology is a brutal thing to contemplate, full of concepts and principles that we would just as soon not know. Contemplating the mechanism of our own minds and gazing morosely on the chemical action and reaction that equate with consciousness and personality, we seem directed toward the dark conclusion that free will is but a concept designed, like Santa Claus or God, to shield us from the unacceptable truth.

The truth, we are terrified of learning, is that we are chaff in the wind—robots that jump on the command of dead puppeteers, chemical wind-up toys full of self-importance that play out their programs and then run down before they have the opportunity to figure out the terrible trick that's been played on them.

Out of this perception there grows the cliché, popular in pseudoscientific and philosophical circles, that the mind that tries to examine itself too closely comes upon a paradox. The instrument of knowing cannot know itself; the mirror of science may be bright with objectivity, but the image wavers and blurs as it is processed through the subjective mind of the beholder.

In short, we can't be allowed to know how we work. It's too grim, too mechanistic, too hopeless. If we knew the truth, we'd simply stop working.

It's certainly true that the common reaction to the devil nestled at the crossroads of our minds is denial. The Thing, the Devil, the Dark Force, the Id—whatever you choose to call it—exudes ugliness. And it's almost as though it doesn't *want* to be seen.

The deep mind responds to being caught in the spotlight by extending a horny claw and pushing a button. Neurotransmitters flow, receptors reconform, electrical charges flash down axons and, presto . . . we are convinced we didn't really see it. We may turn away at that point and leave sleeping devils lie. We order a drink, think about sex, or turn the television on.

These arguments about the paradox would be stronger, though, if the turning-away reaction were more universal. Some people, among them you and I, do not turn away—or, turning away, we remember what we saw and return later for another peek. We are, if nothing else, curious about ourselves.

And curious creatures we are, in every sense of the word. Not only are we the sole animal in all of nature capable of believing in Santa Claus, we are also the only one that can come to grips with the unpleasant truth that he doesn't exist. We are believers in what we want to believe but we are also doubters, capable of looking straight into mirrors. With our big cortexes we can sometimes see even what we are not supposed to see.

And when we practice this human discipline with the devil in our lizard brain, and watch it frantically try to pull the curtain and turn out the light, it occurs to us that there is more than one possible explanation for its actions.

The obvious one, of course, is that we're not supposed to see what's going on in our own minds. In this view, the devil is our friend, so to speak, and is trying to prevent us from seeing the nature of our enslavement, lest the knowledge do us some damage.

But isn't it strange, how frantically the devil is trying to turn out the light—how uncomfortable all this talk makes us? Don't we feel a certain echo of fear, reverberating deep in our brain? Is the devil really a friend, trying to protect us from ourselves? Or might the devil, like certain evil-looking insects who thrive only in the dark, simply be terrified of the light?

Might it be, in other words, that our enslavement to the ancient programs is not quite perfect? Might it be shattered if we saw what those programs were?

This is quite a different notion from the one about the paradox. Implicit in it is a broad hint that, despite the mechanistic nature of our existence, there does exist such a thing as free will.

If we're not capable of seeing our own natures, why does the prospect make us so uncomfortable? If I can't understand what the devil is doing there, and take action to change him, then why is he so skittish about the light? What is he afraid of, if not me?

Might it not be that our conviction that we can't understand ourselves is the last bastion against precisely that understanding?

Might it be that if we knew the mechanism of our obedience, we would gain the ability to disobey?

Is it not after all consistent with the experience of our species that self-knowledge is the essence of power?

As we extend that wisdom into the new science of molecular psychology, we begin to see that the key to freedom is the ability to override commands from below. And the way to override commands is to anticipate them, and arm ourselves against their seductive ways—to understand, in short, what they are and whence they come.

This hope, the hope of a new sanity, phrased in many different ways and sometimes only presumed, brings us to the last battlefront in our revolution. This time, the science is anthropology.

Throughout most of its history, anthropology has seemed at best a fringe discipline, characterized by professors, putterers, and gentlemen graverobbers. It was hardly recognized as a science at all.

But in recent decades, as biologists and biology watchers have sought to flesh out the new understanding of the mind, their questions and speculations increasingly have carried their thoughts, as all biological endeavors ultimately must, to the process of evolution. And as the focal science of human evolution, physical anthropology has by necessity matured and moved to center stage.

The thrust of the new movement in physical anthropology is to seek the roots of human behavior in shards and bones of the evolutionary past. This search, roughly contemporaneous with the development of molecular psychology, has set anthropology on a course that seems destined to meld it finally with the science of psychology.

The first phase of the anthropological revolution was aimed at establishing man's behavioral similarity to other creatures. In the 1960s and 1970s, scientists who studied and compared the psychologies of animals and humans mounted strong arguments that there were many more similarities than had previously been believed.

The parallels between human and animal psychologies, once they are pointed out, are undeniable. Take imprinting, for instance—the phenomenon by which baby ducks identify the first creature they see as mama. Humans, too, can imprint. Consider, for instance, the world of a male human toddler, crawling around on the rug and clutching Mommy's leg . . . and then consider how many such toddlers, all grown up, have powerful sexual fetishes for nylon stockings and high heels.

Human brains, like those of many other animals, contain instructions for pair bonding. We are as territorial as robins, as larcenous as pack rats, and as peer conscious as wolves. We are, in the sum of our programmed actions and propensities, part and parcel of the animal world from which we not so long ago evolved.

This truth has been borne out in recent years by molecular psychologists. In studying the brains of rats and humans, they were surprised to find out what a good model the rat brain was. A human chauvinist will find frighteningly few chemical differences between the mind-brains of a Rhodes scholar and a ghetto rodent.

Establishing the similarities, of course, is preliminary stuff. The real enigma, and the one we all care about, has to do with the differences. Though they may be small, in the chemical sense, and recent in the evolutionary one, they are what makes us what we are. They represent, to touch a cliché grown meaningful in the past decade, our roots.

As we survey the differences between human and rat, certain ones are obvious. There is, for instance, the huge size of our forebrains—and we must mention the opposable thumb. But as we look at man from the point of view of modern social psychology, we find ourselves focusing more and more on our inner conflicts.

We speak of the human dilemma, but never of the dilemma of the rat or the horse. Perhaps this is just because we're not in their skulls, but all the same . . . animals seem to have something we don't.

They, too, of course, have lizards nestled deep in their minds. But unlike us they at least seem to be content in their bondage, and to gain something from it. There is a beautiful consistency that runs through most species and is rarely disrupted. Lovebirds are monogamous, period, and rabbits are not. Rhesus monkeys without exception run in bands, and gorillas do not, preferring family groups instead. Orangutans, however, are loners. Always. Always. Always.

As humans, we can be forgiven for suspecting that with that consistency there comes a certainty, a satisfaction, a kind of peace, if you like. It is almost as though animals know instinctively what they are. And we, clearly, don't.

We have a code of morality, of course—a morality so pervasive, so common to so many isolated societies, that many believe it must have a genetic base. It says, among other things: Thou shalt not kill.

Yet man, of course, is the most murderous species ever to walk the planet.

The code says, and we queue up to proclaim our belief, that we should share with our less capable brothers and sisters.

Yet communist societies based on that ideal are among the most repressive and at the same time least efficient on earth. The freest and most efficient systems, which presumably means those that work best, are based on capitalism—which is to say greed.

The code says, and by consensus we have engraved into our laws, that all humans are by nature entitled to equal rights.

And yet it is our nature for whites to hate blacks, and blacks to hate whites, and Protestants to hate Catholics, and Protestants and Catholics together to hate Jews, and to have that hatred returned, except when they band together in the face of the Moslem hordes. . . .

But in no area of our lives does this excruciating duality between what we think we want and how we behave express itself so painfully, and cause so much personal anguish, as in our sexual behavior.

We seem as a species to want to be monogamous, and to pair-bond for life. When we fall in love, the word *forever* leaps naturally to our lips. We consummate that desire with the ceremony of marriage, and with much ceremony we swear on stacks of Bibles to be true.

And then, of course, we cheat.

Such are the conflicts that distinguish us from other warm-blooded creatures. It is almost as though we were half this and half that, as though the commands of the lizard somehow get bollixed up and confused as they rise up through the higher brains, as though we, alone among all the animals, are trying to march to a cacophony of different drummers.

This is on the one hand the painful nub of our dilemma and, on the other, a clue that could lead us out of the maze.

Anthropologists, following this lead, have discovered that something unusual must have happened to the human line as it budded off from its parent species. There was a terrible event . . . call it a species birth trauma, if you like . . . that disrupted our programming, loosened the lizard's grip slightly, and opened our eyes and minds to the possibilities of complex behaviors.

Their quest to find and identify this trauma was long, convoluted, and vociferously argumentative. It took decades and required the aid of physicists, geologists, and many other specialists.

But slowly, as neurochemists in their laboratories were unlocking the secrets of the transmitter and the receptor, anthropologists managed to reconstruct, in at least its general outline, the tale of man's agonizing and blood-spattered parturition.

Different anthropologists tell the story with slightly different twists, depending on the aspect of human nature they seek to illuminate—violence, say, or man's political nature. The version I prefer probes the origins of an aspect of human behavior that, on balance, probably causes us more pain than organized, armed conflict ever did.

I refer, of course, to the war of the sexes.

The narrator in this case is Helen Fisher, a leading anthropologist, author of *The Sex Contract* (William Morrow, 1982), and one of my favorite interview subjects. But, whoever tells it, the story carries us back some four million years, to the great mother jungle of East Africa and to a species of monkeylike creatures that made its home there.

To those creatures, the jungle was home. Traveling in bands, they leaped from branch to branch, yapping and chattering, grooming one another and eating fruits and insects whenever they were hungry.

Their sexual relationships closely resembled those of monkeys today. They were promiscuous, but they mated only when the females were in "heat" and sexually receptive. They followed their emotions, acted on their instincts . . . and were rarely wrong.

But at the basis of their existence was one fundamental, unexamined faith: the mother jungle was forever. In the end, that was what betrayed them.

The mechanism of the betrayal was simple and has been well documented; it begins with the random drift of continents.

As Africa inched northward into Europe, and the Indian sub-continent collided with Asia, long-established sea currents were pinched off. The sea found new directions of flow, and, as a result, wind and weather patterns were forever altered.

In East Africa, the gentle rains tapered off. In just a few centuries, the trees died; veld grasses grew in their place. Cast from Eden, the animals that would give rise to man scrambled through the parched grass in desperate search of unfamiliar food.

They were tragically out of sync with their new environment. If they dreamed, they dreamed of falling—and of terrible tree-snakes; but in their waking hours the dangers that faced them were dogs and big-toothed cats.

The former occupants of the jungle were accustomed to crossing clearings, when they couldn't avoid it, by running on all fours. But as their world metamorphosed into one big horizon-to-horizon meadow, this proved a mortal weakness. For one thing, it didn't allow them to see above the grasstops. For another, in a bloody, hungry world, the monkey shuffle was just too slow. Stalked by lions, poisoned by unfamiliar snakes and insects, they died in unprecedented numbers.

The high death rate intensified the Darwinian pressures of change, and the animals evolved rapidly from generation to generation, reshaping themselves to strengthen their hold on their shaky new environmental niche.

As the primates struggled to survive under conditions for which they were neither physically nor behaviorially adapted, their worst anatomical drawback was the monkey shuffle. As always, nature provided a solution of blood and gore. For a while the lions benefited, but then, like insects becoming immune to pesticides, the creatures changed.

Within a mere few thousand years, their progeny ran upright through the grass; they could see farther that way and move more quickly.

Bipedalism, since it left the hands free to make and use tools, was one of nature's most portentous experiments. But it required a physical alteration. To allow efficient walking and running, and to ensure stability in the upright torso, the geometry of the hips had to be altered.

There was a trade-off, of course. As the pelvis changed, the birth canal shrank. As it did, the birth process, once characteristically easy and pain free, became increasingly traumatic. The cats ate fewer mothers, now, but increasingly those mothers died in childbirth.

Slowly, the population shifted toward women who gave birth to ever more premature infants with smaller, still-developing heads. Now the mothers lived . . . but their infants died.

The redesign of the pelvis was a mechanical necessity. Bipedalism required it. But if a solution to the premature birth problem was not found, the frightened, maladapted refugees from the forest faced imminent extinction.

Fortunately, the mechanisms of behavior were not nearly so unyielding as the laws of structural mechanics. Behavior can be modified by a few new connections in the mind, or by the increased production of this or that neurotransmitter. The mind is plastic and Mother Nature, as she reshaped the creatures' bodies, also rearranged their feelings.

Today, four million years after the fact, scientists caution against ascribing human attributes to the process of evolution. Nature works blindly, they say, without compassion or intent. Yet she shaped us humans to be sentimental creatures, and we can't help but feel there was something fine and wonderful in the solution that she found.

As the millenniums passed, the miserable, ragtag survivors of the vanished forest, for all their travails, were to receive in compensation the neurochemical blessing that their descendants would call by the name of love.

In the days of the great mother jungle, the prehuman creatures, like most of their monkey cousins, pursued reproductive behaviors that could best be described as promiscuous. They didn't have any choice in the matter, of course. Like all lesser creatures, their sexual behaviors were programmed into their genes and, through their genes, into their lizard brains and ultimately translated into emotional yearnings.

Each inherited program, when evoked by specific circumstances, induced the production of a specific chemical cocktail composed of natural, mind-focusing drugs. Guided by the compelling natural "highs" and "lows," the animals were conditioned to behave however nature wanted them to.

During the fifty million years or so that the creatures lived in the great forest, their promiscuity was constrained by a purely physical reality: the period of heat in the female. She was sexually interested, and desirable, only when she was fertile.

Even so, a certain courting behavior had developed. The male, seeking to incur the attention of a desirable female in heat, offered her something edible.

Such behavior is still seen today in certain monkey species. But for those animals, as for the ancient prehuman occupants of the forest, the offering is of little consequence. The female is perfectly capable of taking care of herself, thank you.

But it does get her attention.

Once the forest had died, however, and the prehumans were cast out onto the alien veld, no scrap of food was insignificant. And so this mindless offering took on a deeper and more important meaning.

The mathematics of genetics were inexorable. The females who had the longest periods of heat attracted more male attention and received more offerings of food. As a result, they and their immature offspring tended to survive.

With the passage of generations, the female period of heat became longer and longer. By the time they had learned to walk upright, they had become, as women are today, desirable at all times.

But as poets have always known, sex was only the beginning of the story.

If a woman could keep a mate, as well as just attract him, he could protect her and bring her food during the long nursing period required by her premature infant. The male would benefit as well. His child, if he protected it and its mother, was more likely to survive in a dangerous world. The human family had begun—and, with it, so had civilization.

If the male stayed around, protecting the female and her child, he could teach that child things—important things, such as how to make a rock sharp by chipping it, where the rabbits were, and how to find water. Suddenly it paid dividends, high dividends in the currency of DNA, for man and woman not just to copulate, but to cling together.

Such was the genesis of infatuation, the forerunner of love.

The mechanism of change was an alteration in the inherited programs of the brain. At bottom it was genetic, but it expressed itself in a change in brain chemistry.

In the ancient days of the mother jungle, the male monkey who offered a scrap of food to a desirable female was rewarded for his behavior by more than just her attention. That attention, which he was programmed to seek, caused his brain to increase its synthesis of dopamine and epinephrine—powerful stimulants with effects similar to "speed" and cocaine. The female, when she took and ate the offering, was treated to a similarly thrilling "high."

As these behaviors became increasingly adaptive, the thrills grew ever more, well . . . seductive. The more smitten the male and female were with one another, the more apt their children were to survive.

With each successive generation, the highs of love grew more and more powerful. In the brain, the adaptive new infatuation programs spread out and masked the old patterns of promiscuity.

One's true love became, somehow . . . more beautiful than all others.

The chemicals of love were powerful amphetaminelike stimulants, and they had important side effects. They disturbed the sleep cycle, for instance, and so lovers found themselves staying up all night making eyes at one another.

They also lost weight. Some of the chemicals in the love cocktail are almost indistinguishable from the ingredients in diet pills.

As time passed and the brain continued to change, the effects of love spread far beyond the merely sexual centers of the brain. The chemicals left no perceptual circuit untouched . . . or unchanged.

Love recast the world in a rosy light, turning winter into spring, spring into fantasy land. Wherever the mind was directed, it somehow always wandered back in the end to bright thoughts of the future with its multiplicity of wonderful possibilities.

It was the human version of nest-building behavior, and it changed everything.

Compelled by the sweet chemistry of infatuation, the prehuman creatures of the veld bonded to one another in a contract of sex, caring, and protection. They chose nesting sites and raised their offspring. Each generation loved deeper than the last. As a result, they were fruitful, and they multiplied.

They did not, however, live happily ever after.

For one thing, the veld was a place of many appetites, and the romantic vow of "until death do us part" often wasn't all that long.

What happened when a male and female bonded, and the female bore a helpless infant . . . and then her male went on a hunt and never returned? The harsh laws of evolution permit only one answer: death. She would die—that, or be forced to abandon her child in favor of her own survival.

The frequency of widowhood presented a major stumbling block for love as an evolutionary strategy. It would be satisfactorily solved, but the solution would reveal nature's careless amorality and set the stage for sexual warfare that would extend into modern times.

The solution was infidelity.

As Fisher explains it, a widowed female was much better off if she'd never been completely monogamous in the first place.

If she'd "cheated" occasionally on her mate, she'd have a lover or two waiting in the wings to take his place if he died.

Cheating had its benefits for the male as well. Bonding made him feel good and heightened his genetic potential. But at the same time saber-toothed tigers liked female monkeys, too, and there was no guarantee his mate would survive. So it was genetically profitable to have his cake and eat it, too, if possible.

From this was born the sexual double standard.

The female was more secure if she kept lovers but was threatened if her man spent too much time with other women. He might, after all, find someone he liked better.

Her mate lusted in his own heart but was threatened if his woman copulated with other males. It was not genetically profitable for him to raise a child shaped by another man's genes.

To keep these mutually exclusive double standards from tearing the bond apart, evolution created two of human nature's most terrible inner forces. One was guilt, and the other was jealousy.

Guilt was a gut-wrenching misery chemical, a "negative reinforcer" that welled up in the brain with each infidelity—or even with the contemplation of it.

Jealousy was an anger chemical. Produced in the brain of the betrayed mate, it led to strong words, cuffs on the ears, and threats to leave. It heightened the misery and insecurity of the guilty party, increasing the production of the guilt chemicals, and thus further reduced infidelity.

That's not to say they didn't think about it, though.

And sometimes, on a quiet and lazy night around the water hole, the ancient promiscuity programs stirred. Across the fire, private signals were exchanged.

The human face is powerfully expressive, capable of transmitting both desire and promise with the twitch of a muscle. Then as now a wink, followed by downcast eyes signifying the guilt that bespoke motive, communicated volumes.

Later, as the band settled down to sleep, a female stood, yawned, and wandered away from her mate and off toward the water hole. A few minutes later a male rose and nonchalantly ambled off in another direction. Once out of sight he changed course and headed in the direction the female had taken.

While the others slept, nature was obeyed. A secret sexual alliance was struck, and, out of the genetics of death and insecurity, the sexual lie was born.

Aside from that, though, the bonding programs worked quite well. As long as the chemicals of infatuation coursed through the brain, the carefully balanced scales of love and promiscuity usually tipped in favor of love.

But how long did the bond last? Certainly not, as lovers are wont to promise, forever and ever.

For one thing, the chemicals of love were stimulants. The monkey brain was still basically a monkey brain, and there was a limit to how much revving up it could endure without beginning to malfunction. Abuse of "speed," the illegal modern equivalent of one of the chemicals in the love potion, will eventually lead to schizophrenic symptoms . . . and a hallucinating monkey would have a very short future.

So nature was stingy with her highs. The prehuman brain probably quit manufacturing the love cocktail as soon as the child had reached an age when its survival was no longer absolutely dependent on having two parents.

In her search for clues, Fisher has studied primitive tribes that exist today. Women in those tribes, she says, nurse their infants for about two years. During that time, they often can't become pregnant again—they are protected by a natural form of birth control stimulated by breast feeding.

The modern two-year-old is still a baby, of course. But on the veld four million years ago, the child of twenty-four months was probably able to fend for himself or herself.

As the child learned to crawl and then to walk, nature could afford to cut back the dopamine dosage in its parents' brains. In two years or so, as the child learned to fend for itself, the infatuation high could end and the bond could safely be broken.

Suddenly the honeymoon was over. Promiscuity between the

mates increased, and new bonds were often formed with other partners. Thus, from the very first, love was a game of musical chairs.

Today, four million years later, scientists like Fisher sift through the lava-covered bones in Rift Valley of Kenya, contemplate those bygone times, and come to the sober realization that they're not all that gone. Today those old behavior programs, formed of the trauma on the veld, are with us still. In the case of the love chemicals, they are the essence of the modern human sexual dilemma.

Today, as in those ancient times, we fall in love and bond. When we do, we are overwhelmed by the infatuation high; it literally changes our minds about who we are and what we are about. Dazzled by the rosy world, swept away by love, we go, two by two, to the altar, and then. . . .

In two years, or three, the earth suddenly shifts.

All of a sudden Mr. Wonderful isn't so wonderful after all, particularly when it comes to picking up his own socks. And does he pay less attention, now? Is he more easily distracted by his job, politics, football? Is he suddenly irritated by habits that, just last month, were endearing?

The honeymoon is over.

The tides of infatuation ebb, and as they do the old promiscuity programs break the surface. One by one, they activate. Ancient chemicals of raw lust seep into the brain. Demons take shape. Stunned, we may be easy prey as they well up from below.

And so, out of the fossil beds of Kenya and the interpretive intellects of anthropologists like Helen Fisher, there crystallizes a picture of the human mind that is altogether consistent with the theory of molecular psychology.

To that theory the anthropologists add the stipulation that the wiring diagram for the chemical engine in our skulls is not and never was a logical one. It was laid down to seduce us into programmed behavior by means of chemical tides that reward us and punish us in accordance with ancient principles that may no longer make sense.

The human dilemma is not that the natural drugs tell us what to think, at least not directly. We can think of things, such as the fact that E equals mc squared, that our ancestors could never have dreamed of. Conscious thought is a mystery of an altogether different sort and is largely influenced by here-and-now social, environmental, and cultural forces.

But the chemicals dictate the shape of our personal agendas, putting us in a frame of mind to work, to love, to bond, to have children . . . and to fight or flee. They may not tell us what to think directly, but they tell us what to think about, and that severely limits our freedom.

Anyone who has ever attempted to study mathematics while in the throes of new love, for instance, has felt the power of the chemical blinders. We try to focus on the open textbook but our minds wander, again and again, to the window . . . and to the lovely, fuzzy daydreams of Miss Wonderful or Mr. Right. Love-sodden brains have little taste for binomial equations.

The work of the neurochemists, of the psychochemists, of the mind-imaging experts, of the psychogeneticists, and finally of the anthropologists tells us, in the end, not only how we love but also why we love.

It tells us whence comes the ancient mystique of the white rose, offered by man for a woman's favor, as a sliver of meat or an edible bug was once offered. It lays bare the mechanism behind the ecstasy of the candlelight dinner, the electricity of the lover's downcast smile, the thrill of the gentle touch of one hand upon another. It tells us why the whispered words, "I love you," compose the most powerful and enduring cliché to be found in all of the many human languages.

And, turning the coin over to the tarnished side, it reveals why, having vowed sexual fidelity to our mates, we're tortured by lewd fantasies of strangers—and why we become miserably jealous when we suspect that similar visions may float as well through the minds of our partners.

It tells us why the sexual lie springs so easily from human

lips, why the eternal triangle is so eternal . . . and why, in a culture that idealizes monogamy, half of our marriages end in divorce.

The saga of the primates in the veld is not a "just so" story, the questions are not idle, and the answers are not romantic daydreams. The issues are serious ones, and, in a society morally, socially, and legally committed to monogamy, they have far-ranging consequences.

A good many of the world's problems, in fact, are caused by the fact that our love lives are houses of cards. Most murders are crimes of passion traceable to insecure sexual bonds. Drunkenness, while a serious problem in its own right, often sprouts from unhappiness in love. And it was love, don't forget, that formed the framework for the schizophrenic fantasy in which John Hinckley shot Ronald Reagan.

In one sense, the cost of love lost is very personal. Divorce leaves at least two victims. As the ex-wife and ex-husband stagger away from the destruction of their romantic dreams, they're dogged by guilt and a nagging sense of failure. Their self-esteem drops, and so does their productivity.

Desperately trying to reassure themselves, they may leap into an inappropriate subsequent marriage.

The agony of broken romance follows the children, too. Teenagers, lonely and insecure, are fodder for drug dealers and police juvenile squads. As their schoolwork suffers, so does the gross national product two decades hence.

So the story of the evolution of love, being worked out by Helen Fisher and others, has a very practical value in today's civilization. If we can understand the forces that break up families, perhaps we can manipulate them socially in favor of greater stability. Or if they can't be manipulated, perhaps we can construct a society in which the inevitable broken hearts and smashed marriages won't extract from us such an awful toll.

The case of love, because it is so fundamental and because the questions it raises are so urgent, is on the cutting edge of the new anthropology. But equally portentous questions, involving other facets of the human dilemma, are being investigated as well.

Are we afraid of spiders, snakes, and big cats? We remember, with a shock, that those posed the chief avoidable threats to our arboreal ancestors.

Why are our teenage years so traumatic? Modern societies ask young people to wait until their twenties to become full-fledged members of their cultures, but is this reasonable? Does this demand that they suppress the unsuppressible, and in so trying do they permanently damage their minds?

Do we automatically suspect the motives of someone with a different color of skin or facial features that seem odd? The reaction goes back to a gene-conserving need to share with those like us, nurturing and protecting them—protecting them, most notably, from people of different stock. Racism, apparently, is built into the human psyche.

Perhaps most tragically, a similar story seems to be developing in regard to warfare. The best-known of these studies were conducted by Jane Goodall, who has spent much of her adult life following groups of chimpanzees as they range through their natural habitats in Africa.

She has recently documented that the animals, which are genetically closer to man than any other species, have inborn programs that prompt them to conduct deadly excursions into neighboring territories. The excursions are so similar to human warfare that contemplating them, in the nuclear age, makes the blood run cold. Are we programmed for war?

Apparently we are. That particular form of madness, far more costly than schizophrenia and depression combined, is "natural."

How the new psychochemical and anthropological knowledge can help us deal rationally with the forces at play in our psyches is suggested by the impact of Fisher's book on the evolution of love. The inner conflicts she described, and the synthesis she proposed to explain them, struck such a chord in the minds of readers that she quickly became a star of the television and lecture circuit.

244

"This kind of knowledge is very psychologically useful," she said in one interview. "Knowledge . . . knowledge often helps. Just explaining why we feel the way we do seems to allow a lot of people to make peace with themselves after broken marriages and love affairs turned bad."

Though her doctorate is in anthropology, many of the grateful letters in her file read like testimonials to a psychotherapist. Thanks to her, her fans say, they finally understand and accept the naturalness of their conflicting romantic feelings.

"And when I give lectures . . . well, for example, I did a radio show recently and a woman came up to me afterwards and said, 'Dr. Fisher, I think I finally understand why I left my husband.'

"I have to admit," she says, "It makes me feel good to know I'm helping someone. That's my mission in life, really . . . my first priority. I want to get this information out, so that people can use it to understand what's happening to them. A lot of things we don't understand, of course. But some are beginning to make sense. The divorce rate, for instance."

The hard lesson she presents to us is that the ancient programs in our brains, and the influence they exert today along the broad front of human romantic relationships, generally conspire to make marriage a chancy business. Many people, perhaps through no fault of their own, will inevitably fail to navigate the rapids and shoals of monogamy.

The fact that past generations tended to have less divorce than today, she says, is probably more due to the growing economic independence of women than changing values.

"I think a lot of women stay in marriages because they're so economically dependent that they can't get out. As you look at the divorce rate around the world, it seems to be extremely high in those societies where females have a great deal of economic power. . . . If they've got a choice, in other words, they're more likely to get divorced.

"And you know there's a lot of stuff about America's endangered children, how you really should stay with the marriage, and this and that . . . well, there's another school of thought that says it's better for everybody if you get out of a bad marriage rather than stay in it. My guess is that many women who stay in it do so because they can't get out.

"Look, I'm just not satisfied with the answers that we have been given for marriage, for divorce, for promiscuity . . . for sexual allegiance. I think there are profound, basic, chemical reasons— biological reasons, evolutionary reasons—that we need to look at. It's just not as simple as people like to think.

"For instance, you see women in America who have one child by a man, break that bond, have a second child with another man, and then break that bond. There may be some genetic logic in that—not today but in the past. It would have produced variability in the population in a time when there was severe selection, as there must have been on the veld.

"If you had children with very different gifts, with three different men, you might stand a better chance of having one of those three children live than if you had all three by the same man."

How an individual should act, Fisher believes, depends on a combination of social circumstance, individual goals, and the strength of his or her inner demons. Some demons, in some people, may be simply overpowering.

"People are wondrously variable. I'm sure you know some men who have never bonded . . . they're the original playboys. And then you see some people who marry at eighteen and maintain that bond for life.

"So lifelong marriage may not be for everybody. Some people seem to have a mental configuration that leads them to both bond and to be promiscuous. One-half of the married men in America are promiscuous, for instance. One-quarter of the married women are promiscuous."

That's not to say that a monogamous relationship can't be maintained, she adds.

"I do not want to encourage someone saying, 'Well, it's programmed in and I can't help it.' We can help it. While these [ancient] behaviors may be powerful, many people in fact resist them quite successfully.

"What I'm talking about are tendencies—propensities. We have a propensity to share, a propensity to communicate with language . . . and we have a propensity to bond.

"Take marriage. Lifelong monogamy may not be 'natural' in the ancient sense, but it's culturally natural today. And culture is a very powerful force. Today we have a society in which 50 percent of the population remains in a marriage for life. Lifelong monogamy is a useful and significant reproductive strategy.

"I'm often asked, when I lecture, about the future of marriage. Where are we going in the future? Where is bonding going as society changes? As women enter the job market, and we get child care centers, will we be going toward a society of total promiscuity —in which there's no bonding?

"People ask about that, but I don't think so. I think the legacy of the veld is too old, and too great. Look around us. People marry who don't really need the bond—who don't have any children and don't intend to. But they bond anyway. People bond in their sixties and seventies."

But there is also a propensity to break that bond, and, in some individuals, that propensity may be stronger than in others.

"Of all the American customs and ideals, I feel that our sexual ideals are among those that are least congruent with our behavior," Fisher continues. "In other words, I think that our natural behavioral patterns do not fit too well with our cultural expectations in this society.

"One of the results is that there are men and women walking the streets today saying to themselves, 'I'm a failure! I've had two marriages, and neither of them has worked.'

"Well, that's probably a natural human behavior pattern, and they feel a little better when they hear what I have to say. I don't think people need to feel failure following a divorce. I think they can choose to work out their feelings of failure, so that they don't have to be unhappy."

247

The important thing, she says, is that people should have the options—and understanding our basic urges may help us see where those options lie.

"I see the human being as being very much like the Stradivarius violin. It has a particular shape, it has a particular size, and therefore particular propensities. But then you pick up the bow of culture and you can play a huge variety of different tunes."

Though Fisher does not endear herself to conservatives by viewing marriage as less than sacred, much of the perspective implicit in her thinking is solidly traditional. On the matter of love at first sight, for instance, the anthropological advice might come as well from a Baptist minister: Stay cool.

The Fisher rationale has nothing to do with morality, of course. In her theory, the infatuation high is induced by powerful drugs, and while under the influence of them no man or woman is fully sane. The first flush of love compels its victim to do something, but it's the wrong moment to join the Army, drop out of college, buy a car, or apply for a marriage license. If the lovelorn male must take some kind of action, it is recommended that he visit a florist.

Beyond the first surges of craziness, the couple wishing to form a lifelong bond should understand, going in, that marriage is a relatively new adaptation and, as a result, that it is exceedingly fragile.

It may not be very romantic, for instance, but newlyweds might find it prudent to reflect at length on the finite nature of the infatuation high. The couple that does so may be in a better position to cope on that inevitable day of withdrawal.

It will be a comfort, when that day comes, to understand the chemistry of why the most beautiful woman in the world suddenly seems to be a bit heavy around the hips and sharp about the tongue, and why Mr. Wonderful suddenly seems like such a slob.

Conversely, the couple that refuses to comprehend that the honeymoon must end will be in a much poorer position to cope when the good-feeling chemicals are withdrawn. In their ignorance, they may be more likely to blame one another for the miseries that follow.

Beyond the honeymoon's end, Fisher says, couples who persevere may discover ways of replacing the honeymoon high with a different, more mellow kind of love. Loving, helping, supporting and nurturing behaviors encourage the brain to produce sedating drugs like the endorphins, similar to heroin and morphine. Thus, the properly managed romantic high inevitably mellows into something equally romantic, and much more sustainable.

"In the end," says Fisher, "I've got the same advice as everyone else. Lifelong marriage is not a natural pattern, and if you want it to work you have to go about it intelligently. You have to work at it.

"But look around you. Isn't that what you see happening? People who have successful marriages . . . they do work at it."

And that may be the advice not only for love, but for war, adolescent craziness, race hatred, and all the other many sorts of "normal" insanity that produces so much human misery.

The truth that finally coalesces about love, and all the rest of it, is that we are the heirs of a race traumatized at birth, born of desperation and fear, reared in violence and bloodshed, steeped in the ways of deceit, evolving at a speed that left our minds full of free-floating bits of obsolete programs. We struggle desperately to live in a world for which we were not made and for which our feelings are not suited, and when we fail we often don't know why.

The human dilemma is finally beginning to make sense. As we reflect on the unhappy fix we're in, it's easy to see why our minds are so delicately balanced, how a warped gene or a multiplying virus or a deprived childhood will push us over the edge. Perhaps the mystery is not that so many of us are insane, but that so many of us aren't.

All this is vague, of course—the molecular psychologists, along with the anthropologists, the psychogeneticists, and all the rest, are just getting started. In the years to come, they will fill in the hazy outlines, and we will have a better feel for precisely what we should do.

But one thing is clear. If we want to stay married, or serve social justice, or lessen the pain of adolescence, or keep the nuclear missiles in their silos, then we'd better understand up front that it's not natural. We're going to have to work at it.

Hard.

And, with the scientist's help, intelligently.

19

THE

APPLE

IS

A

PERSIMMON

A N D S O, slowly, detail by detail, scientific paper by scientific paper, molecule by variant molecule, from exhumed skulls in the rift valley and tagged neurotransmitters at Stony Brook, from patterns that flicker across PET scan screens in St. Louis and new theories that sprout and grow in the minds of bearded psychiatrists in the climbing steel towers of New York City, we are coming to understand the nature of the human species.

We know, of course, that in our ignorance we have much out of place, that we are oversimplifying, and that generations will pass before finally the puzzle is finished. Still, the pieces fit, and, even making allowances for our inevitable mistakes, what emerges makes a certain sense.

As we peer at what we know and think we know, for instance, we can see that our twentieth-century mind is full of fossil footprints. And we can follow those footprints backward and find out where and how it was that the gods played their cruel trick on us.

It happened during all those millions of years that we shivered in the flickering light of the campfire, praying desperately for the sun god to reappear and banish the demons who populated the darkness beyond the mouth of the cave.

We cleaved, then, to a dualistic interpretation of our existence. Our bodies were corporeal but our minds, our soul—whatever human part of us it was that felt the terror—was phantasm.

We had, in our abject ignorance, no other option. We saw in the world around us no clues to the nature of the chemical engines inside our skulls. The strange bumps we heard in the night really seemed to be outside, not inside, and ignorant of the nature of dopamine, we naturally assumed that perception was truth. If we saw demons outside, then by jove that's where they were.

We had no inkling of the cascading reactions that proceeded along the PCP receptors as we painted pictures of mammoths on the cave walls. We had no conception of the endorphin molecule, or the way it mediated the comfort we received in youth by the mother who fed us and later, as adults, by the mere presence of the elder who reassured and protected us—and later, yet, when we were the elder, by the unseen but closely felt presence of God Our Father In Heaven.

We knew that the inanimate world, rocks and water and dead logs, were numb. Trees . . . well, trees were harder to figure. But in any event they weren't like us.

The thing about us was that we had a slippery kind of knowledge we called "feelings." We felt love, and anger, and yearning creativity, and trust. The feelings were powerful and undeniable, and, having no substance, they could be conceptualized only as spiritual forces, given us by the gods. And, of course, when the gods commanded us to do something, we, mere mortals, could but obey.

So it was all okay. We heard the music, and we marched to it, certain in the faith that we would somehow be rewarded—if not in the here and now, then in the afterlife.

This obedience, and the spirituality implicit in it, and the concept of soul implicit in that, and the concept of eternal justice implicit in that, like so many hollow eggs one inside the other, became the foundation of our traditions. Upon it we shaped a long succession of societies and associated ideologies.

In the jungle we paid obeisance to the alpha male of our group, accepting his desires as law; his cuffs and bites were, to us, the epitome of justice. Later on the veld the alpha male became the patriarch, and he ruled by the wisdom of his gray beard.

Finally, with the passage of many generations and the growth of the prefrontal cortex, the patriarchs were inspired by the notion that power, like property, could be passed on to eldest sons. Kings then ruled by divine right while more generations passed. When their brains became addled by inbreeding, their power was exercised by regents and advisers until it was finally seized and held, for a long moment, by merchant princes—who in turn had it wrested from their grasp by union bosses, ideologues, communist insurgents, and the boys of Madison Avenue who had learned the magic of selling soap, cigarettes, and presidents.

Still, in the White House and the Kremlin, at the head table of almost every nation, regardless of who might pull the hidden strings of power, there sat on the throne an alpha male.

In the veld, the alpha male was prosecutor and judge. He pointed the bone at the accused and the indictment followed by the consensus of the mob. We tried suspected criminals by fire; guilty, we cured them of their demons with stones, the garrote, and the noose.

Later we learned to make judgments on the basis of omens and signs, today called evidence, and to reduce the unwieldy mob to a panel of twelve. The procedure grew complex, and there arose a brotherhood of experts who argued each case while an old man in a cloak, an alpha male of the lawyer's band, peered down from a bench above—and we moved on to a therapy of high-voltage electricity, cyanide pills, and the slow drip of intravenous oblivion.

On the ancient veld, old men and women, users of herbs and knowers of phantasms, painted their faces with berry juice and clay and shook their rattles to attract the attention of the gods. They screamed and chanted, and the world indeed did not end after all. They brought back the sun on those fearful occasions when it disappeared in midsky, and they ensured that each night was followed by the dawn of a new day.

With their ceremonies they turned the winter into spring, brought forth rain from the sky, and aided the dead in their terrifying journey to a new life. They were the masters of the unseen and the unknowable, they were shamans, and healers, and preachers, and priests, and then, as one unnumbered millennium followed another and the legends piled up, they wrapped themselves in crimson robes and called themselves popes.

And so it has always been, the mode evolving with time but the thing itself never changing. Barbers became brain surgeons, mule skinners learned to fly jumbo jets, blind roving poets became playwrights and moved to Hollywood to write soap operas or took up the electric GE-tar and sang the ancient song of sex and its overlays of heartbreak and violence.

And always we walked behind the alpha male, and always the path of our history followed the course of least resistance, cleaving to the truth of the emotions long after the environment that created them was forgotten. We wandered this way and that, searching for something we didn't understand, some "right," some "justice," some "happiness," some security that we couldn't define.

We never found it, though, because before the search was complete we always died. The next generation lamented its parents, dusted their bodies with ochre, covered them with flowers, and buried them with vows that they would never be forgotten—and then their sons' sons' sons and their daughters' daughters' daughters, looping around in their own blind wanderings and coming by chance upon those strange unremembered graves, beside a long unused pathway, paused to wonder who lay there and in what strange tongue their epitaphs were encoded.

We lived, we loved, we hated, we gave birth, we laughed, we suffered, we found scapegoats, we conquered and were conquered, enslaved and were enslaved, raped and were raped, until finally, clutching the faith of our fathers that we were part of a greater holy pattern, we passed on into death and nothingness. But in our innocence we were children; we never, never for a moment, understood.

In modern times, for reasons still speculative, we did learn to apply our newfound intellectual ability to the mastery of the corporeal world. That world was, for openers (and to the horror of our priests and the acolytes), round. It was not the center of the universe, after all; the sun was.

No, on second thought, on a few generations' reconsideration, the sun was but a star—and not even an unusual star, at that. It was one star among many, drifting like a speck of dust on the outer edges of a vast whirlpool of stars in a deep black velvet sea as infinite as ever was the ancient night beyond the cave. And as filled, perhaps, with demons.

On the round earth we learned to grind lenses not only to see the stars but to allow the blind to see us, and each other. We captured the wind in sails, and the sea was ours. We imprisoned steam in iron cannisters, and with it, we subjugated continents. With gunpowder we made weak men equal in strength to strong ones and at the same time converted bullies into tyrants. On fabric wings we flew, and on aluminum and titanium ones we flew faster and higher. We built a telegraph, and then a wireless.

We applied our knowledge to build steam automobiles, and then gasoline ones, and then the Hero Henry built the Model T, and the automobile, belonging now to us all, gave vent to our wanderlust. It also changed our sex lives, as bundling gave way to panting struggles in the back seats of Pontiacs and Buicks.

Then, in the darkness of early morning on July 16, 1945, in a remote desert just north of Alamogordo, New Mexico, a pinpoint of light vaporized a metal tower, turned the sand to glass, and in a wink grew large beneath a mushroom cloud. It wasn't the sun, but it was nevertheless dawn, the dawn of a new age.

That explosion seemed at the time to be the defining moment of the twentieth century. Humankind, we were sure, would one day reckon time thereby. With the atom unleashed, the world would be even better yet. A train, we were told, could speed from New York to Los Angeles on the power contained in the atoms of a single ticket stub.

Life went on, though, as it always had, and was good and growing better. Electricity extended our days and warmed our nights. Better and faster automobiles appeared in dealer showrooms. There came the washing machine, the dryer, the garbage disposal, the air conditioner, and, wonder of all wonders, that crowning stroke of kitchen technology, the automatic dishwasher.

Penicillin cured our children of the infections that once killed so many of them, and, as a consequence, we needed fewer and fewer babies. The condom was barbaric and, worse, relied on male control; we sought, and found, the Pill. The Pill freed women from servitude, and a revolution followed.

As our power grew, the pace of change itself changed. We moved slowly and ponderously at first, and then faster and faster and faster and faster.

Somehow, stresses increased, but that was okay—we had Valium, now.

Adolescents who read science fiction looked into the future and saw robots, and their parents laughed at them. But in fact the robots were already here, one in each living room, one-eyed electronic creatures called television sets that had already became babysitters and teachers.

Change had become the new constant. Things were changing so fast that we could no longer define what was happening to us. By the time we figured out the side effects of a new drug, it was outmoded and we were already well into another one. Before we had figured out television, Johnny had a computer. Divorce rates were up, and so were crime rates, and there had been so many changes that we didn't know what the causes were. Valium was rapidly becoming the most frequently prescribed drug in history. A phrase, "future shock," grew from the title of a book. There arose the perception that things were getting out of control.

Progress, once a magic carpet, had somehow become a juggernaut. We began to have some doubts.

Each year, 50,000 Americans were dying on the highways and another 250,000 were being maimed. Divorce rates were up some more, and the curve that described them was growing steeper. Alcoholism was a bigger problem than we had thought, and addiction to other drugs was growing. My God! There were drugs in grade schools!

Mental illness, it seemed, was becoming more common. The television, in teaching us, had taught us that thin was beautiful—and our daughters were beset by a horrible new disease called anorexia, against which the wonder drugs were worthless.

We tallied these things on the latest computers and were horrified by what we saw. Our minds opening, we began to understand, dimly at first and then in consternation, that the environment around us was being slowly poisoned. Or maybe not so slowly. We panicked. Something was wrong, horribly wrong. Dioxin! Three Mile Island!

We were being stalked—by paranoia.

Each evening, on our television sets, we watched the alpha males in Washington and Moscow. Their hairy fingers poised above red Armageddon buttons, they jumped up and down, thumping their chests and screaming threats.

A collective chill ran through us. With our technology we had created the tools necessary to convert life from hell on earth to heaven. But those tools, to be used safely, had to be used with wisdom. And wisdom, founded on self-knowledge, was the one thing we lacked. Our world was an eighteen-wheeler full of dynamite, careening down the highway with the pedal to the metal—and the driver was little more than a monkey driven by a mishmash of outmoded emotions and the mistaken illusion that he was something better.

As early as the 1960s, it was being said that the knowledge we needed now was self-knowledge, that the critical element of control we lacked was control over ourselves.

That perception, voiced casually at cocktail parties by women in sequined dresses, mouthed by long-haired revolutionaries and pinstriped establishment board chairmen alike, reduced first to a commonplace and then a cliché, became the one consensus of what was otherwise one of the most divisive eras in American history.

We had finally, in our eons of turmoil-filled wanderings, arrived at a fork in the road. The low road of uncontrolled, unexamined emotions led through chaos back to the mother jungle; the high road was marked "rationality."

Those were the years in which Solomon Snyder turned his back on the problematic enigmas of psychiatry and chose, instead, the precision of neurochemistry. Dozens of other young men and women, destined to be the greatest biologists, anthropologists, and psychologists of their times, made similar choices. One generation had perceived a need, and their children had moved to meet it.

In the decade and more since Solomon Snyder and Candace Pert revealed the existence of the morphine receptor, the discoveries described in this book have laid the foundation for a new understanding of ourselves—a no-nonsense understanding that we need if we are to prosper (even to survive) during the next millennium.

We know, now, that there is a correspondence between chemical reactions in the brain and the flow of thoughts and emotions through the psyche. They are the same thing, viewed through different lenses. Though we don't yet know what the linkage is between chemistry and thought, there is no longer any doubt that such linkages exist, or that we are defined by them.

We know, now, that memory is encoded in the molecules of the brain. We know that adolescence is a chemical phenomenon, beyond the control of the victim. We know that love can be titrated in a test tube, and that avarice is inscribed in our genes. We know now that nationalism plays out its bloody scenarios across the fields of GABA receptors in the brains of old men long before young ones meet to die on battlefields.

From such knowledge there emerge the first hints of what may be a bold new wisdom. We have engineered plants, domesticated beasts, tamed rivers, and made crops grow where once there was only shifting sand. We have built machines that run faster than gazelles and that fly higher than condors. We have changed the face of the earth and begun to work on the moon. We have conquered the force of the atom.

Now, at long last, we will take the final step and assume responsibility for controlling ourselves. That's the sales pitch of the new revolution.

But first, to use the ancient paradigm, there will be the devil to pay. If we are to understand and use the new knowledge, if we are to harness it to the wisdom we need, we will first have to sign in blood. We will have to turn our backs on the duality and, with it, the faith of our fathers. Molecular psychology represents the most fundamental heresy ever committed by science, and we will have to embrace it.

We will have to look into the mirror, surrender illusion, and make peace with the fact that we're staring at a machine.

We are mechanisms, pure and simple, explainable without resort to the concept of soul. We are wanderers out of the past with no destiny save to move on into the future, no dignity except that which we bring to ourselves by our actions.

That is the central, cold, hard, emotionless truth of the revolution in molecular psychology. If we really desire the safety we seek, the safety from chemicals and radiation and war, then we must renounce the romantic, dualistic view of man.

Each new revelation that appears in the neurochemistry journals—and there are dozens every month—further confirms the sobering notion that every human thought, hope, fear, passion, yearning, and insight results from chemical interactions between transmitters and receptors. The chief difference between us and an Apple computer is complexity.

So what, you ask, of that deep, gut knowledge we all harbor in our psyches, the conviction that we're God's creatures, that we're special, that we count?

Doesn't Snyder feel that? Down deep, in his heart of hearts, doesn't he know he has a soul?

Doesn't Pert, somewhere deep in her heart, know there's a God?

I asked her that once, rather sheepishly, explaining that newspaper reporters sometimes have to ask dumb questions.

Candace Pert, do you believe in God?

My pencil hovered over the pad, ready to record the explosion of laughter I was sure such a question would bring. But she looked back at me and, without cracking a smile, said, "Of course."

I stared at her. Come on, Candace. I know you. You know me. Cut the crap. Give me something that makes sense. Or give me a no comment. I've got a story to write.

"No," she said. "It's the truth. I believe in God."

I asked her again, in a different way, angling to understand what she was trying to tell me. Surely this woman, this explorer of the substance of the soul, this scientific, female Columbus— this woman with the picture of a rat brain slice, opiate receptors glowing, hanging on the wall—surely she didn't believe in God!

"Oh," she insisted, "but I do."

"You don't," I said.

Finally, though, she got tired of the game. "Look," she said. "Of course I believe in God. I evolved to believe in God. I'm programmed to believe in God. So I believe in God. It's easier that way."

And there it is, out of the mouth of my favorite scientific revolutionary, the unvarnished truth. Not only are our most precious beliefs myths, we are compelled to believe in them. Nature has put God in our minds to shield us from the coldness of the fact that we are a gene's way of making more genes, and that the principal thing we have to look forward to, as individuals, is death.

And so, multileveled Mother Nature, wry and cruel but at times strangely benevolent, has inserted a mechanism in the mechanism to prevent that mechanism from fully comprehending its mechanistic nature. Faith itself, in other words, is but mechanism.

But, as Pert tells us, mechanistic or not it is also imperative. At *some* level we will always believe in God, and we will always believe in our own spirituality. To do otherwise would be to give up, to sit down beside the road, and die.

And so it is that to join the revolution, to be part of the future instead of the past, we must learn to let our thoughts run, contradictorily, along both sides of the paradox.

God is one example. As the saying goes, if He didn't exist we'd have to invent Him. So we did. But that doesn't make Him less real.

Children are another good example. They're psychological parasites, and as such they're probably the most awful thing ever concocted by nature. They smell bad, they ooze grape jelly, they're fonts of ignorance. They're selfish, they're violent, they're self-centered, and they embarrass us at every opportunity. The proper treatment of a newborn baby is to drown it, forthwith.

Nature won't have it, of course. We're not only cursed with our burdens, but doubly cursed with the illusion that we enjoy carrying them. So we are made to love the little rascals. They're cute, you know (ours are, that is—the neighbor's children are monsters). Johnny is a chip off the old block, by golly, and we'd lay down our life for him.

So it goes, as well, for our country—right or wrong. And for the automobile company we patronize. And for our football team, and for people who are the same color we are, and who speak the same language, and, of course, for our very own, kindest, and most loving woman in the world, the woman who can do no wrong, that saint on earth, our mother.

Nonsense, of course. Necessary nonsense, to be sure, emotional signposts of our lives without which we would surely be engulfed in psychological vertigo. But nonsense.

Molecular psychology demotes our most precious beliefs and ideals to the levels of crude necessity. It is necessary to believe in God, just as it is necessary to have daily bowel movements. Thus it makes a mockery of our religious beliefs, our country, our deep feelings for our wives and our mothers, our antagonisms, our convictions . . . it strips our justifications away and leaves the mechanism stark naked.

We humans feel as we do not because we are guided by the invisible edicts of the gods, and certainly not because our football team is intrinsically more worthy, or our country intrinsically more just, but because of the peculiar sensitivities, densities, locations, and metabolisms of our receptors and transmitters. Those, in turn, are products of natural selection. Thus the behavior we identify as uniquely human is as fundamentally Darwinian as our characteristically hairless bodies and the distinctive type of hemoglobin that flows in our veins.

When it comes to really important things, in other words, our feelings aren't sacred. I'd feel more comfortable spending an evening with Jerry Falwell than with the Ayatollah Khomeini, but I suspect this is nothing more than social bias—and if we need to deal with the Ayatollah to keep our world from going up in flames, then we'd better swallow our revulsion and cut the cards. And when it comes to arriving at some understanding with the Soviets on the issue of nuclear weapons, we'd better be able to suspend our animosity and find some common causes.

It really doesn't matter, in the end, whether the Soviets are athiests or not, whether they speak a strange language, or whether they have ways that seem alien to us. We mustn't get our necessary illusions mixed up with our brutal realities.

The wisdom of molecular psychology is, first, that it allows us to distinguish between the two. We can begin to say, finally, what's fluff and what's real.

And as for the price we pay for that, a certain rule of thumb seems to be emerging. The more important a belief is to you, the more precious an idea, the more pivotal it seems to your existence, the more it seems to bolster the ascendancy of right over wrong, of justice over injustice, the more likely it is to die in the revolution.

You saw that coming, I'm sure. It's been implicit from the beginning—the first truth had to do with moths and the last one, this one about men and women, was naturally destined to be no different. The apple they talk about in the Bible is really a persimmon. We may not like it, but we're puppets on chemical strings, no different from moths, really, except that the pheromones we so blindly follow are embedded in our very minds—our devils are not outside the cave, but inside our skulls.

It's not the way any of us wanted the world to turn out to be, but we have to play the hand we're dealt.

Many people, of course, will refuse to take part in any such heresy. They'll just fold their cards, toss them on the table face up, and walk away. That's the way it's always been with scientific revolutions, and the difficult and heretical truths they bring.

It was like that with Copernicus, who saw full well the dangers inherent in his new theory and wisely chose to keep it secret until life had brought him safely to his deathbed. Almost everybody, of course, knew instantly that the old man was wrong . . . he must have cooked up his theory in his dotage. How could he say the sun was the center of the solar system? Any fool could see it revolved around the earth! Didn't it come up, circle overhead, then pass beneath so that it could come up again the other day?

Bruno, though—Bruno was a real loudmouth. Copernicus had escaped through the sealed door of death, but in Bruno they had a living heretic, and so they roasted him at the stake. Galileo opened his mouth to defend the new principle, but changed his mind after the priests of the Inquisition conducted him on a friendly tour of the torture chamber.

Anyway, how can the earth be round? Wouldn't we fall off?

Always, as surges of new knowledge transcend our experience, our minds rebel. The human reaction then is to deny, and there are those who to this day, despite the evidence of satellites, stubbornly cling to their faith that the earth is as flat as it seems. There are those, to this day, who believe firmly that the earth, flat or round, was created in six days. There are those, to this day, who believe, without question, that Darwin was a fraud. They will dispense easily with molecular psychology—and perhaps, especially at first, the doubters will form a majority.

But science is not democratic, nor is history, and each revolution is followed by a new world shaped not by the reactionaries but by the insurgents. The denial of unpleasant new paradigms is essentially a sterile process; dualism shaped the world we know and has nothing better to offer. Materialism is the soul as well as the body of the future, and those who are psychologically flexible enough to see the new patterns, and put them to use, will shape what's to come.

20

BRAVE

NEW

WORLD

THE appealing thing about the new science of the mind is that we're clearly going to be able to do things with it. Unlike previous paradigms of the human mind, molecular psychology has utility—and, within that utility, its own cold beauty.

And, as we look to the future, we see the one final paradox: molecular psychology, the most inhuman of all approaches to the human condition, already promises to be the most warmly humanistic.

Crusaders, with their often religious and ethical backgrounds, have long preached that it's wrong to look down on the mentally ill. It's wrong, they've said, to hide them away in institutions, and to forget them. It's cruel to laugh at them. They have preached the gospel that mental illness is indeed an ailment, like cancer or heart disease, and its victims should be treated with kindness and mercy.

And what good did it do?

We gave it lip service at the same level we professed the desirablity of loving one another (and especially one another's wives). Sure, we said, wiping away a crocodile tear, the insane are but victims—and then we opened the doors of our mental institutions and "freed" the inmates to the mercy of the inner-city streets.

At least the crusaders identified the problem correctly. The shunning of mental patients, because it feeds into the idea that the patient (and probably the patient's family as well) is at fault, is central. It ranks right up there with racism as a source of human misery.

Naturally, given the stigma, the mental patient vociferously denies what's happening to him. Schizophrenics commonly fight the diagnosis the same way cancer patients did a hundred years ago, when malignancy was considered a "filth" disease.

The mental patient's mother, father, and spouse also deny as long as they can, and then, when denial is no longer possible, they're often paralyzed by guilt. Thus the stigma translates into an inability to cope.

This inability goes far beyond the immediate family of the patient. Legislators, refusing to confront the problem, have turned their back on the need. The voter, seeking to avoid confronting the insanity in his own immediate family, is not offended.

The bottom line is that a hundred years of preaching, in other words, hasn't made much of a difference.

Molecular psychology, on the other hand, doesn't preach. Schizophrenia, depression, alcoholism, and a long list of "behavior disorders" are clearly physical illnesses. That is not contention, it's fact—fact that can be demonstrated by chemical reactions and PET scan photographs, fact that can be shown in your laboratory or mine, solid, argument-ending fact.

There are, of course, still those who argue in favor of spiritual conceptualizations of insanity, and who invoke concepts like "right" and "wrong" in the process. There are still flat-earthers, too, and creationists and fruitarians. But to make moralistic arguments about mental illness today is to reveal oneself as a fool and a bigot. Schizophrenia is about as moral as a broken leg.

The first contribution of molecular psychology, then, is clearly its power to shift the issue from the spiritual plane to the scientific one. This is why the friends and relatives of mental patients were, after the scientists themselves, the first to recognize the historical importance of molecular psychology.

Today, as a result, they compose an effective and rapidly growing lobby group carrying the news to legislators in their state capitals and in Washington, D.C. Thanks to them, a steadily widening circle of people are becoming aware that there has been a cascade of spectacular breakthroughs in brain science, and that it has now become possible to speak rationally of a cure for mental illness.

The result, at least among those who are privy to what's going on, is a sense of anticipation in the field of mental illness research. This new excitement draws more research money, and, even more important, it attracts fresh young scientific minds.

As the stigma lapses, and fundamental research into the human mind-brain continues to accelerate, dramatic new treatments for mental illness are clearly in the offing.

Some of them will be straightforward drug treatments, potions that cure in the ancient tradition of medicine. For openers, there is real hope that the coming decade will see the introduction of new drugs that will get at the chemical roots of schizophrenia, correcting the withdrawal as well as the hallucinations, without the side effects of current drugs.

More dramatic will be the coming drug therapies for diseases that still don't seem, to most people, diseases at all. There is little doubt that medication aimed at correcting basic defects in alcoholism and hypochondria, and probably in some forms of criminality as well, will sooner or later change the nature of our society.

The uses of such drugs will go hand in hand with chemical tests that increasingly will allow the early diagnosis of mental illness. Given the importance of early diagnosis in physical disease, these tests, in fact, may well be as important as the drugs.

In the process, psychiatry will achieve a new credibility. Today, a patient will usually take his doctor's word when he announces he has located a tiny cancer in a hidden place. He will usually approve radical operations on the physician's say-so.

But a diagnosis of psychiatric illness, because mental disease is so stigmatized, is often resisted and denied until the symptoms become unmanageable. The situation is further complicated by society's longstanding confusion over the differences between the human right to determine one's own destiny and the denial that routinely accompanies most psychiatric illnesses. The result is that the victim, denying that he's crazy, is allowed to get crazier and crazier until he finally dies.

But even if the patient is a minor, and his or her parents are more than willing to take a doctor's advice, they may unsuspectingly get caught up in the tug of war between molecular psychologists and old-fashioned psychoanalytical therapists. The result may be that the doctor's advice is useless.

Mental health advocates like James Howe, president of the National Alliance for the Mentally Ill, complain bitterly that too many psychiatrists and psychologists still refuse to recognize the limitations of talk therapy. Such therapists remain highly suspicious of drug treatment.

As a result, many patients don't get drug therapy until they have undergone years of talk therapy. By the time it's apparent that that tactic isn't helping, they have full-blown mental illness.

The discovery of physical markers for mental diseases, and of economical and trustworthy laboratory tests to detect them, should turn this situation around. As this new technology moves into clinical practice, diagnosis will become much more precise—and more difficult for patient, family, or ultimately a judge to second-guess.

Nobody knows, of course, what the result of early treatment will be. But many psychiatrists point to the success of early treatment of the "physical" diseases and argue that there's no reason at all to think the "mental" patients, who are in truth suffering physical diseases of the brain, won't fare as well.

The new technology, of course, won't be limited to traditional diagnostic and treatment schemes. The psychogeneticists' work, for instance, makes it clear that some hefty percentage of mental patients—and perhaps even a majority—are in truth victims of a more or less straightforward genetic disease of the brain. Many others, with "environmental" forms of disease, succumb only because of an underlying genetic weakness. In such patients, gene therapy may be the answer.

One permutation of that will be prenatal diagnosis, in which the genetic defect is discovered early enough in pregnancy that the affected fetus can be aborted. This may soon become possible in certain quasi-mental genetic illnesses, such as Huntington's disease.

But the more immediate hope is that doctors can transplant normal genes into the brains of already living patients.

The perception that new genes might be inserted into a living brain, and that those genes might actually change the patient's mind in the truest sense of the word, is not a product of some far-out science fiction thinking. In fact, one of the two genetic ailments considered most likely candidates for the first attempts at human gene therapy is a disease of the brain that causes, among other things, distinctive self-destructive behavior.

The disease is Lesch-Nyhan syndrome, a rare genetic condition characterized by a defect in a single gene. Children with Lesch-Nyhan syndrome, like those with other serious genetic defects, generally die at a young age of the metabolic effects of their disease.

Unlike most such victims, however, their intellectual capacities aren't significantly affected much. They are horribly aware of what's happening to them, but that awareness doesn't help them control a strange and bizarre compulsion caused by the defective genes. Before they die they are overcome by uncontrollable impulses to mutilate themselves. If their hands are not tied down, they'll bite off their fingers and tear out their eyes. Tied down, they frequently chew off their lips. Lesch-Nyhan, in short, is among other things a behavioral disease.

A combination of factors, including the basic horribleness of the disease, has caused Lesch-Nyhan syndrome to be targeted as one of the first candidates for gene therapy. Sometime in the next few years scientists at the University of California at San Diego, as well as a group at Baylor College of Medicine in Houston, expect to insert a healthy substitution gene, concealed in a virus coat, into the bodies of Lesch-Nyhan patients.

Will it work? Probably not, at first. But in the long run, most research psychiatrists believe that the difficulties will be overcome. In recent years, in fact, experts have begun to look to gene therapy as one of the best hopes for many of the most severe forms of mental illness—including certain forms of schizophrenia, depression, severe alcoholism, chronic hypochondria, and even criminality.

The emphasis on drug treatment and other "physical" therapies, such as gene transplants or early detection and abortion, has caused friction between molecular psychologists and traditional therapists who deal more with the "mind" aspects of the brain. But for the most part this struggle is a product of misunderstanding: the new science of molecular psychology does not threaten the existence of traditional psychotherapeutic methods.

Some serious psychoses, of the sort that have never been very amenable to psychotherapy, probably will be treated primarily with drugs. But where the brain has been damaged by environment or experience, which must often be the case, the most specific method of undoing the damage will probably turn out to be the talk therapists. And since no drug ever concocted is without side effects, such treatment will be safer.

The role of the molecular psychologist, in such cases, may well be simply that of discoverer.

Molecular psychology offers, for the first time, the opportunity to study and devise chemical classifications for that plethora of personality glitches, aches, and pains once known collectively as "the neuroses." Once the various diseases have been sorted out, treatment can be followed with periodic PET scans or other tests to determine which problem responds best to which therapy.

Once this is understood, psychiatrists will have a solid rationale by which to judge the value of different modes of treatment in various situations. This, if early experiments along this line are any indication, will dramatically improve the Freudian track record.

As we increase the depth of our understanding about the mind-brain, in fact, the talk therapist may even become a more dominant figure.

Perhaps the next generation of psychotherapists, using the new understanding of the mind-brain, will be able to treat some diseases that psychiatrists of today concede almost entirely to the prescription writers.

The bottom line is that molecular psychology will clearly have a revolutionary impact across the entire spectrum of the psychological sciences. In doing so, it will significantly decrease and even eliminate the many costs of mental illness.

The monetary savings will be measured in the billions of dollars. The human suffering that will be prevented is impossible to even conceptualize. The benefits to our society will rival and perhaps even surpass those gained as a result of the last public health revolution—a revolution that virtually wiped out typhoid, cholera, yellow fever, and malaria. For the majority of Americans who are directly affected by mental illness, the change will be dramatic; for the rest, life will slowly grow smoother, calmer, safer, and happier.

But a new understanding of the human mind will by no means be confined to the classic boundaries of psychiatry. The mind is, after all . . . . everything. So the new psychiatry, in the form of industrial, commercial, and political psychology, will wreak its changes everywhere.

There is a consensus in our society, for instance, that our criminal justice system is long overdue for dramatic reform. There is a sense that justice has taken a back seat to process, that the guilty are too likely to walk free and the innocent, though they may escape conviction, are handed into the financial servitude of their own attorneys. Our judges are overworked, our precedents don't apply, our overcrowded prisons are academies for crime . . . the only thing we don't agree on is the basis for change.

Molecular psychology offers precisely such a basis. It gives us a conceptual framework for dealing with the problem, a framework so obviously utilitarian that it's difficult to imagine that it won't be pressed quickly into service.

Most obviously, the new diagnostic techniques should serve to cool off, and eventually solve, the current controversy over the insanity defense. As it stands today, the insanity defense is a game of credibility: Who impresses the jurors more, the shrink for the defense or the shrink for the prosecution?

In either case, the jury is left to muddle over the haunting question of whether, considering that the chap murdered half a dozen people, it really matters much whether he's technically bonkers or not.

The new diagnostic techniques, including PET scans and chemical tests, coupled with realistic prognoses for the various diseases, should restore order to chaos. In the first place, a picture is worth a thousand words; a jury might be totally confused by the semantics of an expert argument, but, given a little instruction, a normal person can see an abnormality in a scanner picture. Marginal cases aside, a blob of yellow, say, is either there or it isn't.

As the various forms of diseases are recategorized in the coming decade, and the best treatment for each form is worked out by clinicians, the rest of us—legislators, judges, cops, and voters—can get a much more practical grasp on what's at stake.

The nature of the crime, be it murder or shoplifting, may not make much difference if the accused is suffering from a clear form of a curable disease. The victim was . . . well, the victim of a psychological accident, and the perpetrator was a victim, too. He or she should be turned over to a shrink, cured, and then set free.

But a different course might be indicated for a person who was obviously and profoundly insane with a disease that predisposed for violence . . . and was incurable. Protection of society might demand that such a person be locked up for life, even if the crime of which he was accused was relatively minor.

As the new psychiatry develops, there is also likely to be a major breakdown, or at least a dramatic blurring, of one of legal psychiatry's major principles. Classically, mental illness, such as schizophrenia, has been one thing and "antisocial personality" quite another. If you were mentally ill, you deserved to be acquitted. But if you were antisocial you were just . . . well, mean. And you deserved the slammer.

Likewise, a depressed woman who killed her children and then lost her nerve before she killed herself might be acquitted on an insanity defense. But a male violent alcoholic who killed a man in a drunken rage was a murderer, pure and simple.

As we come to understand the genetic underpinnings of at least some types of alcoholism, and even some sorts of criminality, the distinction between the crazy and the merely mean appears to come apart and our sense of justice becomes less and less clear.

Clearly, as such knowledge accumulates, our current framework for judging guilt and innocence in such cases will have to change as well. In some fashion, the outcome of the legal process must be made to square with our new perception of psychological reality.

Beyond the shifting sands of culpability, the new technology may have some very practical uses in the legal establishment. Lie detectors, for instance, are currently inadmissible as evidence because they are perceived as unreliable.

Another half-dozen generations into the PET scan revolution, though, and it may well be possible to administer and read brain scans in such a way as to detect lying with a high degree of confidence. Such a lie detector process would put lawyers and investigators out of work and speed up trials while at the same time improving the odds of convicting the guilty and acquitting the innocent.

The prison system will also benefit greatly from the new psychology. As it stands now, drug abuse is rampant. Corruption is the rule. Violence is the ethic. The social system inside the walls, far from teaching social values, reinforces criminal behavior by rewarding bullies and converting the meek to serfs and servants. Not only do prisons fail to rehabilitate, they are the colleges of crime, and, by any rational estimation, the system is a shambles.

Applying the principles of molecular psychology to the problem brings about some uncomfortable juxtapositions. Despite a gut feeling that prompts us to refer to a mass murderer as a "madman," we seek today to make a sharp distinction between the criminal and the insane.

There are valid motives for the distinction. One of them, for instance, is that any blurring of the distinctions might conflict with the continuing attempt to combat the prejudice that would paint all schizophrenics, for instance, as dangerous criminals.

Even so, criminality and insanity are categories that just won't stay separate, and any major improvement in the prison system must somehow come to grips with that.

The most obvious (and in some ways most informative) example involves alcoholism, now known to be a metabolic disease with genetic foundations. An estimated 50 percent of prisoners are alcoholics, and most of them committed their crimes while under the influence. If prisoners addicted to "hard" drugs are included, it's fair to say that the vast majority of people in the nation's prisons are addicts.

To ignore this fact, as we do, is in keeping with our traditional approach to mental illness. That is to say, we lie to ourselves.

Addiction, of course, is not the only answer—there clearly are no single answers. Some of the most violent criminals, for instance, may be victims of what is essentially "emotional epilepsy."

Practical distinctions will always be made, of course, between the mentally ill person who is violent and the vast majority who aren't. But as we come to better understand the complex function of the human mind, and to appreciate and categorize its many aberrations, our prisons will surely come more and more to resemble mental hospitals.

Already pilot programs in federal prisons, for instance, have demonstrated that treatment with antidepressant drugs can greatly reduce the incidence of violence. And in recent years, courts, faced with crowded prisons and the grim statistics on recidivism, have begun to experiment with various "drug punishments," such as chemical castration for rapists, in lieu of incarceration. As more behavior-controlling drugs become possible, that trend is certain to grow.

But while the new science of the mind is ostensibly aimed at the pathologies of our culture, understanding insanity implies a grasp of the normal as well. Our new knowledge, once absorbed, will also be put to work in our collective and even individual decisions.

At this moment in history, for instance, the citizens of this country don't have much more confidence in the educational system than they do in penology. The shoddiness of our educational system, in fact, is one of the firmer shared convictions of our society.

The situation, though, is a bit like that in penology. While we may agree that Johnny can't read, we argue like fishwives about why that's so. Some people think it's because he watches too much television, others blame it on government edicts that forbid him to pray in homeroom. Others say he can't read because his teacher can't either, and for that matter neither can Mom or Dad.

Molecular psychology, as it reveals what's really going on in the human mind, will surely provide us with some solid answers.

We liberals may chuckle at the notion, for instance, but it may turn out that the fundamentalists who drive around with "KIDS NEED TO PRAY" bumper stickers have a point. Kids may indeed need to believe in God, the same way they need to believe in the infallibility of their parents. Intellectual honesty is not independent of age and sophistication, and experience with the new psychology so far contains broad hints that no ideology is completely wrong.

Beyond such volatile issues as prayer in school, there are hundreds of practical educational questions that could take decades to work out—or could be solved in a few months with PET scanners or other appropriate technology. For instance . . . are examinations fair? Just what is the most efficient class size for learning English? Is that optimum size different for math? Which textbooks are best? How can educational computers best be used?

And how about teen craziness? What does that first flood of hormones do to a child's ability to absorb history? Should fourteen-year-old boys be spared mathematics until they adjust to their new testosterone levels? Or is it English that suffers most from the chemicals of puberty? Would the problem be solved with teen marriage, coupled with salaries for staying in school? Or, perhaps, should adolescence-preventing drugs be designed and administered to all students until the day of their graduation?

Molecular psychology will not solve all the educational enigmas, of course, but it will be a powerful tool in the hands of educational theorists and philosophers. With it, experts may well be able to end the interminable arguments and make quantum jumps in the efficiency of the learning process.

Then, of course, there's also the question of educational screening, one of the areas of the educational establishment with a long psychological tradition. Might a seventeenth-generation PET scanner, for instance, separate out the students who will make the best doctors? Might the PET scan pattern of a top-ranked engineering student be quite different from that of an ace history student? Might it be, as many suspect, that our university system is grossly inefficient simply because it tries to drive too many square pegs into round holes?

Beyond the educational system, the new psychology might be useful in screening applicants for jobs. Are there, for instance, "bully personalities" who are fundamentally good people but who should under no circumstances be given a police officer's badge and gun? Could we keep officious people out of social work, liars out of journalism, sadists out of dentistry, charletans out of pulpits, and pedants away from lecterns?

Today reporters clamor for a would-be president to release his income tax returns. Might the press corps of the year 2000 demand that a candidate publish his PET scans and brain-gene profile? And might a population accustomed to molecular psychology back up that request?

Another obvious arena for the new science is domestic relations —a turf already being worked by scientists like Helen Fisher. If her view is correct, our new understanding of the mechanism of love should help us think the problem through much more effectively than ever before.

The new understanding that lifelong marriage may not be the "natural" pattern may relieve people of the guilt that accompanies failure. On a broader scale, such knowledge should lead us to reevaluate whether or not we want monogamy to be the standard. If we do, by revealing that it's a delicate institution, the research should spur us to make laws that would nurture its success.

A love potion, in light of recent experience, is not wild speculation. It might help us preserve marriage. Equally valuable would be a drug capable of breaking the spell of love, a sort of "antilove potion," so that divorces could be clean, without bitterness.

As the ability to understand our minds grows, and the technology for changing them keeps pace, the mavens of the mass media won't be left out of the revolution. Writing, singing, dancing, directing, and similar arts are in essence aimed at programming the human mind, making it run its ancient programs on cue and feel what the artist intends for it to feel. New insights into how the mind works are destined, inevitably, to yield better drama—and more powerful soap commercials.

The possibilities go on. Might students not benefit from memory-enhancing drugs? Intelligence boosters, given judiciously to scientists and diplomats handling international crises, might help us cut the risks we face.

Or do we need drugs for all that? Once we understand and identify the genes that lay the foundation for our intelligence and creativity, why not use our newfound genetic engineering abilities to make us all smarter and more insightful? Why not turn the drudges of the world into geniuses instead?

If we are prepared to take strong measures so that men and

women will not have to suffer schizophrenia and depression, why should they endure stupidity?

And might it not come to pass, as our understanding of ourselves deepens and matures, that we may finally become smart enough, insightful enough, understanding enough, to grasp the one goal that we have for so long sought, but that has always eluded us? Might we not, by engineering ourselves, finally find peace?

We could go on, and on, and on, and on. But clearly this new science is so promising, so potentially powerful, so pregnant with dreamy scenarios, that if even a tenth of them come to pass our society will be forever changed.

The future, through the eyes of the molecular psychologist who is not afraid of honest speculation, and of human dreams, will be a spectacularly different place from the present.

It's not just that mental hospitals will be few and far between, or that their inmates will rarely stay for more than a day or so. It's not that prisons will be more humane on the one hand and more effective on the other, or that few inmates will return. It is not just the new level of stability that will be achieved.

It's not just that there will be fewer drunks on the road or fewer thugs on the streets. It's not just that fewer depressed people will abuse their sick leave, or that factory morale will be better.

It's not just that our children will be better educated. It's not just that our managers will be more savvy, our voters more discerning, our politicians more astute, our generals more decisive, our teachers more caring, our cops more honest, our garbage collectors more cheerful and optimistic.

It's not just that profit margins will improve, or that our wages will be higher, or that their value will be more substantial, or that the things we buy with them will be far more likely to perform as advertised.

It is not just these things, but all of them and thousands more, some large, some small, all playing one upon the other in a dramatic synergism. Though we may debate the precise process by which this will occur, the new psychology seems fated to yield a new sanity, a new and better oil for the social and economic machinery.

It will be a far different world from the one we know today—and a far better, and more efficient, one. Who but a carping fool or a flat-earther would question it?

But it is not, of course, going to be that neat and simple. The same scenario that makes the heart beat with optimistic anticipation also touches another, more skeptical part of us with a cold hand.

The civil libertarian in our minds looks this gift horse in the mouth, and remembers that Mussolini, too, made the trains run on time. What price, in freedom and justice, will we have to pay for this brave and efficient new world?

21

A

NEW

NIGHTMARE

THE doctors and scientists who sought to work out the mechanisms of pain in the 1960s and 1970s had in mind humanitarian goals. And surely that work will pay off as they would have wished, with cures for addiction and psychosomatic pain. Surely, as the revolution proceeds, there will indeed be clinics where kindly doctors soothe the agony of an endless line of patients with intractable back pain. But the lessons of history require us to consider, as well, the potential for abuse.

In this sad world, only a small minority of humans ever have the privilege of voting, even in ignorance, for their leaders. Most bear the yoke of dictators. There are still dungeons, we know, and torture chambers. There are reports of sadists who clip electrodes to nipple and clitoris, who beat men senseless with hoses and pipes, who win political arguments efficiently and offhandedly with a bullet behind the ear of their opponent.

Dreams or no dreams, this is the real world, and the observer who attends neuroscientific meetings finds himself in the company not just of researchers, writers, philosophers, businessmen, politicians, and journalists but also of military men.

They don't advertise their presence, of course, but you can identify them by their well-clipped hair, modestly priced suits, and military shoes. They take copious notes but rarely if ever make presentations; when asked, they readily admit they're from the Defense Department, but when queried about their interests, their answers are bland. Usually they say they are merely researchers doing their military service and trying, in the interim, to keep current in their science.

It's a legitimate answer, and it may even be true, but the presence of these men seizes the imagination and leads it down sinister pathways. What, one is compelled to ask, would be the meaning of psychochemical warfare?

The answer triggers a cascade of visions, each worse than the one before it. I see a weapons designer taking intelligence enhancers, a prisoner of war being interrogated in a PET scanner, an odorless gas that produces terror and panic in the minds of enemy soldiers, a drug that induces blind obedience in infantrymen.

But the potential for military abuses of the new technology pales beside that offered by the realm of politics. The super political commercial, carefully crafted by technicians to make the brain juices of the audience move in sympathy to the image of a would-be president or senator, only begins the list.

What, one asks, will the Soviets make of this new technology? Communists traditionally have defined those who disagree with the system to be deviants and therefore insane. Such people generally ended up in mental institutions for "treatment." This policy, though, has been largely mitigated by the fact that Soviet psychiatrists generally aren't any more effective in changing behavior than American ones.

But what will it be like, a few years hence, when the secret police have scanners to identify banned thoughts and drugs to change minds?

Consider a loyalty drug in the hands of a dictator in Nicaragua or Chile, or a truth serum that really worked in the clutches of a Ferdinand Marcos or an Ayatollah Khomeini.

And what then, of the much-publicized breakthroughs in the understanding of pain?

Consider, if you have the stomach for it, an antiendorphin, a drug that would do the opposite of morphine, opening up the mind's pain filters instead of closing them. Think of an agony as intense as heroin is blissful.

Think of that compound at work, deep in the thalamic neurons, creating the agony of the stake but denying the welcome death that the stake has always finally offered. Imagine the torture going on, and on, and on, not for minutes but for hours, ripping apart the psyche and recasting the mind in another image.

And then remember, as you read on, that while science is a force of great and shining power in the modern world, it has also proved itself time and time again to be almost totally bereft of morality. And consider that such pain would leave no welts, no bruises, no revealing marks of any kind.

It is not difficult to extrapolate from the age of molecular psychology into horror scenarios that begin only a few years hence. Clearly, the future is fraught with moral and ethical unknowns. But such extrapolations, though very possible and perhaps even inevitable, have the ring of science fiction about them. In this future-shock world of ours, truth often seems more like fantasy than impending reality, which makes it all the more difficult to confront.

But in this case the future lies dead ahead, clear to any who care to see.

One of the most obvious of the dilemmas facing us involves the forced treatment of mentally ill patients. Today we find the concept of involuntary treatment for diseases of the mind to be an abhorrent necessity even when the patient's own actions show that he is a danger to others. When patients who do not pose threats to society refuse to be treated, a common occurrence among drug addicts, alcoholics, schizophrenics, and some manic-depressives, we often honor that refusal—even though we know full well that the mental patient's inability to see the nature of his own disease is one of the hallmarks of insanity.

This reluctance stems from the individual's sacred right to his individuality. The fellow preaching on the street corner, for instance. Is he really a schizophrenic, like the shrink says, or is he just seeing the world differently? What about the right winger who's obsessed with a fear of communists? Isn't that protected by the Constitution? They don't send the guys with the nets after William F. Buckley, do they? What about the housewife who's down in the dumps over the world situation? What could be more legitimate? Maybe she doesn't need tricyclics . . . maybe the world needs Thorazine! And who's to say that Aunt Sarah's hallucinating when she talks to God? Lots of Baptists talk to Him every day, and they don't get locked up!

This careful attitude is justified by psychiatry's perceived inability to make distinctions between the pathological and the merely unusual. But as we begin to rely more on physical determinants of brain disease, such as skin cultures and PET scans, and less on subjective assessments and opinions, we will confront an altogether different situation.

If Aunt Sarah really is sick, undeniably sick, then what right do we have to deny her treatment just because she's out of her head and thinks the doctors are after her?

The truth is that we're already backing away from the libertarian practices of the 1960s and 1970s. Increasingly, we're requiring drunk drivers to attend AA meetings; increasingly, companies are threatening to fire alcoholic employees unless they "voluntarily" undergo treatment. Courts often force drug addicts into treatment programs and now may also give rapists the choice between prison and chemical castration. There is an increasing willingness to broaden the use of blood and urine tests to catch drug users.

As our diagnostic abilities improve, we may find ourselves asking why we should pay special teachers to teach children who have difficulty learning because of a treatable mental illness. Why not just treat the mental illness?

Why should we allow depressed mothers to raise children who, as a result of that rearing, are likely to pose expensive problems for the rest of us?

Why should we allow a schizophrenic to remain a burden on society?

The discovery that many mental illnesses may be genetically determined, at least in large part, carries with it considerable promise. If we can identify children with acetylcholine super-sensitivity, we may be able to save everyone a lot of trouble by pretreating with lithium and preventing the manic-depressive behavior from ever manifesting itself. Ultimately we may replace the defective gene.

But, at least until our ability to detect such diseases is matched by our ability to cure them, the technology poses questions that are clearly destined to pit the rights and needs of society against the rights and needs of individuals.

"It's going to be a real can of worms," acknowledges one clinical scientist. "Take Elliot Gershon's work, for instance . . . do we want a person with acetylcholine sensitivity, who may become a suicidal depressive but hasn't yet . . . do we want such a person to be an airline pilot?

"That's one side of the coin. On the other side, the sensitivity doesn't mean he will necessarily develop the disease. He may have resources in himself, or in his environment, that counterbalance the susceptibility; he may never develop depression, gene or no gene. So can we in good conscience deny him the right to be a pilot?

"Or what happens when we find that one type of schizophrenia is genetic, and find a marker for it? Do we want to let the person with that trait join the Army and learn to use weapons? Do we want to give him training in killing?

"That's the problem. Do we dare use this information? Do we dare not use it?"

The anguish in store is illustrated by the search for a marker for Huntington's disease, the genetic illness that lies dormant until middle age and then strikes—driving its victims insane and then killing them.

The Huntington's situation is in one respect more straight-forward than that of acetylcholine-sensitive depression. Huntington's disease is strictly genetic; a person who inherits the gene is doomed, regardless of the environment. But the disease has always had a different, and even more terrible, ambiguity—the son or daughter of a victim wouldn't know whether or not he or she had the disease until middle age.

The wait, in itself, is excruciating. The potential victim watches his afflicted parent die horribly, so he knows what may be in store. The odds that he'll die the same way are fifty-fifty, but to find out he has to wait until middle age.

In the meantime, there's the question of children. Should he have them? If he has the deadly gene, and he does have children, then they too will have to suffer first his death and then the uncertainty of their own future. But if he doesn't have children, and finds out later that he doesn't have Huntington's, he will have forgone the pleasures and rewards of parenthood in vain.

Since the advent of recombinant DNA technology, scientists have been working to find a marker. If one could be located, and a test devised, Huntington's disease victims could learn their fate early in life; affected fetuses could be detected in the womb and, if their parents chose, aborted. In that way, scientists hoped, one of the most heartbreaking genetic diseases known to man could be wiped out.

The work has been successful. The scientists haven't yet located the bad gene itself but they've pinpointed another gene, a normal one, that's on the same chromosome as the defective gene.

This should lead to the identification of the defect itself in short order; in the meantime, it gives medical technologists the ability to identify victims of the disease before it strikes. No longer does a potential victim have to live the first three decades of life in ignorance.

But doctors, while hailing the work as a major advance, worry that the discovery—along with others pending in a variety of mental diseases—has brought their profession to the brink of an ethical abyss.

Susan Folstein, a Huntington's expert at the Johns Hopkins Medical School, worries that the information will be used to discriminate against people who carry the deadly Huntington's gene.

Employers, for instance, could save on medical insurance by asking potential workers whether they had the gene in the family, requiring those who answered "yes" to be screened, and then denying employment to anyone who tested positive. Insurance companies, likewise, might deny coverage.

Historically, she adds, people with Huntington's are victims of a double enigma. One, they have a genetic disease. Two, it is a mental illness. In her mind, at least, that leads to the fear that society will pass laws aimed at eradicating the gene—and the victims along with it.

"You know, the Nazis just killed people. I know of one case of Huntington's disease that they just plain killed. A family member of one of my patients . . . her aunt.

"The hospital wrote a letter to her [aunt's] brother, saying that she had died and would he please come and collect her belongings. So he got on the bus and went to the hospital—and there she was! Living!

"The next day she was really dead. It was an administrative error; her death was scheduled for the wrong day.

"So all of those things went on in Germany, and you can't forget that."

The doctors' discomfort with the implications of the test are shared by some of the people at risk for the disease. Many sons and daughters of Huntington's patients have declined to be screened. They don't want to know. Others want to know, but don't want other people, including their spouses and children, to be told. Doctors are asking one another whether they should go along with such requests for secrecy . . . or if, ethically, they have a choice.

Such dilemmas will become increasingly commonplace if, as expected, the next decade sees the discovery of a long series of genetic defects that predispose to mental illness.

The type of gene-linked "violent" alcoholism identified in the Swedish population, for instance, might well be detectable in children. If it is, such children could be warned not to drink, of course—but the chances of teenagers taking such a warning seriously is questionable at best.

The tempting option, of course, will to be to require such children to take a drug like Antabuse, which triggers violent vomiting if alcohol is injested.

The ethical ice will grow even thinner as, inevitably, scientists find markers for genetic brain diseases that predispose toward criminality. Lacking a cure from the field of genetic engineering, for instance, what should be done with a child who, according to his genetic profile, is destined for a life of petty crime? Would the answer be different if the crime wasn't petty, but major?

The question of criminality prediction, of course, carries us beyond the rather limited area of genetically determined mental illness. Mind-scanners, combined with other techniques, should be able to tell us much about the criminal mind—whether the criminality is genetic, environmental, or a combination.

Though there's nothing in the literature to suggest that molecular psychologists will be able to predict specific criminal actions, such as murder, researchers probably will be able to forge links between such acts and certain psychochemical patterns.

With the use of a combination of tests, chemical and psychological ones as well as PET scanners, it may well become possible to predict, for instance, that a certain person has a fifty-fifty chance of committing an act of violence in the foreseeable future.

Obviously such information would weigh heavily, say, in bail hearings. Persons accused of violent crimes might be kept locked up if molecular psychologists testified that they posed a significant danger to society.

But what if such information became available before he committed a crime of any sort? Should men with certain sexual disorders be identified and chemically castrated before they commit rape? Should someone be incarcerated, though totally innocent, on the basis of something he might do?

If not, what of the rights of his luckless victim? If it boiled down to a question of statistics, as it well might, what would the cutoff be? Would a man with a 90 percent chance of committing murder be locked up, and one with an 89 percent chance turned loose? What role may molecular psychology one day play in the parole process?

What will happen when law enforcement agencies apply the mind-scanners to the problem of lie detection? Will suspects one day be questioned with their heads in scanner doughnuts? Will witnesses testify under a scanner helmet instead of an oath?

Outside the interrogation chamber and the courtroom, scanner evaluations might well eliminate, from potential police cadets, those applicants with a flair for the brutal. CIA operatives might have to undergo periodic scans to make sure they haven't become double agents.

As we follow this line of reasoning, the questions become increasingly intriguing. Could loyalty be determined by means of molecular psychology? Honesty? Diligence? Intelligence? Sexual deviance?

Do good physicians have certain mind-brain characteristics in common, and, if so, should candidates for medical school be determined not by grade point average but by scanner results? Might potential pilots, crane operators, stockbrokers, and journalists be chosen by the same means?

The new diagnostic and scanning techniques will be used in conjunction with a whole pharmacopoeia of ever more specific and powerful mind-altering drugs. Such drugs, developed to treat the mentally ill, will also be useful in general society.

The memory enhancers, already the subject of experiments at the National Institute of Mental Health, are a good example. They may be the forerunners of whole categories of compounds that boost the human ability not only to remember but also to learn. Smart pills, as a result, may find a place in the lunch bags of grade schoolers.

Recent work with the brain's PCP receptors suggests that creativity enhancers are also possible. They may become as common in artists' lofts and screenwriters' garrets as steroids are now in weight lifters' gyms.

And, in a world increasingly accepting of the use of chemicals to alter the mind, what of addictive drugs? As sweetly horrible as heroin may be, may not someone one day concoct something even worse?

Is that not already beginning to happen in the covert "designer drug" industry, in which manufacturers stay one jump ahead of the law by inventing drugs that have not yet been outlawed?

And, if new drugs are that easy to invent, the mind wanders back to the secret agencies of the government, to the CIA and military intelligence bureaus.

What are Soviet neurochemists up to these days, and what's the news from China? Are there neurochemists in Nicaragua, in Peru, in Brazil, in South Africa, and what are they thinking, what are they doing?

Is the revolution really that far in the future? Or are we already embroiled in it?

And is it the millennium, as we so desperately hope, or the apocalypse?

22

AT

THE

CROSSROADS

A s we stand at the crossroads of history, on the threshold of self-understanding, we hesitate. On the one hand we see the possibilities for a cure for mental illness and a better understanding of the human condition, while on the other we see that the new technology contains within it a vast potential for what can only be called evil.

We are made doubly hesitant by the essentially alien nature of the new truths. We can understand easily enough that there is a receptor for the good feeling of a mother's love, and another for the anxiety we feel when we see a spider. We can marvel at the dopamine system, and the way it filters our reality, and we can grasp, with some thought, how it might be that a genetically damaged pain filtration system might produce a child in constant pain, and how that pain might be assuaged by alcohol.

But when we put it all together, what we get is nothing less than weird. We think and, as we think, our thoughts are accompanied by the wash of complex chemicals against receptor fields, both causing and reacting in a cascade of existence measurably chemical yet palpably spiritual. We are caught up in a swirl of paradoxes.

The end result, however we handle it, leads us to a fiction coupled with truth, a new kind of duality. Mental health, on the one hand, may require a belief in God. Survival, on the other, may dictate a compromise of His principles in negotiations with the Ayatollah—a recognition that the Ayatollah's God is every bit as powerful and valid as our own.

Ultimately, as we poke through the new science of the mind, we realize that there are as many realities as there are chemical combinations, but that we have only one safe default position. That position is a fundamentalistic belief in reality, as represented (at least in principle) by science.

This attitude isn't new. Most of us, regardless of which church we go to, have already tacitly if not overtly adopted science as our religion. We go to the doctor first, and visit the faith healer only when medicine fails.

Whenever possible, we accept what the scientists say as more or less true and then, shrugging, go on with our daily lives. There are bills to pay, shopping to do, meals to prepare and eat, children to raise, bosses to satisfy. We haven't the time or the energy, let alone the training, to follow out the many-layered permutations of Candace Pert's belief in God. She opened the issue, let her figure it out.

But . . . remember what happened the last time we did that.

Early in this century the fact that E equaled mc squared was no state secret; in fact, the expedition to South America that detected the bending of starlight and proved the theory of relativity in 1919 was openly reported in the scientific press and wasn't totally ignored by the popular media. Einstein was even destined to become something of a baggy-pants public hero.

Yet most people had been schooled in the doctrine that atoms were indivisible, that time ticked steadily from Genesis to Armageddon, and that the shortest distance between two points was a straight line. They believed these things, in an everyday way, the same way we believe in the spirituality of the human mind.

And what the heck, relativity didn't have anything to do with the price of corn on the Chicago markets.

So the legend grew that it took a genius to grasp Einstein's work and, not being geniuses, our parents and grandparents were relieved of the responsibility of considering what might happen if m were somehow converted to E, as the equation clearly implied it might be. And so when the day of trinity arrived, and the New Mexican desert was bathed in the light of a new dawn, they were caught unaware.

Given the unexpected power of the technology, and our lack of preparedness, we were captured by the immediacy of the thing. The atomic bomb meant sweet victory. It meant American men did not have to wade ashore amidst desperate gunfire on the beaches of Japan. That was good, and we rejoiced.

Our joy carried over into the postwar years as we contemplated Pax Atomica and found it sweet—until the Reds got the bomb, too. Even then, magazines and newspapers extolled the virtues of the atom, predicting an age of free energy. The power inherent in an apple could carry expeditions to the moon and Mars.

But those were dreams founded in ignorance and innocence, and when they didn't turn out to be exactly as advertised we inevitably became bitterly disillusioned. Slowly the image of the atom, once the symbol of hope, became the sign of death. The pendulum swung, hard left, and a backlash grew first against physics, then against science in general, and finally encompassed even the precepts of rationality.

By the 1960s, the revolution was in full swing and we embraced astrology, Tarot cards, acupuncture, hypnosis, and faith healing. In Amerika, as it was sometimes spelled then, we threw rotten eggs at scientists. We traveled to India to take our wisdom at the feet of gurus.

In the 1970s, we still accepted an annual highway death rate of 50,000 without a whimper, but a minor nuclear accident at Three Mile Island, in which no one was killed, fueled a hysteria that all but destroyed the nuclear industry. When physicists announced that they were nearing break-even on a prototype fission reactor, the news was greeted with catcalls and protests— fusion, fission, smission . . . who knew, or cared?

"No nukes," the placards read, but few of the young people who carried them had any knowledge of the science they were protesting; few of them, if questioned, could have described the second law of thermodynamics. In their ignorance of the science they hated, they were loose cannon. The breeder reactor program died, but the Peacekeeper missile was approved and built.

Now, even after the accident at Chernobyl, public opinion seems to be swinging back in favor of nuclear power. Will it stop swinging at a moderate point, or will it go to the opposite extreme?

We muddle through, somehow.

In the forty-odd years since Hiroshima and Nagasaki were destroyed, nuclear weapons have not been used again in anger. In fact, while terror has reigned, and while soldiers have died by the hundreds of thousands in places like Korea and Vietnam, it has nevertheless been the most peaceful forty years in all of modern history. Since World War II, far more people have died on the world's highways than in combat.

Perhaps a nuclear war in the immediate future will change this equation, and perhaps it will not. For a while, it appeared the Chernobyl accident had proven, by hideous example, the protesters' case. But what lasting effect on public opinion has the Chernobyl incident really had?

I am not extolling the virtues of nuclear power. I am pointing out that even today most citizens of the United States and the Soviet Union, and of the more minor nuclear powers, are abjectly ignorant of even the fundamental concepts that underlie the age.

We, the citizenry, got a late start—and we never caught up. We never had a prayer of adopting sound, shared attitudes through which we could control events. To this day public opinion remains volatile and emotional; we are still playing Hamlet with the atom, maybe this and maybe that and maybe something else.

The practical result is that we are all disenfranchised. The revolution is still in the hands of scientists—and they, each intent on his or her narrow projects and goals, having no outlet for peaceful research, are purchased individually by politicians and generals.

Can we afford to let that happen again?

For the past decade I have been privileged to watch, up close, the birth of the new science of the mind. This naturally led me to the study of molecular psychology itself, and to an interest in the general statistical and scientific information involving mental illness.

But my experience has not been antiseptic. I have seen, during this same time, the brutal reality of insanity. I have conducted in-depth interviews in mental hospitals, in psychiatric prison units, in prisons. I have visited the mentally ill in dingy walk-ups in alleyways, and in therapy sessions.

I have also, like you, lived my life. I have committed my share of emotional stupidities, and paid for them on the installment plan. I have watched people I loved die of alcoholism. I have seen my marriage dissolve, and with it my own innocent dreams. Helplessly, I have watched friends founder and sink into the cold, smothering sea of depression. I have watched helplessly as my own children underwent the agony of adolescence.

We don't normally look directly at the common horrors of our lives; they are too close, and we don't dare. But what, oh Lord . . . what if our agonies could be alleviated?

I subscribe to the notion that knowledge is power, and dream that molecular psychology will part the clouds and bathe the vale of tears with a new sunshine. I have a dream that the endless chain of pain, inflicted by father upon son and mother upon daughter, can finally be broken—and that our children do not need to repeat, once again, our mistakes.

But coins have two sides, and my dream sometimes fades into a nightmare.

In that nightmare, we turn our backs on the new knowledge, choosing by default to remain ignorant. As a result, the revolution in molecular psychology grows and blossoms in obscurity.

The nature of this refusal varies, in my nightmare, from group to group.

Some, inevitably, simply deny. The Ayatollah Khomeini, Jerry Falwell, and the Reverend Moon predictably go on peddling their myths. Bunkum has always attracted an audience of shallow fools, and so it will. But the sizes of the audiences vary from time to time, and in my nightmare the audiences are large and powerful. They become mobs, running through the night with ropes and torches, hunting witches.

Philosophers, of course, object to the materialism inherent in the new science. They point out, accurately enough, that the connection between chemical reactions and thoughts is unproved. In this way they will be correct: biological theories are built not of proofs but of patterns.

The political right will by nature be opposed to the new view of man, on the grounds that it is simplistic and, even if it's not, that it is inimical to all concepts of morality and responsibility. The left will continue to attack psychogeneticists as neo-Nazis, and will hold to their view that drug treatment is but a cheap substitute for social justice.

And so it will go. But this is not what terrifies me.

The kernel of my nightmare is that the rest of us, you and I, those who have the interest, the intelligence, the literacy, and the openness to read this far, will shrug and turn away. My nightmare is that we, the powerful and educated minority that the pollsters like to call "opinion leaders," will go about our lives, as we always do, above it all, engaged in our own everyday problems, trusting the scientists to somehow work it all out.

Because the bottom line, the thing I know absolutely for certain, above all else—and the reason I wrote this book—is that they'll do no such thing.

They are interested, as they must be, in the reaction of chemicals, the publication of papers, the reorganization of academic departments, and changes in obtaining grants. Neurochemists are not social philosophers and do not claim to be. They are scientists.

They're good, too.

And so molecular psychology will forge ahead, and the revolution will gather steam. The discoveries will appear, at an ever-increasing rate, in the journals. Mental illness will continue to break down into ever finer and more specific categories. Markers will be discovered, early treatment will be undertaken, and more drugs will appear.

And, in my nightmare, the difference between what they know and what the rest of us know will widen.

From time to time, as the thrust of the research becomes ever clearer, there will be protests. Do we really want to know what makes us tick? Do we really want mind control? Are we ready, yet, to deal with it?

Such questions will be heard, perhaps, by reporters and an occasional politician. They will be batted around, thoughtfully, in editorial columns and perhaps even in congressional hearing rooms. Various authorities will worry that scientists, each of whom is totally invested in his own project, are not likely to ask the hard social questions raised by their work—and that none of the rest of us is competent to.

But the protests will originate from the camps of the anti-scientific right and left, and as such will have little credibility. The scientists will point out, quite accurately, that benefits will accrue not only to the mentally ill and their families but also to society as a whole. They will present witnesses to illustrate the suffering, and sheets of figures to document the potential economic benefits. Their arguments will be overwhelming, and we will proceed.

And that's the bottom line, in my nightmare or out of it: molecular psychology will proceed regardless of protest.

For one thing, the revolution's international; it proceeds not just in the United States but also in England, France, Italy, Australia, Switzerland, Sweden, Germany, India, Japan, the Soviet Union, and Mexico.

And so in my nightmare the revolution will fester, as did the revolution in physics, in the obscurity of the arcane.

And then one day we will be rudely awakened to reality by an army that marches across the globe sustained by artificial courage, armed by scientists who invent weapons while under the influence of intelligence enhancers, supplied by automatons who work long hours in munitions factories for the reward of a chemical called something like "Heaven."

When I stumbled into my ringside seat at that historic press conference in 1973, my first reaction was fascination. Here, to judge from what was being said, lay the key to the mystery of the human psyche. It was the story of my life.

But as I struggled to make it sound believable, I fell far short of my goal. Molecular psychology is at least as complex as physics, and—as in the early days of physics—it flies in the face of common assumptions.

My story, limited by time, space, and talent, made the front page of the *Evening Sun* but did not convey the historic nature of the discovery. Surrounded as it was by stories on politics and violence, my too-qualified claims for the epochal nature of the discovery got lost in the everyday hype of the media. Horrified, I watched the discovery of the morphine receptor slip quickly into oblivion—almost without mention of its world-shaking implications.

It was then that my nightmare first occurred. In it, the revolution marches on, out of sight and out of mind. Blinded by our own prejudices and our own everyday priorities, we don't awaken to the new reality until events have overtaken us and it's impossible for us ever to become master of the situation. In the years since, as I've watched the science unfold in an obscurity that approaches secrecy, my fears have intensified.

This, then, was my motivation for writing this book. In it, I have attempted to lay out for you the nature of the revolution and to demonstrate to you, by the march of discoveries, that molecular psychology is very much a reality of today's world—and that it will define tomorrow's. Psychiatry is no longer a joke, and those who continue to laugh are fools.

True, on any given day progress seems slow—especially to the victims of mental illness. But as we look back over the past decade we can see that the knowledge is growing exponentially. Our children will not see this as slow progress at all. With the hindsight of history they will label it for what it is: an explosion without precedent.

This revolution, because it entails the control not of things but of people, represents a sea change in human history. The events that flow with the tide, as they unfold slowly at first and then ever more rapidly, will destroy not only our perceptions of ourselves but also the traditional, commonly understood social understandings that form the foundation of our society.

In the reformation that follows, nothing will remain unchanged —not our families, our sex lives, our educational system, our criminal justice establishment, our medical system, our political establishment, or our means of warfare. Of such upheavals are nightmares, and dark ages, constructed.

But so, too, are dreams—and I have a dream to match the nightmare.

History need not repeat itself. Caught unaware by the revolution in physics, and living as a result under the shadow of the atomic cloud, perhaps we have learned something.

Molecular psychology is knowledge, and knowledge is power. With openness, intelligence, wisdom, sensitivity, and good will, we can apply that power in the cause of freeing ourselves.

First, we can free the insane from the chemical chains that bind them. We can free criminals from their prisons, and make them good citizens. We can free alcoholics and drug addicts from their perpetual hells.

Then, as we come to understand the nature of the ancient demons that inhabit all our skulls, we can free ourselves.

We can, as we decipher the meaning of adolescence, restructure our educational philosophy to better reflect human nature; in the process, we will become ever wiser. We can use our intelligence, memory, and creativity-enhancing drugs to boost these efforts.

As we come to understand the nature of love we can sign a permanent peace between the sexes; with such disarmament we will be calmer, less full of guilt and hatred. Our children, spared the turmoil of our makeups and breakups, can grow to adulthood as stronger and more secure people.

As we reconstruct our society to better reflect who we are, our factories can become more humane and our workers, as a result, more productive. We can make our roads and streets safer, our opinion leaders more thoughtful, police officers subtler, voters more knowledgeable, politicians more open, writers and philosophers more insightful. . . .

If the nightmare is a vision of hell, the dream is a glimpse of the millennium. One is darkness, the other is dawn.

The struggle between the two is the single facet of the human experience that will not be affected by the revolution in molecular psychology. There will be choices, many choices, along the way, between light and darkness, knowledge and ignorance, good and evil.

In the decade and more since I've been following this new science as a journalist, I've thought a lot about what those choices should be—and arrived at precious few firm convictions. The questions of forced treatment for mental patients, of psychochemical screening of potential police officers, of the proper use of mind-scanners by parole boards . . . these are not questions that one human being can answer in a vacuum. They are social questions, and they must be answered by all of us.

But it is my place, in my role as technological Paul Revere, to say that those choices are about to be presented, and that they must be made. And it is my place to insist that we must not make them, as we made the choices that shaped the nuclear age, by default. The science of man is far, far too important to be left to the scientists.

Different societies will choose differently, of course. And, as always, there will be struggles.

If historical pattern is to be trusted, there will be many mistakes made and many abuses perpetrated. Intelligence enhancers, as they become available, will certainly be used, by someone somewhere, in the design of ever more terrible weapons. Workers will be pacified, and converted to slaves, by drugs. As sure as the chemicals of curiosity flow in the brains of scientists, and one discovery follows another, fearless armies of automatons will one day march in lock step.

As an observer of this new science since its birth, I can't offer any suggestions to prevent this. We couldn't stop this science even if we wanted to, and, given its power for good, I for one wouldn't want to try.

To counter my own nightmares, I personally rely on my dreams —and on the yet undiscovered receptors that mediate the human emotion called "faith."

I have faith that workers who come by their happiness legitimately and constructively will in the end prove more efficient than those who find it in a pill. I have faith that enhanced intelligence will lead not to the design of better weapons but to disarmament. I have faith that armies of automatons will be no match for free men and women who oppose them out of choice.

I have faith that we do not need to learn the lesson of the atomic age twice—that we will pay attention to this new science as it develops, deal with its enigmas and paradoxes, recognize the force it embodies, and teach our children what they need to know as we send them forth to meet the future.

This book is dedicated to that faith, and to the proposition that a species capable of looking deeply into the mirror of its own psyche is able also to think carefully about what it sees, and to draw intelligent conclusions, and to act upon them.

And survive.